SEVEN DECADES

Arthur J. Wohlmut

VANTAGE PRESS
New York

FIRST EDITION
All rights reserved, including the right of
reproduction in whole or in part in any form.

Copyright © 1998 by Arthur J. Wohlmut

Published by Vantage Press, Inc.
516 West 34th Street, New York, New York 10001

Manufactured in the United States of America
ISBN: 0-533-12365-8

Library of Congress Catalog Card No.: 97-90318

0 9 8 7 6 5 4 3 2 1

Contents

Preface		v
Part I.	Survival of the Meekest	1
Part II.	To Rebuild Life under Freedom	139

Preface

This is an account of happenings over the span of seven decades. It encompasses events in war and peace, in tyranny and freedom, in sadness and in happy times.

Mine and Georgine's sons, their wives, and our grandchildren may therefrom develop their own views and understanding of that part of the past that went by before their young years. They may ponder on the mystery by which one event follows or causes another in the complicated web of one's fate. If external forces interfere, they can be overcome in order to steer back to the chartered course. Only the weak are tempted to follow the crowd that has no individual face or shape.

It is my hope that some of those who read my lines may find new strength in their noble belief in liberty. But for those who abhor freedom and work toward its destruction I can only express sorrow and disdain.

Part I
Survival of the Meekest

1

The room was lit only by the twilight of the approaching night. My mind slowly drifted from the body and wandered down the long past. My head was gently sinking like a dry leaf gliding to the ground in a soft breeze. Time became endless as the twilight retreated into darkness.

At first my mind remembered nothing about the body slumped in the chair. What kind of person had he been? Had he led a God-fearing life, or had he perhaps been a scoundrel, a thief, or even worse? Had he had friends and made others happy, or had he been despised or rejected? Or had he been respected, liked, or even loved?

The room became colder as the faint moonlight tried to penetrate the heavy curtain. I yearned for someone to cast judgment on the man I might have been, but the room remained enveloped in silence. I could have been anyone. Destiny leads men sometimes on a safe path in a given direction free of complications, but it may also be affected by thousands of seemingly unrelated events that also touch those who happen to pass by. Whether prearranged by some unknown power or fallen into place at random, the past cannot be erased, as it is written in indelible ink. Every single event in my life that had followed a previous one and preceded another one probably changed only lightly the course of my life, but together they were all part of a force that had dictated what role I, a mere speck on the earth, was to play over the years. My early youth came first to my mind. The clarity was almost frightening as it evoked moments of pain of a time that I could now relive but that could no longer hurt. Those involved appeared before me as if alive. They walked by as shadows. Only some of them showed their blurred faces. We communicated without a sound being uttered.

2

The scene was a village in a former province of the old Austro-Hungarian monarchy shortly before the outbreak of the First World War. The region was called Bukovina, and lay on the Russian–Romanian border.

My origin in this remote corner of Europe was due to my father's occupation. He had become a respected customs officer in the service of the Austrian emperor. In his profession he had been assigned frequently to posts in various parts of the empire that stretched over vast areas from Central to Eastern Europe. During his assignment to Bukovina, he married my mother, a lovely girl with a pale complexion and beautiful dark hair. Two sons were born out of the marriage: Bruno, two years my senior, and myself.

Father was proud of being a customs officer, a profession that commanded considerable respect in the local community. He ranked equally with the schoolmaster, the mayor, the physician, and the police chief. His duties included the supervision of a rather large plant for the production of spirits, a state monopoly on which heavy taxes had to be properly collected. In his dashing uniform he carried himself always erect, his mustache well groomed, and his eyes benevolently yet firmly scanning the surroundings. In his home town back in Bohemia where he had been raised, there had been little opportunity for a good education. He had spent hardly five or six years at the small local school. Higher education had not been a frequent occurrence during the years of his youth, at the end of the nineteenth century. He always strived, however, to rise above the average and had never ceased to read and learn. At an early age he had developed a keen sense of honor, self-discipline, and appearance. He had a rare gift of communicating intimately with both people and nature. On his walks he often approached complete strangers and was in no time engaged in a warm and friendly talk. At other times people came to him with their own problems, expecting warm words of encouragement and bits of wisdom in return. On frequent occasions he would pause suddenly in his walk and stand still for a few moments to admire the beauty of the countryside, the sky, a flower, or a bird. Although I was only a child then and had only recently taken my first steps, he carried me for short walks and taught me to admire nature's wonders.

Through perseverence and sheer determination he had managed to pass the rigorous test required by the royal commission before being accepted into the ranks of the prestigious Austrian customs force. Having achieved this, he was assured of a lifetime of security, regular advancements, and finally, upon retirement, a comfortable pension. There was no doubt in anyone's mind as to the safety and perpetual prosperity under the monarchy. This was Central Europe's golden age, with the emperor being the guarantor of peace, joy, well-being, and confidence in the future. Vienna was Europe's center of music, the good life, and pleasure. From there prosperity had spread to all corners of the monarchy, including the faraway Bukovina.

My mother was not in good health. Her pale complexion somewhat distinguished her from other women in the community, although they, too, avoided exposure to sunlight, as the custom of that time demanded. She easily became tired when Father took her to any official function or for a social visit or when we had guests. I remember her face clearly but anything else about her only vaguely. Father told me years ago that she was a slim, strikingly pretty woman. As was customary in those days, she was always in the shadow of her husband. I do not recall whether she ever held me in her arms or talked to me. In my dreams I see the silhouette of a woman who was my mother and who was near me during the first years of my life. Beyond that her picture becomes vague and distant.

The house we lived in was modest but comfortable, considering this part of Europe, the time, and the circumstances. Even after so many years I remember it distinctly. It was next to a dusty town road, across from the school building. The school appeared to me enormous compared to the other houses. Ours had a large courtyard that was separated from the road by a heavy wooden gate. From the courtyard we walked through a small entry hall to a rather large kitchen. There was no running water in town. It had to be fetched from a well in the yard. Mother had some help in her kitchen chores, as she was too weak to manage the household alone. Meals were prepared on a huge ceramic oven with an alcove in the wall that remained warm and cozy during the nights. I remember that an old woman used to crawl up into the alcove and sleep there on occasion, but I do not know who she was.

From the kitchen, where we also had our meals, we entered into a huge adjoining room that served a dual purpose: as a sitting room when we had guests and as a bedroom at night. There were cabinets with pieces of china and glassware, ornate vases, and figurines and a respectable table with heavy chairs. Two ornamental wardrobes stood in the corner, next to the beds and lamps. A door led to a smaller room, the furniture of which was less impressive and therefore not meant to be shown to visitors. Finally, from there a back door led to the outside garden, next to the road and the entry gate. The garden did not deserve the name. Aside from a few wildflowers and small trees, there were weeds everywhere. It would have been difficult to water the garden by carrying buckets from the well in the backyard. As a result the garden was usually covered with a blanket of dust from the road except during the rainy season.

The town, or rather the village, was not far away from a mountain range covered with a deep forest. The stream running through the village originated from there. Its water was crystal clear and ice cold. The riverbed, covered with pebbles like little gems, shone through the fast-moving water. Under the large rocks good-sized fish sought security. I remember that we used to wade into the water armed with a large stone and by hitting the rock under which the fish were hiding with a sharp blow sometimes succeeded in stunning them so that we were able to catch them with our bare hands.

The villagers sometimes encountered packs of wolves in the hills. When some of the men were attacked, the story would spread like wildfire. We children were frightened by the wolf stories, which might have sometimes been exaggerated to impress upon us that the wolves would get us if we misbehaved. Children in those days were held to strict rules of behavior.

When we had guests, the conversation among the adults always had a serious tone. We children knew that we were expected to sit motionless at the table without uttering a single word unless in response to a direct question. Even then, the parents usually took over and answered properly all questions themselves so that no social blunder would be caused. It was considered rude and uncalled for if, during the visit, we expressed the need to go to the bathroom. When chocolates and sweet cakes were passed around we craved them terribly, but we had been trained to politely decline a second helping even as our eyes were begging for more.

The wolf stories had a big impact on me during my first years of life. Like most children, I feared darkness. When night set in and the dim light made objects hardly recognizable, I used to see all kinds of suspicious shadows lurking in every dark corner. I was particularly scared when the wind whistled past the windows or the rain hammered on the roof and walls. One night fear gripped me so much that I could not fall asleep for hours. Suddenly I had the distinct feeling that something was moving at the base of my bed. A silhouette of a wolf, a real wolf, was staring at me with its glittering eyes and white teeth shining in the darkness. He nodded to me and whispered to come with him. The image then dissolved and nothing remained any longer in the darkness at the base of the bed. I heard strange noises around the house and spent the rest of the night awake, gazing into the darkness, soaked with perspiration. I was not older than three then, but the incident left a mark on me and haunted me for years thereafter.

3

Out of the blue the fate of nations and millions of people changed when, in the summer of 1914, World War I erupted following the assassination of the Austrian archduke and his wife in Sarajevo, Serbia.

I was not yet two and Bruno four years old then. For us the war signaled the beginning of many upheavals in our lives. What would the future have brought us otherwise, had we the opportunity to live normal lives and grow up as sons of a respected customs officer in a peaceful and prosperous empire? We would have probably been raised in comfort, received a suitable education, and been given positions in some minor government offices. Our lives would have continued similar to those of our parents and other royal subjects. Instead, we found ourselves on a road filled with fear, poverty, malnutrition, hatred, disease, and drama, in a world torn by conflicts and disasters.

For a year or so my father stayed with us, having been assigned to duties in our region. Then he was suddenly recalled for a special assignment back to Bohemia, which was also a part of the empire. He had to leave in haste, with hardly any time to say good-bye. Bukovina had still not been seriously touched by the war, but conditions in Central Europe did not permit Mother, Bruno, and me to travel with him. Consequently we were left behind. Father thought that the assignment would be a short one and that, in any event, we would be safer in Bukovina than in the western part of the empire, where the war had originated. He was convinced that the combined Austrian and German forces would be well capable of protecting our area. His travel entailed a long journey by train, the only means of transportation available at that time. Because Mother was ailing, a long trip would have been, in any event, too strenuous for her.

Shortly after my father's departure in 1915, the war suddenly reached our town. From then on Mother's health deteriorated rapidly. She grew weaker almost by the hour. She must have had great concern about Bruno's and my future in a strange land, without father or close relatives. I still see her as she lay in her bed, to which she had now been permanently confined. Her white face on the pillow and her pale arms stretched over the blanket contrasted deeply with the semidarkness of the room, in which the curtains had been drawn to afford her some measure of comfort.

One evening she suddenly rose in bed and cried out in agony and pain as if calling for help. A few days later she was no more. Someone lifted me up and told me to kiss her good-bye. I did not understand or cry when some good neighbors took Bruno and me to the village cemetery for Mother's burial. Someone was holding my hand as I stood there watching the simple wooden casket being lowered and the dry grass gently swaying in the breeze.

4

During military operations the front line wavered back and forth. Austrian armies advanced and retreated against the Russians. At first the Austrians over-ran Galicia, Bukovina's neighbor to the north, to protect it from the czar's armies. On their way, endless columns of men and arms passed through our village. Then, in 1915, Russia was successful in defeating the Austrian forces, pushing them as far back as the Carpathian frontier of Hungary. The combined Austro-German troops then mounted a counterattack and drove the Russians out again of Galicia at a Russian cost of 1 million men. However, in June of 1916 Russian armies under General Brusilov started a major drive against Austrian lines and within a short time had taken most of eastern Galicia. Later that year, Austro-German forces counteracted by occupying Romania. In their operations, large sectors of armies from both sides moved through Bukovina as the fortunes of war kept changing.

The military actions affected life in our village immensely. Endless troop movements over the dirty country roads took place. Camps were set up everywhere. The sounds of heavy gunfire and marching boots and rolling equipment drawn by horses filled the dusty air.

We did not fully realize the gravity of our situation, with Mother gone and Father in a faraway country. For a short while some of our good neighbors looked after us. They brought some scraps of food from time to time while we stayed alone in our silent house. As the fighting and troop movements became more intense and as the sound of guns got louder and closer, most of the local population left, mostly in haste. Only a few elderly people, some of them invalids, remained in a remote corner of the village. Bruno and I, only about five and three years old then, could not think of a place to hide. We had no one who would take care of us. Our house became our shelter at night, while during the day we roamed through the village, which began to look like a ghost town with its destroyed or burned-out buildings. I can still sense the odor of the charred ruins and the musty smell inside the abandoned houses.

Bruno was the leader. I followed him wherever he went. Together we spent a great deal of time in search of food. We ate whatever we could find in the dried-out fields and gardens, and in the abandoned buildings. Scraps of food that had been left by the armies that had passed through the village were most welcome to us. Sometimes a single soldier, probably reminded of his own children back home, would look at us and hand us a piece of bread or throw us an open can containing some leftovers. One day a cook in a Russian regiment signaled us to come closer. He offered us some rice porridge from a huge kettle that he was about to clean. Another time some Cossacks with big black mustaches played and joked with us when they camped in our backyard. They lifted us in their arms and put us on the backs of their small horses to sit there for a while. One of them reached into his pocket and brought out two pieces of hard lump sugar for us. We had been craving something sweet for a long time. This was a real treat. The Russians used to hold small lumps of sugar between their teeth, sipping hot tea through them.

There was a wooden tower in the center of the marketplace, located in an open field. Its bell used to signal the villagers whenever a fire had broken out and at other times of danger. When the battlefront approached for the first time, the bell could be heard far away. Now only the tower's charred structure remained. We used to sneak inside, climb the shaky remains of the old staircase as high as we dared, and with the ground far below us and the sky above our heads, watch in silence for hours. Smoke was rising everywhere. We could see soldiers as soon as they appeared on the horizon. Then we watched them coming closer, covered with perspiration and dust, marching in disarray toward the battle line or back in retreat and despair. We were fascinated by the endless lines of vehicles and guns pulled by horses. Bruno and I huddled together on the shaky steps of the tower, scanning the countryside from the village to the horizon. Occasionally an automobile, making a terrifying noise and carrying come important commanders, passed by. The sight of an automobile at that time was an unusual experience, which impressed us very much.

Everywhere along the roads and close to campsites one could see the rotting remains of slaughtered animals, with clouds of flies feeding on them. A choking stench filled the air.

We became obsessed with ammunition. Neat little white boxes containing abandoned ammunition could be seen everywhere. This tempted us to experiment. Crude wooden crates with heavier shells were of particular interest to us. We collected them secretly and dragged them into the shed at the corner of our backyard until we had no more room for more. Whenever we got hold of small-rifle ammunition, which happened frequently, we placed single shells on a stone and from a distance of only a few feet hurled medium-sized rocks at them until they exploded. The idea, of course, came from Bruno, as I would never have taken such an initiative. Once he gave the signal to go ahead, I followed without hesitation.

Bruno, being almost two years my senior, naturally was much bolder than I. As the war went on, he led the way to abandoned houses and ruins as if on an exploration trip for unknown treasures. Often we found things that we foolishly considered as being of great value, such as a broken mirror, an armchair, or even a cupboard. We then dragged them, no matter how heavy, into our backyard, to hide them in the old shed. We perfected our clandestine actions in a way so that we remained unobserved by the handful of old people remaining in the village.

Our will for self-preservation made us mature fast. It did not strike us then that without father and mother, or any other guardian for that matter, our situation was pitiful or at least unusual. We accepted it as if we were an integral and natural part of our lives and as if this were to remain our fate for the rest of our days.

The conditions brought about by the war deprived the village of even the crudest sanitary facilities. The moving armies left decaying cattle carcasses, broken equipment, open fires, and latrines everywhere. Hunger forced us to eat anything we could lay our hands on, regardless of the dismal hygienic conditions. Unripe fruit picked from abandoned gardens or the ground was just as welcome as rotten turnips from unattended cellars or fields. We gulped them down without hesitation. Soon I developed a serious case of dysentery, a disease that had assumed epidemic proportions among the soldiers. Even under reasonable medical treatment they remained incapacitated for long periods of time, unable to join the fighting forces. In many instances the disease was fatal. I, being so small and undernourished, suffered immensely, passing blood day after day. I became so weak that I could hardly stand on my tiny feet. The pain was unbearable. It is hard to imagine that I survived, deprived of the most basic medical assistance and care.

One day, Bruno, too, got terrible stomach aches. Rather than squat by the roadside or behind a bush as usual, he decided that what was good for the armies was good for him, too. He chose a regular open military latrine, of which there were hundreds in the open fields. They consisted of rectangular holes, the size of which was prescribed by the proper military manuals. The holes were several feet deep. Over them were strategically positioned narrow elevated planks on which several soldiers at a time could sit and simultaneously attend to their needs. At his age Bruno was far to small to deposit himself comfortably and securely over the narrow plank or to find solid support for his short legs and small feet. For a few brief moments he swayed desperately back and forth, but finally he could no longer retain his balance. He plunged, headfirst, into the deep mess, which was truly of international origin, from both friend and foe who had passed through the village. We had no extra clothing for him to change into. In fact, we slept in what we wore all the time. While he shivered in his nakedness we tried to wash his pants and torn shirt in a nearby creek, but with only limited success. Although he scrubbed his head and body thoroughly in a desperate effort to cleanse himself, it took weeks before all evidence of his misfortune was gone.

I recall another time when in search of food we came upon a huge melon behind a dilapidated fence. We were anxiously looking for some means to open it and enjoy its contents but could find none. Then Bruno got an idea. He took a loose plank from the fence and handed it to me. An old nail was still stuck in it. He grabbed the melon in his arms, rather than leaving it on the ground, and directed me to hit it with all the force I could muster. I swung hard but, unfortunately, misjudged the distance and hit Bruno instead. He started to bleed profusely, and I stood there motionless, not knowing what to do or say. He did not blame me. He only clutched his head with his little hands, accepting the blow stoically, as if it were a predestined and unavoidable event. When he finally started to stagger away, I followed him silently and helplessly. Up to this day, many years later, a scar still marks the head that has had more than its share of pain.

Until that time I had never heard of any human being able to fly through the air. True, Bruno and I had been told children's stories of flying bats and dangerous monsters. One day, however, I observed a huge object slowly crossing the sky from one horizon to the other. It seemed to take hours. I shall never forget the deep impression and awe this left on me. I felt as if some monstrous creature or object had crossed the heavens. The heavy sound, coming in waves, heightened the awesome effect. I could not imagine in my wildest dreams that anything or anyone could really float through the air so close to heaven. As it happened in the late afternoon, the sky was red and the whole countryside looked mysterious and weird.

I was even more awed when a few days later a slim man in a black leather suit and a cap with goggles appeared among the soldiers who camped in our yard. Some of them whispered with great respect that he was the pilot of the monstrous flying machine that I had seen earlier. To me he looked devilish and utterly mysterious. I could not associate him with reality. Where was the world heading?

In general, I had considerable fear when I saw new soldiers coming through the village. I was constantly worried that they might harm us. Sometimes a single sentry worried me more than a group of soldiers. When a guard was pacing back and forth some distance away, his rifle over his shoulder, I always hid behind a boulder or a tree. Watching him sometimes for hours, I hoped he would leave so I could be on my way again. Some of the men were rough characters in both their language and action. Some others, however, were gentle and their eyes showed warmth. This was comforting even if they spoke a foreign language.

Bruno did not mind the soldiers so much. This sometimes got him into trouble. Once some German-speaking infantrymen camped nearby, their rifles neatly stacked in groups of three, with the bayonets pointing skyward. The rifles were loaded, of course. After all, the war was in full swing. Bruno sneaked up to the rifles unobserved. He could not help touching and manipulating a few of them. In the process he tried out a trigger. The resulting loud bang of the exploding shell caused an immediate general alarm, with hundreds of men running in all directions in great confusion. This time Bruno was fortunate to escape and avoid severe punishment.

He was less fortunate on another occasion. One day we saw an elegant open automobile approaching from the distance. The unusual sight fascinated us immensely. Clouds of dust surrounded the vehicle. The roaring of its motor became louder and louder. Soon we could recognize the silhouette of the chauffeur and of some high-ranking Russian officer, most probably a general. Only a general could have at his disposal such an automobile at a time when few were in use. The car passed by. Both the officer and the chauffeur were looking stiffly ahead, not paying the slightest attention to us little children at the roadside near the gate to our home. All of a sudden Bruno, on some strange and unpredictable impulse, lifted a good-sized rock from the road and hurled it with all his might after the car that was now about thirty feet away. He could not have meant to hurt anyone or to cause damage. Fate would have it that the rock landed in the middle of the windshield of the open automobile, instantly shattering the glass and probably hurting the occupants.

Rather than escaping through the alleys between the ruins, we stood there in terrible shock, unable to speak or move. We heard angry shouts and swearing as the car abruptly stopped. At the officer's order the driver jumped out and with his pistol drawn searched around, ready to kill anyone who wanted to harm his master. Under the circumstances it could have been assumed that in his rage he would kill Bruno without the slightest hesitation. After a second or two, however, he decided against shooting a child. In his uncontrollable rage he gave Bruno a terrible beating, punching him with his fists over the whole body and head until Bruno's face was covered with blood and he had dropped to the ground.

After a time that seemed endless, during which I stood helplessly near him, Bruno crawled away slowly and with great difficulty, like a beaten dog to lick his wounds. Again he was remarkable. He did not cry out in pain or complain. The ordeal most likely caused or at least contributed greatly to the hearing problem that has troubled him ever since and has become more pronounced over the years.

Although he often ran into problems and painful experiences through his own doing, Bruno always took the consequences like a man. To me this seemed the right behavior and proper attitude of a person who was my older brother.

On another occasion, when some cavalrymen had tied their horses in a neat row to the large schoolyard fence, Bruno snooped around and walked close to the horses' behinds. One of them became nervous, jumped around, and suddenly kicked its hind legs with great force into Bruno's stomach and chest. He landed several feet away in great pain, clutching his body with his little hands. He lay there for some time without uttering a sound. Only a strange grimace testified as to his terrible suffering. Again, I stood by in silence, not knowing what to do or say, but I was certain it would be better if we were not seen. We crawled into the darkest corner of the yard and waited there for a long time until his pain subsided somewhat. Then, in the evening, we sneaked out furtively just as the soldiers started to water and feed the horses.

I do not recall having spoken more than a few words with Bruno during all those long months. Even earlier, when we were still with our parents, we only talked when spoken to. This affected mine and Bruno's behavior toward each other. We grew up in the belief that children were not supposed to say or discuss much, even among themselves. And so now, in the middle of the war, without parents and friends, we found it even more proper not to talk much. We held onto each other day after day, hardly uttering a word but somehow, deep down, aware that either of us without the other was bound to perish in the world we lived in.

We were unable to openly comfort each other. The very thought of doing so never occurred to us. Also, we never gave any thought to the future, not even to tomorrow or the day after. Our memories of the past faded away almost painlessly. We did not search for the reason why we had been thrust among soldiers, ammunition, guns, smoke, dust fires, the sounds and smells of a real war, and old villagers who had not enough strength to flee. We could not help but wonder, however, why we were the only children among grown-ups, but then we accepted the thought that life is simply such.

We never found out what happened to all our neighbors and acquaintances who had left the village in haste. They, too, had never dreamed that the empire that had given them a feeling of complete and unconditional security as well as an assurance of a happy future would one day collapse, shattering their lives and dreams. Those who may have returned to the village later after the hostilities ceased must have despaired at the sight of the ruins of their homes. The war brought with it a great number social and political changes that would, in the coming years, affect every family in Europe.

It took a long time before the sound of guns in our region subsided. Armies finally started on their long way home. There were no victors, only tired and beaten men. They walked like shadows through the village, many of them in bandages and limping, carrying their rifles and other belongings without pride. Their torn uniforms covered with dust and dirt and their eyes buried deep in their drawn faces were witnesses to their past ordeals.

The few old villagers crawled out of their hideouts, their faces showing sparks of hope and expectations of better days to come. Some of them brought to the road buckets of water, from which the soldiers drank eagerly. Bruno and I sat at the dusty roadside watching column after column pass by. In our minds for the first time a distant thought came up as to how we would survive tomorrow without the familiar war.

Gradually more civilians returned to the village, looking for their relatives and belongings among the dilapidated buildings and ruins. Amid their walls a musty smell lingered for a long time. In my later life, whenever I encountered that musty odor in an empty, rotting building it brought back immediately memories of the days of my childhood in the war-torn village.

One night, when we were huddled on our dirty cots, a silhouette of a man appeared in the doorway. He stood there for some time watching us in silence. Then he came close, bent down, and gently touched us, stroking our thin, little faces. His hand felt warm and kind, a touch we had long forgotten. The room was dark and we could not see him well, but we knew it was someone who cared. After all these long months during which we had drifted aimlessly in a cold and strange world, our hearts filled with warmth. We all sat there on the cot for a long time holding each other and knowing that a new episode in our lives was to begin. For us, Father would from now on be our big brother and take care of us. He was heartbroken to hear that Mother was gone but thanked the Almighty for protecting his two small sons during these trying and dangerous times.

In October of 1918, Czechoslovakia became an independent country. Prior to that time two of its western states, Bohemia and Moravia, inhabited by Czechs, Moravians, and a substantial minority of Sudeten Germans, had been ruled by the Austrian Hapsburg monarchy. Slovakia, in the eastern part of the country, had been under Hungarian rule for some one thousand years.

So, in 1918, with Czechoslovakia's independence from the Hapsburg rule, we returned to Bohemia, the home of my parents and grandparents, and settled in a small town on the southern border of Bohemia.

Father remarried. Our stepmother was a strange, cold person. We children never experienced motherly love or care. She had no friends in town, partly because she only spoke German, a language that was despised by the Czechs due to the long rule of the Austrian Hapsburgs. While other children ran around and played in their casual clothes, Bruno and I were frequently required to wear strange city attire and walk along with our parents, to the amusement and ridicule of the other children. This often kept us away from the other youngsters. Later I managed to get closer to them. I was more outgoing than Bruno, who, mainly due to his hearing defect, was never fully accepted as one of them. Sometimes, to my later regret and shame, I sided with the other youngsters rather than with Bruno, despite our many traumatic experiences together in our younger days.

At one time Father was assigned by the government to a customs outpost in Slovakia. His absence from our small town lasted for almost a year. We missed him, as there was now no one to whom we could turn for love and understanding. Our home's atmosphere was cold, as our stepmother was unable to express any warm feelings or even smile. In Father's absence she sometimes insisted on accompanying us on our way to school. Before entering the building we had to kiss her hand in front of all the children, to our greatest embarrassment. It exposed us to a great deal of ridicule and laughter.

During our early years, when we had the misfortune of having lost our own mother in the middle of the war and when we had experienced its horrors, Bruno and I suffered from lack of both food and love. Now our stepmother was a cold person unwilling or incapable of showing any affection or even providing us with nourishing and tasty food. We longed for basic foods such as milk, butter, fruit, and meat that were well provided in other families in the neighborhood. We were not even allowed to take any food from the pantry, not even a slice of dry bread, without permission. Sometimes, when Mother was out, Bruno and I got so hungry that we risked stealing two small slices of bread, which we then shared. We broke each slice in half, each hand holding one part, and we pretended that the left piece was a juicy sausage. We chewed each bite slowly and with great delight, as if participating in a serious religious rite. From time to time we also stole a little bit of sugar, for which we had an uncontrollable craving.

There was a considerable difference between Bruno and myself. He disliked discipline and hated school. My life style, on the other hand, was guided by my parents and aimed at acquiring a good education. Bruno's rebellious nature reminded me of our younger days during World War I, when he often had acted on impulse, disregarding any consequences, thereby getting himself into trouble. Before finishing his tenth school year he got, one day, into an argument with Father, who reprimanded him strongly for not wanting to develop into a serious and responsible citizen. That night, after everyone had gone to bed, Bruno collected his meager belongings and left home. He confided in me but asked me to keep our conversation to myself.

The next morning our parents were shocked. They had no idea what had happened or why. I kept silent. Soon I learned that Bruno was living in a shack in the back of a home belonging to his friend's parents. He could not stay there for an extended period of time. My parents did not find out about his hideout but finally became aware that he was alive and somewhere in town. It was not necessary, therefore, to report the case to the local police. Bruno had no financial means whatsoever. He searched desperately for a job to survive. With his unfinished education and without any work experience he suffered for a long time during which he was literally starving. At that time a young man could not hope for a decently paid job unless he first went through an apprenticeship. Bruno was finally hired by a small transportation company. His duties consisted mainly of delivering packaged goods to neighboring towns on the company's bicycle. His weekly income was pitiful. It was not enough to buy a decent meal or any article of clothing. He lived for a few years on bread and a little milk that were left three times a week at the door of his room by the milkman. Bruno considered himself lucky that the company let him stay in a small room in the huge warehouse.

At that time I was studying business administration and business law at an academy of commerce in a nearby city. Bruno's little room was not far away from the railway station where I had to board the train every weekday early in the morning. I had to get up shortly after four o'clock in the morning, as the train ride took about one and a half hours. In winter my room was ice cold. Each morning I munched on a slice of dry bread and sipped a cup of black coffee. Shivering, I felt my way through the corridor and staircase of the unlit apartment building, through the dark backyard, and towards a huge wooden gate that I had to open with a key as large as my hand. At one time, when the shopkeeper who had lived downstairs lay dead in the house, I trembled with terror. In the complete darkness I managed to open the large gate to get to the street leading to the railway station. Before getting there I sometimes managed to sneak to Bruno's door, and without waking him up I left a slice of bread there, hoping it would help him supplement his meager diet.

These became years when Bruno and I developed an increasingly brotherly relationship. Without openly talking about it we both felt the revived love for each other that was a special gift bestowed upon us by fate. We believed that it would further blossom and last throughout our lives.

When I completed my education, Bruno and I were forced to part. My assignment took me to a mining town in Moravia where my knowledge of business and languages was appreciated. I earned an excellent salary at the local mining company. This assured me of good prospects for the future. My income was higher than that of Father, who had worked many years for the government. My good standing allowed me to intervene on behalf of Bruno, whom I suggested as my substitute during the two years I was called to spend in military training service. The company accepted my offer. For Bruno this was his first decent and well-paid assignment.

5

When in 1933 Hitler assumed power in Germany, not many statesmen took him seriously. Czechoslovakia knew better. Her people and government were aware that the coming years would bring an ever-increasing tension between the two nations.

The Czechoslovakian republic was only fifteen years old, but it was well on its way to international recognition and respect due to its democratic political system, sound economic policies, and achievements in industrial fields. A relatively small country, it ranked seventh on the world scale of industrial development. Its international trade was blooming. Stretching some six hundred miles from west to east, it was regarded as a bridge between the West and the Soviet Union. Belonging to the Slavic ethnic group, the Czechs sympathized with their "Russian" brothers even if the Soviet communistic regime was alien to them. Its real friends and allies were Western Europe, particularly France. The latter's friendship was most valued, since France had been one of the great victors over Germany in 1918. The Czechs had for centuries been leery of their aggressive and powerful German neighbors.

Hitler's rise to power was a cause for preparing the strongest possible defense. Morally, the Czechs had already been preparing themselves during the preceding years. Beginning with their independence, their educational system, the press, the publications, and their politicians had been stressing over and over the past historical oppression and dangers from Austria and Germany. Now, in 1933, a new and urgent emphasis on the growing danger resulting from the political changes in Germany had become necessary. Defense preparations had to be stepped up dramatically.

The Czechs now became superpatriots who were ready to sacrifice anything, including their lives, to prevent another occupation of their country, this time by Nazi Germany. They relied heavily upon their mutual defense treaty with France and the Soviets but also on their own determination and military preparedness, which they continued improving vigorously. Elaborate defense fortifications were constructed along the borders facing Germany. Rigorous training of the armed forces and reserves was introduced.

My two-year compulsory training took place in Bohemia starting in 1934, while Bruno substituted for me at the mining company in Moravia. I had to endure several months of hard schooling and exercises in a reserve officers academy, followed by active duty at a border battalion. This was an elite group especially trained to watch and defend a section of the Black Forest line on the southwestern border of Bohemia. Our insignia was two black dog heads, one on each side of our uniform collar. We were very proud to wear it. The hernia operation I had undergone only a few months earlier was never used as an excuse for avoiding our heavy exercises. I would have felt unpatriotic had I complained of pain or fatigue when our officers drove us relentlessly across freshly plowed fields. Our tired bodies wished desperately to revolt against unending jumps and leaps against an unseen enemy. We simulated attacks and defenses while carrying heavy machine guns on our sore shoulders. My weight was barely fifty-five kilos. With half a machine gun weighing about twenty-five kilos on my sore, bony shoulders I was running forward, taking cover, jumping up again, hour after hour like all the other men. Sweat was pouring from our tormented bodies when we finally returned to the barracks for some food and a little rest.

Later on, our machine guns were mounted on mules. For weeks we practiced mounting and dismounting the guns and bringing them into firing position instantly following orders. We reached a point of perfection, being able to do so almost blindly in a matter of a few minutes, day or night. The mules were ideally suited for long exercises and marches on the narrow border mountain paths. During the marches absolute silence had to be observed. Men and mules walked in a long single line behind each other. When at night the leading officer stopped to listen at any suspicious crossing in the forest, the dark figures of men behind him kept bumping their bowed heads into the mules' rears, not having heard the signal.

We used to spend two to three weeks at a time close to the border on plains, mountain crests, or forests. Our rigid training called for disregarding any discomfort. Often we slept in the open, with rain pouring down on us, or in small farmers' sheds on barren and cold floors. At times we huddled in the forest in our small tents or under the protection of trees. No rest was afforded us during these exercises. It was difficult to sleep anyway. Early before dawn we were up again. The mules were fed first. Then we sipped hot black coffee prepared in our field kitchen and each ate a slice of bread, a ration of which we carried with us at all times. A hot meal was given to us only at night.

After the simple breakfast the machine guns were mounted again. Another seemingly endless march followed until our bodies would ache from sores and pains or from simple physical exhaustion. At the same time we grew stronger and more confident in our ability to take the punishment. We became familiar with the border assigned to us. Soon we recognized every strategic hill, crest, path, creek, building, and even tree that we might have to defend one day.

A few months after I had been drafted, the world was shocked by the assassination of Yugoslav's King Alexander in the autumn of 1934. Countries friendly to Yugoslavia dispatched small contingents of their military to Alexander's state funeral in the capital city of Belgrade. I was chosen to be among about a hundred soldiers representing Czechoslovakia. Live ammunition was handed out to us before departure, just in case. Rather than travel through Hungary, which was not considered a friendly country at that time, we traveled to Yugoslavia by train across Czechoslovakia, and then south through Romanian territory.

At the funeral we marched in perfect formation, armed with rifles and new steel helmets that had just come out of production, past an honor tribune where dignitaries from various foreign countries were assembled. Among them were French president Albert Le Brun, who stood next to Reichsmarschall Hermann Göring. The latter, more than twenty years later, committed suicide by poisoning after he had been sentenced as a Nazi war criminal at the War Crime Tribunal in Nuremberg to die by hanging.

In my earlier years I had always been underweight. Now, the fresh air, regular exercise, and adequate military food in the barracks strengthened my muscles and added weight to my body. I felt better than at any time in the past. My promotion to second lieutenant, with good pay, was a reward for my perseverance and determination not to give up. While I used to be a shy young man, I now felt confident of myself to give orders that were followed without question. I could now face people without fear or embarrassment. I had a good feeling that with the men trained as well as I had been and with help from France and the Soviet Union we could face the German danger.

With the clouds of a new war appearing on the horizon it did not occur to me that there might be a certain similarity to the events around the outbreak of World War I that ultimately had changed the map of Europe in a manner no one could have expected. Our friends and allies were strong enough, I reckoned, to impress upon the Nazis that it would be utterly foolish to even think of embarking on a new large-scale military adventure.

Having completed my military training that year, I returned to my civilian job in the small mining town where I had been previously assured continued employment. Bruno, who helped out during my two-year absence, was offered a steady job, too. This seemed to be a most ideal situation for both of us. Unfortunately, his hearing problem, from which he had suffered since childhood, had further deteriorated. He was too proud and embarrassed to openly admit it, but his handicap was obvious to everyone in the company. In spite of that, Bruno tried desperately to hide it. When his boss gave him specific instructions or dictated a letter to him, he could often follow directions only half way. To make up for this he tried harder. This must have caused him a great deal of mental stress.

Bruno was ashamed of his handicap. Only old people were generally assumed to be short of hearing, and this would put him in such a category. Although at the time a hearing aid gadget was an unknown thing, even if it had been on the market he would not have worn it, as that would have meant an admission of his problem.

It was painful for me to watch helplessly as he struggled throughout the days to be effective and recognized. As time went by, his perseverance, pleasant personality, looks, and high intelligence gained him admiration and recognition in the company.

Those around him liked and respected him. His sense of humor was remarkable. He was good-looking—and certainly aware of it—and intelligent far beyond his simple education. He took great care of his outward appearance, spending more time than was necessary in grooming himself. His looks were important to him, something he seemed to have inherited from Father, whose government services required it.

As Bruno and I both worked in the same company, to me it meant the start of a joyous life for us. That this would be the case was my firm belief at a juncture of my life when I switched from a military to a civilian existence that was full of promise for the future. To my great disappointment and concern, however, Bruno's behavior toward me seemed to have changed dramatically without any apparent reason. He showed signs of reluctance and insecurity while talking to me. While he seemed appreciative that I had been instrumental in securing an excellent job for him, certain small things in our relationship hinted strongly that not everything was all right.

It did not take long before the reason came to light. During my two-year absence I had been exchanging letters with a young girl whom I had befriended before my departure for military service. Her letters had been warm and encouraging. Her mother and older sister had been very good friends of mine for the previous six years. I had been looking keenly forward to my return and courting her earnestly. A happy civilian life awaited me, I thought with confidence. Furthermore, I had expected that my return would draw Bruno and me even closer together.

I was sadly mistaken. In my absence Bruno also had become attracted to the girl. In fact, he fell in love with her. The situation became unbearable. It affected us deeply. The girl had become a beautiful young woman, although only sixteen years old. She was fully aware of our rivalry but did not find it necessary to make a decision one way or another. On the contrary, she seemed to enjoy keeping us in the dark.

Bitterness crept into our lives. Memories of our former brotherly love faded fast. We could not sleep or work. Our lives seemed shattered. A solution had to be found, because we could work together at the same place no longer. I knew one of us had to take a drastic step. It could only be myself. For Bruno to leave his job was, in my view, unthinkable.

One day, with a heavy heart, I decided to move on, leaving Bruno and the girl behind. I succeeded in securing for myself an important position in the Prague office of a major oil company. On a gray day I left the little mining town without even a handshake. As the small local train was leaving the station in the cold morning hour, the town slowly faded into the disstance and then disappeared behind the hills. The people whom I had loved were no longer a part of my life.

My Prague assignment brought great responsibilities to me. My duties consisted of preparing material for the agenda of several oil companies that were associated in a mutual oil cartel. My boss, a director of our company, attended the weekly sessions. Sometimes he asked me to accompany him. Later, when he was away traveling, I represented the company at such meetings.

My heavy responsibilities helped me to overcome, to some extent, my past disappointment, but sadness lingered in my heart. I spent some two years alone, without seeking friends. My work absorbed most of my thoughts, but inside I was filled with bitterness. Gradually, as time went by, I tried to look back at past events with a more open mind. Some doubts crept into my mind as to my attitude in the past. This must have happened to Bruno, too. In the meantime his company had also moved from the little town in Moravia to the capital city of Prague, while the mining operations remained, naturally, in the country.

One evening Bruno knocked at the door of my apartment. From the expression on his face I could feel that the peace offer he made to me came from his heart. At first I hesitated. It had been so long since we had parted that the man before me now was almost a stranger. It took several weeks during the coming weeks before we felt and acted like brothers again. Our grievances faded gradually away, and our brotherly relationship slowly reverted to what it had been prior to our feud. A great burden was taken off our chests. It would have been sad to continue living with bitterness in our hearts and disregard the tragic days we had spent together during World War I.

The girl who had been the cause of our grievances also had moved to Prague some time ago to pursue her studies. She lived with her relatives. I had seen them socially on several occasions, but not a word was spoken about the past. Later she married a physician, but the marriage ended in divorce. She seemed unable to settle down. A restless life and misfortunes followed her. Her son underwent an operation during which one of his legs had to be amputated. She herself was later stricken with breast cancer and operated on, but the disease finally took her life. Her mother, a friend of ours from the days we had worked in the mining town, was arrested by the Nazis years afterward as a Czech patriot and had to spend several years in a concentration camp. Her niece, Irena Barnášková, also our friend, later was beheaded by the Germans for having aided British and American airmen stranded in Czechoslovakia during the war. I learned about the execution from the official newspaper and had the sad task to inform the stricken family.

6

Back in 1938, after Hitler's Munich speech in which he launched a brutal verbal attack on Czechoslovakia and its democratic leaders, war seemed imminent. He demanded an immediate inclusion of the Sudeten border regions of Czechoslovakia into the German Reich, after a barrage of crude propaganda by his press and radio about Czech "atrocities" against the Sudeten Germans. Many books have been written about these tragic events and the Munich Agreement, which demonstrated to the world that none of the Western powers were prepared to go to war to save a "small country" and its democracy.

I was among the mobilized Czech units that were rushed to the assigned border sections in the fall of 1938. We marched day and night. At the start, our determination and enthusiasm were boundless, but they abated as we listened to the radio broadcasts describing the negotiations between Neville Chamberlain and Hitler. Soon it became obvious that at this critical moment we Czechs would have to face the huge German war machine alone, isolated from our former friends and allies. Prime Minister Chamberlain reasoned that a small, relatively unknown country should not be the cause of a war. Besides, he argued, Hitler's territorial demands were restricted to the small Sudeten border areas.

When all was over, only tears and a deep disappointment remained with us in the cities, villages, fields, and forests. Our friends had betrayed us. The morale among soldiers sank to a low point. Some of them felt it was utterly futile to continue carrying their arms and equipment.

We received orders from our government and the top military command to retreat from the border defense line in an orderly fashion so that the German troops might fill the evacuated strips of land. This meant falling back a number of kilometers every day. As we did so we watched with sadness the Germans advancing and occupying our strategically vital border areas.

In our retreat from the border my soldiers considered it a hardship to carry, under the sad circumstances, their arms and equipment. They would have been willing to dump them right there on the very spot, keeping only their light personal belongings. I, on the other hand, felt responsible for army property that, I thought at that time, we would have an occasion to use in later years. I made a fast decision. At my order a farm wagon was commandeered and loaded with all the arms, ammunition, and equipment that we could put together in haste. No horse or motorized vehicle was available at that section of the border. We solved the problem by pulling and pushing the vehicle up and down the long hills and through the villages toward the interior. We looked like emigrants from our own land. This was Sudeten territory. We were watched by its inhabitants who were standing alongside the road to greet the victorious German soldiers who were only a few kilometers behind us. Ours was a grotesque picture of an army beaten before even a single battle. But we kept our heads high. None of the onlookers made any sign of contempt.

As history has shown, Hitler did have additional territorial demands. As a start, in March of 1939, his troops moved to occupy what had been left of Bohemia and Moravia, the western regions of Czechoslovakia. It could not have been defended anyway after the surgery performed by the Nazis in 1938, with the acquiescence of our former friends and allies, that had left our country a crippled, diseased body without limbs. Slovakia, the eastern region, retained some kind of autonomy at the cost of becoming subservient to the Reich.

It was a cold and rainy March day in 1939 when tanks, camions and motorcycles loaded with heavily armed Germans drove through the streets of Prague. I stood on the pavement of Wenceslas Square among Czech citizens watching helplessly. These good, peace-loving people did not deserve such a cruel fate. In spite of the drama developing before their eyes, most of them still carried hope that evil would not prevail for long and that one day the country would be free again. Now, several decades later, it is sad to realize that they have not had a single day of freedom since Hitler marched into Prague. After him it was no longer fascism but an evil equally devastating and brutal: the communism of the Soviets.

In September of 1939 the Nazis crossed the Polish border. The country soon lay in ruins. Not to be shortchanged, the Soviets moved on Poland from the east, dividing the loot. A German-Soviet pact was concluded. It did not, however, prevent the Germans from invading the Soviet Union in June of 1941. The Polish and Soviet populations suffered indescribable hardships throughout the war. England and the United States fought the Nazis on the western and southern fronts, also sacrificing the lives of their soldiers. The heroic deeds of the seamen trying to supply the Soviets with badly needed war matériel through the icy northern waters of Europe and under constant threat posed by the great numbers of German U-boats, can never be forgotten.

In past history, countries have been occupied and conquered by foreigners, some of them at times of colonial expansions considered pioneering adventures and heroic deeds. Such consequests in past centuries often did not give rise to massive objections, although native populations were subjected many times to abuse and terror. The twentieth century, however, did not seem to have a place any longer for territorial conquests. And yet Hitler, in his thirst for power and world domination, supported by his initial successes in the Reich itself, decided that the moment was opportune to reach out and conquer, in order to fulfill the destiny providence seemed to offer him. His superior army, navy, and air force seemed to be guarantors of certain and infallible success.

During these trying times Bruno and I were drawn even closer together. Through friends in his company I met and subsequently fell in love with Georgine, a lovely and intelligent girl. She had graduated from a teachers college and was determined to pursue her career. However, in February 1940, only a few months after the German invasion of Poland, we got married, oblivious of how the war might affect our lives.

Our marriage was performed in the beautiful quaint chapel of Saint Mathias on the outskirts of Prague. The countryside was covered with glimmering snow. Georgine's and my relatives attended the romantic ceremony. For my father this was the first time he looked closely at my bride. In a familiar gesture he took her gently into his arms and then nodded to me, stating, "Good choice!" This pleased both Georgine and me very much. It added a spark to the touching ceremony.

Unfortunately, Georgine's mother had been confined to bed due to a serious illness. She could not witness the wedding in the chapel. At home, after the rites, Georgine and I held hands and knelt at her bed. With tears in her eyes she blessed us solemnly. Her good thoughts and wishes would carry us over many hardships during the years to come. She died only a few months later.

On June 29, 1941, one week after the Nazis marched against Russia, our son, Peter, was born. Georgine and I had walked to the maternity hospital through the darkened streets of Prague the night before. He was a tiny, premature baby. When I arrived the next morning, the nurse identified me as his father due to Peter's and my thin faces. It took Georgine a great effort over a number of years to overcome his fragile health and weight problems caused by the difficult wartime food supply conditions.

About three and a half years later, in December 1944, our second son, John, was born. On the night he was born, Allied airplanes bombed the city. Georgine and newly born baby John had to spend hours in an underground shelter, together with other patients and hospital staff.

Bohemia and Moravia remained occupied by the Germans for six years, until May of 1945. No nation or people who have never been overtaken and subdued by enemy administrators and soldiers can imagine the ordeal and persecution such an occupied territory must suffer. No words can properly describe the physical pain and mental anguish. It is not only the physical wounds inflicted upon the population, including food deprivation, enforcement of strange, brutal ordinances, widespread political arrests, and mass executions, but also—and perhaps mainly—the terrible mental pain and hopelessness that grip the whole nation. Ruthlessness and terror were called for against any who would dare to oppose the occupation. This was the situation that prevailed in Czechoslovakia for six long years.

All the industrial, commercial, and financial enterprises of any significance for the German war effort were transferred into the hands of German managers. Most of them came from the Reich, in spite of the fact that there were many capable Sudeten Germans, formerly Czech citizens, available. They had hoped that the important positions would be allotted to them as a reward for past efforts to be incorporated into the German "Fatherland." In the majority of cases they had to be content with lower assignments. They exercised, however, strong power over their Czech coworkers and made their lives utterly miserable. There was great unspoken hatred between the two groups.

The Czechs could now show their hatred openly. They expressed it mainly by way of passive resistance. The Germans were aware of it. They could not very well change it, but they would not tolerate any visible or spoken expression of resistance or dislike. There were many occasions when this required a good deal of willpower and self-control by the Czechs. They prayed and hoped for the smallest sign of German weakening on the battlefield. Instead, the first years brought only heartbreaking news. The fall of Poland, the invasion of France, and the fall of beautiful Paris, the country and city that had been cherished by the Czechs for decades, brought despair to them. The unceasing German air raids in the west and the victories in the east deepened the gloom.

On the other hand, each of these successes was the cause for celebration by the Germans in the country. Usually a speech by the Führer himself followed. Employees were ordered to assemble in plants and offices. They had to listen to the fiery speeches transmitted through loudspeakers. Only the German faces glowed with enthusiasm, admiration for their beloved Führer, and an unshakable conviction that the hour of final victory was at hand. When the German anthem concluded each speech, the Germans stood at rigid attention, with their right arms raised in the Nazi salute. For the Czechs who were forced to be present it was a time of desperation, depression, and mounting doubts that the German war machine could ever be stopped and freedom for their country restored. And when the German anthem was played the Czechs stood silently behind the rows of their German coworkers without raising their arms in salute. This was generally tolerated, with the exception of a few plants and offices where the German administration insisted on the Nazi salute.

In the Prague offices where I worked, my Czech friends and I quickly sneaked behind the rows of Germans whenever we were ordered to participate in the celebration of a victory. This helped us to hide our deep disappointment at the endless line of successes. On one occasion the whole Czech group around me, following my example, quietly left the room through the back door while the anthem was played. The consequences could have been serious. The German in charge of the company, a comparatively young lawyer from Hamburg who was lucky to avoid being sent to the front, had to display a strong disciplinary hand. He called me to his office and warned me of severe punishment. He was aware of the trust I enjoyed among the Czechs, so I had to think fast. I defended the group by stating that we had listened throughout the speech, but when it was over we considered it important not to waste any time away from our work. It was difficult for him to seriously object to my argument, as it was his duty to see to it that work for the war machine was interrupted as little as possible. At the same time he insisted, however, that this should never happen again in the future, as it would result in dire consequences for us. I suspect that he was anxious not to disturb his own cozy position with a possible investigation that would have involved the Gestapo. Had the man in charge of the company been a Sudeten German, this surely would have happened.

My responsibility in the company included a liaison between our oil refinery in Moravia and the German *Mineraloel Beauftragter* in Prague. His was a function established by the occupation authorities and could be loosely translated as "high commissioner for the oil industry." He was to see to it that the manufacturing, distribution, transportation, and storage facilities were utilized at their maximum capacity at all times. His demands were constantly accelerated or switched from one plan and process to another, in line with the military situation and needs or as the result of the bombing and destruction of some of the oil installations anywhere in the Reich or occupied territories.

After the meetings at the offices of the high commissioner I had to convey instructions to our plant which was run, naturally, by German engineers. Instead of instructing them under my signature that a certain action should be taken to implement an increase or a fast switch from one product to another I found a convenient way to circumvent my direct involvement. This I did so that in my written or telephone messages to the German plant management I always stated that "the commissioner desires" these actions be taken and that "he deems it essential" his instructions be followed. Throughout the war I got away with this tactic, which in fact was a way of shifting all the responsibilities that may have fallen on my Czech colleagues or me to the Germans. This was also a way of avoiding anything that would have tainted me as assisting the war machine.

This system also worked the other way around. Whenever there was a problem, such as nonfulfillment of the expected plant production, I conveyed the related explanations to the commissioner's staff as the plant management's answer, word for word.

Some of the lesser positions at the plant were occupied by Czechs, as the Nazis could not afford to replace all of them. The plant was comparatively old, with the exception of a few important additions and renovations undertaken by the Germans to boost the output of some high-quality lubricants needed for their planes and tanks. It was not unusual, therefore, to experience breakdowns or slowdowns in the old part of the plant. This always took some time to overcome, thus creating undesired shortages and disruptions in the commissioner's plans and expectations.

The repairs could not always be sped up, because essential replacement parts were unavailable at a short notice or could not be located due to the special sizes or material quality. It was understood among the

Czechs that to ensure that our "silent tactics" worked well without endangering our lives it was imperative that absolutely no leak occurred. Our group consisted of about two dozen unquestionably loyal people whose goal was the same as that of thousands of patriots at other plants and offices: namely, a clever sabotage of the industrial production to somewhat hasten the final German collapse. My group relied on my connections with the Prague resistance movement and on my keeping the group advised of preparations for the takeover of the offices and the plant when the time came. I had to travel to the plant from time to time. As the war progressed and the Allies began to demonstrate that their victory indeed could be won, our hopes gradually rose. Even so, we had to exercise extreme caution in our daily conversations and dealings, as the occupiers became even more ruthless when things did not go well any longer.

Every radio owner was ordered by the Germans to affix a notice on his radio set, a stern warning that listening to any foreign broadcast was punishable by death. At one critical point in their war efforts they even ordered the removal of the shortwave part of the sets. This did not prevent the Czechs from learning about important events through clandestine radios and word-of-mouth reports. Every morning, as soon as they arrived at their workplaces, they mutually exchanged the news they had learned during the night. This could only be done by whispers and when no German was around.

Travel to the plant now became more time-consuming and dangerous. A previous eight-hour trip by train now took twice or triple that time because of frequent Allied attacks on trains. Train engines were particularly vulnerable to attack by air. Once their numerous steam pipes had been damaged by "enemy aircraft," the engines had to undergo difficult and time-consuming repairs.

As soon as Allied aircraft approached, an alarm was sounded and the train, wherever it happened to be at that moment, had to be evacuated without delay. Even before it stopped, passengers leaped out of the carriages and ran as far as possible from the rails. The train continued only after the danger had passed and the passengers had slowly drifted back. The action always caused a delay of several hours. Whenever the Allied airmen succeeded in damaging the engine, a rather hopeless situation developed, since it was difficult to remove the engine from the tracks and replace it. The Germans were furious, but we enjoyed it tremendously despite the great inconvenience.

Only a few months before the end of the war did the Allies commence bombing the Czech oil installations. After several attacks on them, our plant in Moravia remained the only one still undamaged. One morning, finally, air-raid sirens sounded there. I happened to be at the plant on my monthly visit. The announcer stated that "enemy aircraft are approaching from the south." He then repeated at regular intervals the time margin remaining before a probable attack on our refinery would take place. Permission to leave had been officially fixed at five minutes, but when the time became shorter than ten minutes the manual workers and clerical employees, including myself, decided not to wait any longer. Everyone fled, either through the main gate if it was close to his working place or simply over the refinery fence to gain time. My close friends and I ran across the fields to an elevated place several hundred yards away from the plant. We hid inside a large drainage pipe under the road.

From there we could safely watch the coming attack, which was most welcome to us. While the American planes and their crews were the German's archenemies, we greeted them in our hearts as our best friends and heroes. We were extremely happy to hear the roaring noise of the bombers. They were now fast approaching. The first formation was already overhead. The whole sky vibrated under the power of their engines. Soon they started to descend in preparation for the attack. The noise was deafening. They had hardly reached our position when the first bombs fell with frightening whistles, followed by explosions. A tremendous crater opened before our eyes, between us and the plant. To our dismay, the first bomb fell not more than one hundred meters from us, leaving a gaping hole in the soft ground. Another one hit a brick kiln that was very close to our shelter. A few women who had been hiding there came running into our shelter, some bleeding from superficial wounds caused by flying brick fragments.

We gazed in disbelief. Numerous bombs were dropped thereafter. They caused tremendous shock waves, noisy explosions, and fires. Not at the refinery, which remained intact and unattacked, but in the town of Ostrava, some two kilometers away, which was devastated to a great degree. The loss of civilians and property was considerable. Our disappointment was painful. We could not understand why the mission had failed. The plant must have been easy to detect from the air, being situated away from the town and living quarters. Perhaps, we tried to convince ourselves, the bomber crews had been tired after hours of flying over enemy territory under heavy fire. Our only consolation was that the other oil refineries located in different parts of the country had been hit hard and rendered useless for some time.

A grave event shook the country in May of 1942. While the Nazi terror had been severe since the beginning of the occupation on a regular basis, this time it affected the whole nation at once, like lightning. It happened on a warm morning when two Czech commandos, who had been parachuted into the country with a few other men from England, succeeded in their mission to attack the German *Reichsprotektor,* Reinyard Heydrich. He was generally known as the ''Bloody Dog'' or ''Butcher of Prague.'' He was Hitler's favorite and Himmler's aide before he was appointed to the Reich's governor for the protectorate of Bohemia-Moravia. During the first three days of his bloody reign he put ninety patriots to death. Thousands of executions of workers and members of the intelligentsia followed upon the least suspicion of disagreement with the new German order or of sabotage. He also sent thousands upon thousands of Czechs and Moravians from the ranks of former political or civic leaders, as well as prominent personalities from every town and village, to concentration camps in order to remove them from the political scene. This included for instance, the former Lord Mayor of Prague, Dr. Peter Zenkl. (It is interesting to note that in spite of his six years suffering in Nazi jails he was later arrested by the secret police of the Communist ''liberation regime'' installed in Prague by the Soviets after the war.)

On that fateful spring day all hell broke loose. As Heydrich's chauffeured car had to slow down to make a sharp turn on his way to the offices at the historic Prague castle, one of the commandos got into a preselected position from which he could freely fire his automatic rifle at the Nazi staff car. In spite of all the careful preparations, the commando neglected to release the safety catch and failed to fire a single shot. A few painful seconds followed. In desperation, his compatriot tossed a hand grenade under the vehicle. The explosion mortally wounded the *Reichsprotektor.* Heydrich suffered from massive internal wounds. None of the specialists who were sent on orders from the Führer to attend to him were able to save his life. He died in agony a week later. Hitler, the Nazi officials, and the Gestapo were enraged. They ordered a nationwide manhunt for the assassins, who after their attack escaped on bicycles through the small side streets and across one of the bridges spanning the river Moldau.

When the news of the attack reached the nation the same afternoon, an ominous silence fell over Prague. A strict curfew from early evening until the morning hours was ordered. The military and the Gestapo were instructed to shoot without warning anyone found out in the open or even visible in a window after six o'clock in the evening.

I rushed home after work. Our apartment was empty. Georgine and our little son, Peter, had left for the country one week earlier. Food in the city had been so scarce that we thought our son had a better chance for survival in the village where a related family lived. Georgine's loving and courageous nature and her dedication to our family would be proven many times throughout the difficult years that followed. Without her love and devotion our family would not have survived as a unit during the trying times and upsets in our homeland and in the foreign, faraway lands. Our home, whether we lived in comparable luxury in Prague before we were hit with disaster or later in desolate and dirty camps, was always kept clean and afforded us badly needed comfort and security. Even when there was almost no food available, Georgine managed to put together a meal as if by a miracle. Politically she always stood with me, even if it meant persecution and suffering for her. We were aware that our lives could have been easier had we forced ourselves to pretend acceptance of Nazi doctrines and later of communist teachings. Through mutual love and support we kept our heads, ideals, and conscience high and clear. We were determined to do anything to bring up our children the same way and let them, in the years to come, taste freedom as fully as possible under the given circumstances.

Now, on the night of the assassination, I was alone in our apartment. Wartime regulations required a complete blackout in the streets. There was a standing order that no light could penetrate from the inside of the homes. Every window, therefore, was equipped with special drapes made from heavy dark material. In addition, to be on the safe side, we used only dim lighting in our home.

It was difficult to sleep. Also, it was out of the question to try to communicate with my brother or friends on the telephone. No matter what we would have talked about, even only mentioning the attack could have been interpreted by the authorities as condoning the events of that fateful day.

Toward midnight there was suddenly great activity on our street. Sharp orders in German and the noises of rolling and stopping vehicles echoed through the darkness. Obviously, the military and the Gestapo were conducting brutal searches from house to house. Our area was under suspicion of hiding the assassins, as we were less than two kilometers from where Heydrich had been hit. When the search units reached our building and the troopers rushed from door to door kicking them open, yelling and cursing, I thought the end had come for all of us. It was indeed the end of some of the building occupants. Among screams of those who were beaten up or otherwise mistreated I could hear vulgar shouts and commands by the officers and the Gestapo men.

Several people were dragged out of their beds and thrown into waiting vans. Some of them were taken because they could not, in their fright, promptly produce their identification papers or could not explain their presence in the flat, others were Jews who somehow had survived the previous waves of deportation to concentration camps, and still others were unfortunates who could not readily answer some questions. Any weapon found would seal the fate of its owner.

When the men reached our apartment I was near the door, which they pushed in with brutal force. I had not switched on the light in the entrance hall, for fear of possibly violating orders for total darkness. For this I could have paid dearly if the Nazis supsected foul play on my part. After cursing me, they pulled the switch and examined my face. My identification papers were in order. I had a card stating that I was a "National of the Protectorate Bohemia and Moravia." This differentiated the Czechs and Moravians from the Germans, who enjoyed special privileges.

They pushed me aside and made a brisk but thorough search of the apartment, looking at places where I could have hidden a weapon or even someone connected with the attack on Heydrich. The terrace and its overhanging roof were searched thoroughly. As luck would have it, only two weeks earlier I had hidden a pistol with ammunition in our apartment but then decided that it would endanger not only me but also my wife, Georgine, and Peter. With the pistol placed under the seat of Peter's pram, Georgine and I had pushed it toward the river embankment, which was paved with large rocks. We sat down on the bank, lifted Peter out of his pram, and took out the pistol, which I had wrapped in wax paper. Removing one of the rocks between us, we inconspicuously dug out a hole, placed the pistol in it, and covered it with the rock. I intended to come back one day to reclaim it at the appropriate time. I found out later that someone, hopefully a good patriot, had dug out the gun and removed it. If my pistol had been discovered by the search commandos that night, my family never would have heard of me again. My heart was pounding.

It was a great relief when they finally left. Although the building suddenly became quiet, the screams and cries sounded in my head for the rest of the long night, keeping me awake.

It was in the early-morning hours when salvos of rifle fire sounded in the distance. A period of indescribable terror began throughout the country. Every newspaper was ordered to publish every day, for more than a month, names of citizens who had been shot in connection with the assassination. On some days this included names of whole families, including infants, wives, parents, and grandparents. The fabricated reason for every execution: "Guilty of approval of the attack on the *Reichsprotektor*."

We were on the edge of a breakdown. Every morning we looked at lists of citizens and entire families who had been shot. Altogether this amounted to about two thousand souls! We could feel the torment of those condemned to see their innocent children, spouses, and other relatives await their deaths.

When among those executed appeared the name of someone who had been a friend or acquaintance this was even harder to accept. One day when I looked at the first page of my newspaper I recognized the names of eight former officers under whom I had served during my military training at the border. One of them was a major to whom, during our border exercises, I once had to make an oral report. In the darkness I erred, reducing his rank by oversight. For this he scolded me in front of the battalion, but later he called me to his quarters and joked about it. Now he was dead, together with his colleagues. His former rank made no difference any longer.

As part of the brutal retaliation, the Nazis wiped out an entire village, called Lidice, near Prague. Without proof, they accused its inhabitants of abetting the commandos sent from England to carry out Heydrich's assassination. All men over sixteen years of age were shot on the spot. The women were deported to Germany and the children scattered over the Reich to be brought up as true Germans. In my office, this caused great sadness. A German superior, a very well educated and seemingly gentle person, remarked to us, "This is war!" without feeling any remorse.

It took weeks before the commandos involved in the attack met their fate. In the meantime, photographs of a bicycle, a raincoat, and an attaché case were circulated among the population to review and perhaps recognize as having belonged to the two men or their sympathizers. The pictures with a stern warning were shown aboard trains and buses and in offices, factories, homes, and public place, including theaters, and parks. Those forced to view the photographs were ordered under penalty of death to declare whether or not they had ever seen or heard of the objects in question. Anyone who happened to have been close to the place of the attack and had witnessed it or had even only heard of it from his neighbor or friend or who had observed anything suspicious was commanded, again under penalty of death, to come forward immediately and make a detailed report to the Gestapo. This forced many to do so and sometimes involved their closest friends and acquaintances, as the latter ones might already have gone to the Gestapo out of fear for their own and their families' lives.

The terror was indescribable. Fear was spreading into every family. In spite of it, for a long time no one disclosed the location and the names of the group of men that had been sent over from England to perform the patriotic and dangerous assignment. They found shelter with and advice from the well-organized underground. Most of those who sheltered them at one time or another later lost their lives in retaliation. They included brave men, women, girls, and boys.

One day, after the daily executions of whole families had reached some two thousand persons, someone fearing for his life disclosed that a suspicious bicycle smeared with blood had been seen in the center of Prague on the day of the assassination. The Gestapo followed the lead like bloodhounds and finally found out that the bicycle, which had, in fact, been used by one of the attackers in his escape, had been removed and hidden by a young girl whose parents had been assisting the paratroopers hunted by the Nazis. She and her family were found by the Gestapo. All of them, as well as others who had assisted the group, in the end paid with their lives. The hunt was accelerated when one of the men who had been dropped from the plane missed a clandestine meeting with a representative of the underground. In desperation he walked aimlessly in the streets, unable to find a safe hiding place. He knocked at a few doors, but those who heard his plea were scared to death to offer him shelter. They took a grave risk for not reporting it to the Gestapo. The man continued drifting through the streets. He knew he could not stay in the open any longer without looking suspicious. In desperation, he finally went to the Czech police station. The Gestapo was informed without delay. They had no difficulty finding out the names of his friends and the details of their mission. While he had no knowledge of their hideout, his information was very valuable to the Gestapo, and it hastened the end of the men involved. After the war this man was condemned to die for his betrayal by the newly established Czech government.

The underground leaders became desperate in their efforts to find a suitable and safe hiding place for the group, as their ranks were diminishing due to arrests and executions. One day a seemingly good solution was found. The group was clandestinely transferred to an old church in the center of town, not far from the river Moldau. There in the cellars were numerous crypts and recesses carved out of solid rock. Only a small opening from the center of the church floor offered a way down into the crypts. The sole light reaching down to the cellars came from an opening about twenty by forty centimeters leading to the street level on the side of the church.

For several days everything worked out well. Food and messages were supplied to the group through the parish office above. The calm did not last, however. In another part of Prague among those arrested was a teenage boy whose parents were directly involved in hiding the group. At first he resisted for hours, but the brutal interrogation and torture by the Gestapo proved finally beyond his strength. Now the whole Nazi administration and the Gestapo, together with the armed forces stationed in the city, went to work.

I was in my office, only a few minutes away from the church. Drawn by an unusual activity in the center of town, I moved closer to the church area, not knowing that it had become a hideout for the patriots. When other curious people and I came closer we were stopped by a cordon of elite SS German men standing, with their arms drawn, around the city block in the center of which was the church. We could not see the church clearly but soon deduced what this was all about. The sounds of exploding hand grenades and shells fired in rapid bursts told us the story. It was the hour of truth for the brave men inside the church.

From the reports that reached us later we learned that it took the Germans many hours to put an end to the drama. The first battle took place in the upper part of the church, where two of the men had been positioned. The Nazi losses were numerous, as the patriots occupied advantageous positions. When the resistance in the inner church finally ceased with the death of the two men, the next step for the Germans was to penetrate down to the crypts. Orders were given to several soldiers. Each of them lost his life as soon as he tried to slide down the rope suspended for such a purpose. Then an appeal was made for volunteers. Only a few diehards raised their hands. They, too, met a sudden death in their effort. Soon a pile of bodies lay on the floor below the opening. The soldiers had been easy targets for those hiding in crypts and around corners. A barrage of hand grenade explosions followed from the top. This, too, had no effect. No more volunteers could be recruited by the Nazis. The deadlock was most embarrassing to the hundreds of armed men equipped to the teeth who had been charged with the liquidation of the resistance. After several hours of shooting that had brought no victory, the deputy *Reichsprotektor,* Frank himself, arrived at the scene.

The resisters were aware that this could not last forever. Their ammunition could not last too much longer. Under no circumstances would they fall into Nazi hands. That would have meant torture and certain death. Their end came when after a heroic battle the Germans successfully flooded the crypts and further defense proved impossible. Only then did the resisters point their guns at their own heads or hearts.

The nation was saddened and shocked by the events. Thereafter deportations and executions continued on a regular basis, even if at somewhat a lesser degree. The brutal actions left deep wounds and resentment in the minds of the nation. A hatred of everything that was German was now ingrained in every citizen. It grew larger with every day of occupation. Punishment for the crimes must come one day, they swore to themselves. Later, during the first few days after the war, when lawlessness prevailed in the cities and villages, they kept their resolution.

When the tide of war began turning in favor of the Allies, the citizens' faces brightened. Their desperation and depression began to vanish. Great expectations could be read in their eyes. Good news arriving through broadcasts from abroad spread like wildfire. The occupiers' faces grew longer. They mirrored a serious doubt as to the possibility of a Nazi victory, in spite of the unceasing official propaganda to the contrary.

7

After Hitler's suicide even the die-hard Germans in the company realized and accepted the fact that the end of their dreams for world domination had come. Pretending to go on official business visits, they headed toward the western border of the country and across to Germany. There, with the U.S. troops rapidly moving eastward, these Germans hoped to find some measure of protection. The Soviets moving in from the east would treat them mercilessly. The Germans aimed for towns they had lived in before they had been appointed administrators in occupied territories.

The others who had occupied positions of lesser importance and had not committed openly harmful acts against the Czechs stayed. During the war they, too, had dreamed of the important positions they would be awarded upon victory. Their cheer on occasions of Hitler's triumphs in France and North Africa, on the seas, and in Eastern Europe now changed into disappointment and deep melancholy. The more moderate ones now openly expressed their resignation to the approaching, and for them unfortunate, outcome of the war.

The time appeared ripe to me to begin preparing for an orderly transfer of the company's management to the prewar executives. The company's owners were residing somewhere abroad, out of reach of the occupiers. Their actual whereabouts were unknown. Making contact with them was not feasible. A few former managers had escaped before the German armies entered the country in March of 1939; others had been imprisoned in concentration camps. While we were anxiously awaiting liberation, we were apprehensive as to the political and economic conditions that would prevail or be forced upon us after the war. In any event, developments proved that the re-installation of former company and plant owners and their previous executives and trustees following the end of the war would not be permitted.

The British Broadcasting Corporation, whose daily news and announcements now circulated among the Czechs almost freely, made it clear that the wartime Czechoslovakian government in exile in London had been concerned that the political and economic system after the war would have to be quite different from the one that had prevailed prior to the Nazi occupation. This ultimately proved to be true. As we then learned, the members of the exile government, who had spent six years in England organizing and preparing for the official takeover of the country's affairs in the spirit of traditional democratic principles, had suddenly been called to Moscow. It was officially announced from there that the Czechoslovakian industries, businesses, and private enterprises in general would be nationalized. The political system would be such as to conform with the interests of the Soviets, in whose area of interest and influence the country would fall. This was in conformity with the decision made at a conference among Stalin, Churchill, and Roosevelt. Only years later it became known that a member of the American entourage had, in fact, been working actively to please the Soviets. The result of the conference caused horrible pain and suffering in many European nations and to millions upon millions of decent, freedom-loving citizens.

The changes that had been announced as to the future of the nation strongly occupied my mind. Surely, I reasoned to myself, this was something to be concerned with in planning from an organizational viewpoint. Several democratic countries had previously nationalized some of their important industries and enterprises. In our own country the railway and postal services had always been state enterprises. This, I thought, should not cause any undue hardship to the nation and its citizens. In any event, I speculated, the executives who had been persecuted by the Nazis would be able to return and resume their former positions. All the regular employees, I thought, would be able to continue their work without interruption, although they would be working for the government rather than for the prewar owners. However, these thoughts seemed insignificant in comparison with the overwhelming expectation that the country would soon be free from Nazi occupation and that it would renew its traditional role among decent and civilized countries.

In my company I was respected as the leader of the clandestine resistance against the Nazis dominating our industry. My close friends and confidants and I had managed throughout the war to slow down production in our plant while, at the same time, the Germans had to be led to believe that efforts were being made to maximize output. This required constant dangerous and skillful maneuvering and also kept us in perpetual fear that our game would be discovered, bringing disaster upon us and our families.

Throughout the war I had kept in touch with a certain Smejkal, an executive director of the large Zivno Bank. He had been on the board of directors of my company before the conflict and was expected to rejoin the board as soon as the war was over. In clandestine meetings I shared with him all the information I had access to through my company and my personal contacts. This included interesting items I had learned in meetings with partisans in the other Czech oil companies. Smejkal, in turn, kept me informed of political events and plans for the future to which he had access through his important underground connections. Our agreement was that I would be ready at any given moment to receive from the underground specific instructions pertaining to my sector of responsibility.

On Saturday, May 5, 1945, as soon as the city awoke, the certainty that the end of the war was near could be felt in the air. U.S. forces were making rapid advances. They were expected at the outskirts of Prague momentarily.

I rushed to the Zivno Bank early in the morning. Director Smejkal was already in his office. Excited men and women kept coming to his desk. After short exchanges of words and handshakes they were leaving with specific instructions pertaining to their roles in the coming hours. Smejkal's telephone was ringing constantly. He kept busy giving short instructions or personal advice. Due to pressure of time he could not spend more than a few moments with me. The forthcoming nationalization of industries and businesses would adversely affect our previous plans that had been under careful consideration and preparation for months. However, we agreed that we would have to improvise for the moment.

He asked me to return to my company without delay, take over its affairs, protect its assets, and see to it that management would be handed over, if possible, to the prewar senior executive, who had been interned by the Nazis for the last five years but who should be available at any moment. In fact, the executive concerned had at that moment already arrived in Prague, having taken advantage of the growing confusion in the political detention camps caused by powerful armies moving into Central Europe from both east and west. Smejkal also told me that he had received reliable information that U.S. tanks on their drive from the west had reached an area not more than two hours from the city. Consequently, he added, the plan for the long-awaited uprising against the occupiers had arrived. His friendship, patriotism, and dedication to our roles in the events before us gave me full confidence that I would not fail in what I had to do.

I learned only later during that fateful day that Smejkal died two hours after I had talked to him. On his way to the Prague radio station, which had been occupied the same morning by Czech patriots, he was struck by a German bullet, not far from the Gestapo headquarters.

Having left the bank, on rushing to my office I observed that the city was already in turmoil. Excitement about the approaching liberation could be sensed on every street. Citizens rushed to comply with instructions that had long been in preparation by underground cells. I saw several German officers being stripped of their handguns. They protested strongly, but to my surprise, violence was avoided as they surrendered their weapons. A streetcar full of German militiamen, who had been sent out by their units to protect the safety of their countrymen, was stopped by citizens demanding their rifles. The men appeared greatly confused. They looked at each other, not capable of deciding one way or the other. A few of them were ready to shoot it out, but the majority hesitated. Taking advantage of their momentary weakness, the patriots ordered them off the streetcar and stripped them of all their arms. Other civilians rushed to the scene and eagerly received the available rifles and ammunition. The wave of the Prague uprising was no longer under control.

Upon arrival at my office I called my loyal friends together to share with them Smejkal's instructions. Then I designated one of the senior members of the staff to take the necessary steps to ensure the return of the company's former top executive who had arrived from the detention camp but had not yet joined us. The Germans working in the company had not come to the offices that day. I also made arrangements through the limited communication means available to have the company's assets, particularly our oil refinery in Moravia, protected as well as possible. I myself intended at first to stay in my office, but events outside in the street were happening so fast that I could not remain inactive. We were all gripped by the excitement of the hour, just as every other true Prague citizen was at this historic moment. My closest friends decided to follow me, go out into the open, proceed to a previously designated arms cache on Spalena Street, and take part in the uprising.

No one had any doubts that this would be a rather short demonstration and that after six long years of suffering and underground preparation we were ready to contribute to the liberation—if only in a small way.

As my group proceeded through the narrow streets leading to Spalena Street we were suddenly stopped by a burst of machine-gun fire on Jungmann Street. We hastily took whatever cover was available but kept moving forward slowly. We finally took refuge in a passageway of one of the buildings. It was lined with small, elegant shops. Here we felt reasonably secure, at least for the moment. To find out what was going on, I crawled forward on the dirty ground in my light-colored raincoat, which I had earlier tightened with a belt around my waist to look like a true revolutionary. A few meters to the left from the entrance to the passageway was an immobilized truck that was being fired upon from the opposite building. I recognized the structure immediately, having walked by it many times before. It was the Prague headquarters of the famous Skoda armament works. Its importance obviously called for the presence of the Nazi military.

On closer inspection of the truck I recognized that it carried a light machine gun on its open platform and a great deal of ammunition. There were also some rifles protruding from under a gray blanket. Crouching behind the front wheel, out of reach of the gunfire coming from the Skoda building, was a young man. With his left hand he was making efforts to bandage his badly wounded right wrist. His face twisted in pain as he signaled to me that his hand had been smashed by gunfire from the building. He was fortunate to have managed to jump off the vehicle and take temporary shelter behind its wheels. He pointed to the machine gun on the truck, which he insisted must be saved at any cost. His injury prevented him from doing so himself.

The young man expressed sadness for not being able to use the gun that he had been hiding in his partisan group throughout the war. He asked me by way of signals if I knew anything about weapons. I nodded, to his relief. My two-year prewar compulsory training in the Czech army now bore fruit. I was quite familiar with the various weapons that I had to use during military service. In fact, during maneuvers we had used live ammunition in our machine guns, firing tracer bullets only inches above the heads of infantrymen advancing before us. I instantly recognized the weapon on the truck as the light Z machine gun, a very effective and easy-to-handle gun. It was only slightly heavier than an infantry rifle. Each magazine had twenty bullets that could be fired singly or in bursts.

I made a fast decision. As soon as the firing from the opposite building abated, I jumped out of my shelter. With a few short leaps I reached a safe spot behind the rear wheel of the truck. Several seconds later I lifted my head cautiously to pinpoint the exact location of the gun and ammunition. Then, with all the determination and speed I could muster, I leaped over the edge of the truck's platform, grabbed the gun and several magazines, and swiftly landed back on the ground behind the wheel. The firing from across the street intensified for a while, then subsided. I signaled to my friends in the passageway to make room for my return. They moved farther back, leaving an opening for me. Pressing the gun and ammunition against my body, I leaped forward as forcefully as I could and reached safety.

None of my young friends were familiar with any weapons of the former Czech army, since it had been disbanded six years ago. Even I was somewhat doubtful of my ability to handle the weapon without refreshing my memory. To do so, I went down on the ground, loaded the machine gun, and fired a few single shots. It worked. As there were no other suitable targets, I aimed at a newspaper displayed in the window of a tobacconist's shop, which was now deserted. My boldness surprised me, as I had always considered myself a law-abiding citizen respecting private property. For the first time that day I realized that the uprising had abruptly affected my sense of material and even human values. Suddenly I became a participant in happenings in the midst of which I found myself without perhaps my own actions. I was being carried along by the wave of the coming liberation from the oppression and fear that had been reigning for the past six years.

Shots were now heard inside the Skoda building. It seemed that the Czechs working there were able to engage the Germans in a skirmish. Someone opened the entrance gate. Two civilians armed with rifles signaled to me to come to their assistance. I nodded in agreement and ran across the street into the now-open building. Martin, the partisan whose machine gun I now carried, followed me shortly. Despite his serious wound, he stayed with me for the duration of the uprising. On the ground floor of the building he received attention at an improvised first-aid station.

I placed my gun strategically over a low partition overlooking a long corridor from which a wide staircase led to the upper floors. After a short exchange of fire, several Nazi officers leaped across the narrow corridor onto the stairs while one of them covered the others with rifle fire. They all escaped to the higher levels of the building. Soon thereafter they were disarmed by the Czechs who were determined to defend the building during the coming hours until the first U.S. tanks arrived from the west. My presence was no longer needed.

Martin and I proceeded in the direction of the center of the city. We reached the main plaza, Wenceslas Square, without incident. We passed a film crew taking shots of the uprising events. They asked us to retreat several steps and then advance again so that they could get a good view of us, civilians, carrying a gun with the intention to take part in the uprising. We willingly obliged. Sporadic shots were being fired in the adjacent streets. On several spots fires were lit to burn Nazi pictures, books, and propaganda material. Flags with swastikas were added for good measure. Czechoslovakian flags were hoisted on some buildings, but some houses appeared lifeless, with all doors and windows shut. Their occupants were uncertain as to the reaction of the Germans, who were still masters of the city. In fact, more and more retreating troops arrived in the city as Americans from the west and Soviets from the east and north kept advancing. A substantial number of the Germans belonged to the elite SS formations. They had six years of intense fighting on various fronts behind them. No wonder that the Prague citizens who had felt their iron fist during the occupation feared them immensely. Some of them dared to peek at the SS men only from behind window curtains.

It was now noon and a beautiful day. It could not have been nicer for the occasion of greeting the first U.S. tanks, which we were convinced would arrive momentarily. And if not the tanks, U.S. warplanes should have been seen over the city to assure us that our Western friends were at hand. Gradually a painful thought began creeping into our minds: what if the Americans should for some reason be delayed or stop their advance?

At first, we dismissed our fears. We could not imagine that we would be left abandoned at this critical historic hour, to be exposed to the brutality of the SS troops. But as time went on, this proved to be the case. We felt suddenly alone, although the uprising was gaining momentum and could no longer be stopped. More doors and windows throughout the city closed. Those who still had an opportunity to retreat to their homes did so in haste whenever the situation permitted. Families tried to gather their members to be together during the uncertain hours to come.

Fortunately, Georgine and our two little sons, Peter and John, were in the country. I had no means of communicating with them or comforting them. I was alone in the city, separated from them, and suddenly thrust into events over which I no longer had control.

After lingering for some time at Wenceslas Square we heard a burst of machine-gun fire from the vicinity of the Central Post and Telegraph offices on Jindrisska Street, one of the thoroughfares crossing the square. The square itself was now almost empty when shots rang out from some buildings and their roofs. Their origin could not be determined. There was no longer a clear distinction between friend and foe. Any shot could have come from either one. The echoes resounded from the buildings around the square, making it impossible to pinpoint the direction from which single shots had been fired. It became clear, however, that after their first surprise and confusion in the earlier-morning hours the Germans had regained confidence and were proceeding to reinforce their hold on the city.

Renewed shooting sounded from the vicinity of the Central Post and Telegraph Office Building. Martin and I decided to investigate. We could no longer stay in the open square. It was an impressive structure: the communication center not only of Prague but of the whole country. Aside from major government buildings, the Central Post Office, the Central Railway Station, and the Radio Building were usually the principal structures in most European capitals. The Prague Post Office handled not only a great volume of mail but also all the telephone lines connecting the country and foreign lands. During the war it was the key point for communications between government institutions and civilians and, to a great extent, for contacts between the various government military units. It also took care of a great number of money transfers on a daily basis, because payments of all sorts were done by means of postal orders. Private checking accounts in banks were not at all common. Without these services, communications and the nation's life in general would slowly come to a standstill.

The Czech postmaster general in charge of this important center did not greet us with enthusiasm. Being fully responsible for keeping operations in perfect order, he was very vulnerable should any damage occur to the building or its precious equipment. Any act of sabotage that he did not try to prevent with all means at his disposal would mean his immediate execution, particularly at this time, when the German government and troops in the city greatly depended on uninterrupted services. Observing that I was armed and that my partisan friend had a bloody bandage attached to his wrist, the postmaster declared categorically that as long as he was in charge no one was going to use any weapon in the building. Many of the postal workers, however, expressed satisfaction on seeing us. It must have given them a token of security at a time when shots were ringing in all directions. I assured the postmaster that I was taking over the responsibility for the building. He meekly objected, but I could sense that he accepted my decision with a certain degree of relief.

I ordered the main gate, made of wrought iron, and all side doors leading into the building be locked immediately. Volunteers were posted at all strategic places.

An ominous silence was falling over the city. The joyful expectation expressed earlier that day had disappeared from the faces of its citizens. With a few exceptions the streets were empty. From time to time someone inched his way cautiously along the buildings, using every door or niche for cover from stray or direct bullets. Streetcars and buses ran no longer. Not many cars operated during the war, but now they were nonexistent. If a motor vehicle showed up at all, it sped through the streets and one could be sure it carried German officers, soldiers, or Gestapo men. This was the hour of truth. The city began to feel the impact of events.

U.S. tanks that had driven as close to the city from the west as twenty kilometers not only discontinued their drive but also followed orders, as we learned from the revolutionary headquarters, to withdraw a considerable distance westward, so that the Soviets would not be offended. After the bitter disappointment at Munich in 1938 this was another Czech tragedy to which the free world leaders had given their seal of approval. This time it was not for Hitler's benefit but to please another bloody dictator: Joseph Stalin.

A life-or-death situation now existed between the citizens and the Germans. Any armed citizen felt an obligation to take advantage of it, as otherwise he would become a target himself. Individuals were forced to make a fast decision: try to withdraw to the safety of their homes and families there, awaiting the outcome of this uncertain and dangerous situation, or join the dedicated patriots in their fight against the occupiers knowing that although the end of the war was near, lives could be lost during the last hours of the conflict.

Gradually it became clear which buildings or parts of the city remained in the hands of the patriots and which had developed into a stronghold of the occupiers. In some sectors the situation could not be clearly defined. Some basements may have been held by Czechs while the upper floors and or roof was occupied by Germans, or the other way around. The situation became further confused as firing increased. A shadow behind a curtain was sufficient reason for a sniper to send a bullet through the glass pane. Some civilians rushing home were caught by stray bullets or well-aimed shots from unknown windows, balconies, or roofs. In some instances Germans hurled hand grenades from upper floors down on passersby sneaking along the buildings. There was no mercy to those who were caught unprepared or by surprise, friend or foe.

With the danger spreading over the city, in their shelters people prayed and hoped for survival of their families. A growing number of determined citizens, however, gathered whatever arms they could put their hands on. They manned strategic positions throughout the city, including the bridges across the river Moldau. Some had received instructions from the provisional resistance headquarters, others simply followed their instincts or common sense. They elected their leaders sometimes on the spot, positioning themselves in familiar areas or wherever they could be of best service. Gradually these groups made contact with one another either by telephone or through messengers, many of whom were to lose their lives in their assignments. The post office was able to render invaluable assistance by acknowledging and relaying messages and by advising group leaders when, where, and how to get in touch with their neighbors and resistance cells.

I concluded that the reason for having been thrust into the middle of these events was not so much courage as having tasted the strong air of approaching freedom that had prevailed that morning in the city. This was due to the unfortunately false news of an early arrival of the first U.S. tank units and the comparatively bloodless initial actions of the citizens. I had always wanted to be on the side of the just and honest. Now I felt good that I had not betrayed my principles. I could not, however, help having great concern about my family. Georgine, with our four-year old son, Peter, and six-month old John, seemed to be comparatively safe at our uncle's home in the small village where they could get better food than in the starved-out city, but it was difficult to estimate what might happen when the Soviet soldiers reached the village from the east.

The Czechs had taken over the main radio station, situated about a kilometer from the post office. They now regularly broadcast the latest news. We kept listening attentively. In the beginning the announcer had been as optimistic as we had been about the Americans, but as time went on he could no longer hide the truth from us. He urged the citizens to stand up against the occupiers, to fight them whenever and wherever opportune, and to build as many barricades in the streets of Prague as the available material would permit. He also warned about the rapid buildup of strongholds by the Germans, who were applying their well-known precision and organizational talents to this end. In a dramatic manner the announcer began to appeal to the Allies at regular intervals in English, Russian, and French. He desperately called for help in the struggle. Prague was only minutes away from the nearest Allied units by plane, but the appeals for assistance remained unanswered.

In the post office we got ready for whatever might come. I ordered that telephone lines connecting any government offices or their operations be cut off. The same was done with units of the German military command posts. Although they would have access to substitute means of communications such as shortwave radios, our action would cause them considerable confusion or, at least, hamper their operations.

A small committee was formed and made responsible for food supplies and sanitary services. This was essential, as the several hundred postal workers could no longer leave the building. Provisions had to be secured for their stay, the duration of which could hardly be estimated at the moment. A hidden passage leading from the cellar to a neighboring hotel was found and secured. The front of the hotel faced Wencelas Square, and the rear was connected with the post office. A makeshift kitchen to provide soup, warm beverages, and simple meals got under way.

Martin and I had to make a decision as to a plan of action. From the window of the upper floor we surveyed the two streets merging at the corner of the building, Jindrisska and Panska. About two hundred meters to the right, on Panska, stood the imposing structure called the Petschka Palace, which had been converted into Prague's Gestapo headquarters at the outset of the war. A young SS officer was standing in front of the palace, partly obscured by an entrance pillar. Because of our difficult firing angle he was out of reach of our gun, although we would have liked to aim at him, remembering the thousands of Czechs who had been tortured or lost their lives at the hands of the Gestapo.

Closer to our view, also to the right but diagonally across the street, was the National Bank building. The Germans had put in effect emergency measures to protect strategic buildings in the city. The National Bank was guarded by three men in uniforms. They did not belong to the SS units but nevertheless presented considerable danger to the post office and its employees. If they were to be reinforced, which we suspected could happen at any moment, an attack on the post office could be expected at any time.

Martin insisted without hesitation that I open fire on the three men at once. Although shots were being fired at this point with increasing intensity all over the city, I could not easily overcome my strong resistance to firing at human beings. I forced myself to remember the faces of my friends and acquaintances who had been executed by the occupiers in cold blood and the thousands of others who had lost their lives either in the Gestapo building, in front of the firing squads, or in concentration camps. I recalled that whole families, parents, grandparents, and even small children had been wiped out under the pretext that one of the family members had aided the enemy or approved of the assassination of Heydrich, the Butcher of Prague.

We opened the window overlooking the National Bank. I prepared the machine gun and aimed at the three men stationed at the entrance. The angle was somewhat difficult, as their position was below me and to the right. Martin became impatient with me when I hesitated to pull the trigger. Several postal workers who stood close behind us also urged me to fire. I realized that I could no longer stall, but in my desperate effort not to waste lives I shouted at the Germans across the street. They lifted their heads and listened. I urged them to lay down their rifles within ten seconds, failing which I would fire. I shouted as loudly as I could in German, counting slowly to ten. The men pointed their rifles in our direction, but their position behind the entrance structure was as disadvantageous as ours.

At the sound of "ten" a burst of bullets left my gun. Two men fell to the ground wounded. The third man quickly took cover inside the bank. A short while later the two wounded men were dragged inside by their comrades. The bank's big door remained closed from then on. The street along the bank was now deserted except for the lone officer on duty at the Gestapo building.

The post office was now firmly under our control. It was time to move on. I made sure that the building would not lack a determined defense and command post. This was facilitated by the arrival of a number of new men with arms. One of them, later identified as Captain Elias, took charge when I transferred my duties to him. At that time no one was concerned about the political affiliations of the men risking their lives for the common cause. It would have made no difference had he told me that he had been sent by the communist underground movement that had kept itself separated from the mainstream and received orders from abroad. This I learned only later.

Together with Martin I scanned Jindrisska Street, which ran parallel to the entrance. To the left, a short distance away, we could see a small section of the now-empty Wencelas Square. To the right, about a hundred meters away, the street was dominated by a tall, imposing stone tower that had been there for hundreds of years. It appeared to have been planted right in the center of the street, but this was an optical illusion. In fact, before touching the tower the street split into two parts, one circling the structure to the left, the other to the right. Whoever controlled the tower would be the master of the entire street, with its post office, including the section of Wencelas Square into which the street led.

Somewhere between our position and the tower, on the left side, was a narrow alley called Nekazanka, well known to me from my frequent strolls through the inner city. At the far end on the right side of Jindrisska, obscured from our view, was the Catholic church, of which the tower was a part. Also to the right were the quarters of a small contingent of Czech police forces who, like their colleagues all over the country, were entrusted by the Germans with keeping law and order. In numerous cases the police had helped Czech patriots to cover up anti-Nazi activities. They were all considered absolutely loyal to the cause of the nation. On the other hand, they had no choice but to denounce their fellow citizens, as they themselves would have risked their own and their families' lives when there was no other way out.

Having surveyed the situation through the windows, I sat down for a while to gather my thoughts. Notwithstanding the constant sound of shots coming from all directions, my situation still seemed unrealistic. I would not have dreamed of standing up to the Gestapo or the soldiers openly had it happened only yesterday. This was even more true with respect to the dreaded SS storm troopers. Their presence in the country demanded blind obedience to the Nazi cause from the Germans and fearful respect from the Czechs. A wrong smile, an uncalled-for gesture, the exchange of news about German retreats on the fronts, an act of sabotage, or an unfriendly expression related to the occupiers would have meant immediate arrest and, in most cases, execution. Today, only twenty-four hours later, I was in an open rebellion against them. It dawned on me only now that if caught I would have no chance of survival. It was too late to turn the clock back.

With a gesture of urgency, my friend Martin woke me from my deep thoughts. He insisted that it was again time to go on. He pointed to the tower, stressing that this would be an excellent vantage point. From its top we could not only overlook a great portion of the inner city but also observe some more distant areas around and beyond the river. We would also have control of the side streets around the tower and the post office.

I nodded that I was ready to move on, thereby shedding any last bit of hesitation that had still lingered in my heart. Before leaving the building I made several telephone calls. I called my brother, Bruno, to learn about his safety at home and to assure him of my well-being and plans. I also telephoned my stepsister, Melitta, who had decided to stay in the city office of the company she worked for. My father, who lived with his third wife in the country, did not have a telephone. I had no means to get in touch with him.

The sentry opened the iron gate of the post office. We stepped into the deserted street. Every building looked suspicious, but the street leading to the tower appeared lifeless. We inched our way toward the tower, keeping close and almost glued to the walls of the buildings. I clutched the machine gun under my arm, its muzzle pointed to the ground. About halfway to our destination our hearts almost stopped in disbelief and shock. Right at the foot of the tower, which we had hoped to reach within minutes, a line of uniformed men had suddenly formed across the width of the street. And then six SS officers with drawn pistols, intermingling with a half a dozen Czech policemen, began moving in our direction, their goal apparently being to impress the civilian population in this area.

This was an unreal situation. Next to every German in his grayish-green uniform was a Czech police officer in his dark blue outfit. Our momentary confusion was complete. Facing the approaching enemy would have called for my throwing myself to the ground, loading the machine gun in haste, and firing. I could not and, in fact, did not do so. How could I fire at any Czech policeman who during the war had suffered as much as we did?

There was no time for logical thinking. Our confusion and fright dictated we avoid a confrontation, if still possible. The nearest exit was Nekazanka Street to the left. We could not turn back, so we leaped into that street, running virtually for our lives, with the gun partially hidden under my raincoat. We expected a burst of bullets aimed at us, but nothing of that sort happened. The men in uniform either did not observe that I was armed or they realized that from that distance they could hardly hit a fast-moving object with their pistols. It was a great relief that shots had not been exchanged, for it would have caused me nightmares all my life had any Czech policeman lost his life.

Upon arriving breathless at Nekazanka we stormed into the first open door at the corner building. We were concerned that the SS officers would follow us momentarily. We locked the door and barricaded it with pieces of furniture that we found in the entrance hall. When nothing happened in the next few minutes we went upstairs and found ourselves in the well-known Prague café the Dutch Mill. Surveying the street below, we saw the German and Czech officers patrolling it on their way back to the tower. This was a momentary relief but also a warning that the Germans were serious in their efforts to control the city, including our sector.

We watched the officers until they reached the vicinity of the tower. The Czechs then returned to their quarters, which now were almost opposite our hideout. The Germans disappeared to the right of the tower and took up stations on the upper floor of the church. One of the occupants of our building lent me a pair of binoculars. It was still early in the afternoon and the sunlight was bright, so I could recognize soldiers behind every curtain of the church windows. I also observed that there was a guard at one of the openings at the top of the tower and several more on its ground floor. We realized now how lucky we had been in having been stopped by the line of officers before we ever could reach the tower, as we had no idea earlier that it and the parish represented an awesome stronghold of the enemy.

The Dutch Mill café had, on the second floor, two alcoves reaching into the street. They permitted me, whenever it seemed safe, to scan the street in both directions and observe any action taking place there. The tower was on my left, the square on my right. Between my position and the square was the post office with its iron gate. We found ourselves now halfway between the post office and the tower with the church. The latter was held by a considerable number of SS men, while the post office was in the hands of the patriots. There was a question in my mind as to the key position we were occupying. If the SS men were to launch an assault at the post office from the tower, it would be our duty to try to stop them before they could reach the iron gate and force their entry with hand grenades.

With this in mind I telephoned Elias, who was now in command of the post office building, and advised him of our position and determination to assist to the best of our ability. I also gave him my estimate of the strength of the SS troops, adding that their attack could probably be expected.

We started to prepare for the defense of the Dutch Mill. We went through the whole building to familiarize ourselves with the layout. The occupants were notified that we were taking over the building for defense purposes and were asked to move into the basement, which they did without protest. They took with them blankets, pillows, and some simple pieces of furniture to make it more habitable. Each of them brought some food and personal belongings. All in all about thirty inhabitants moved down into the cellar and established themselves there as best as they were able to do. Among them was a middle-aged German man in civilian clothes. He was frightened. No one dared any longer to go out into the streets, where friends and enemies faced the same danger of being shot at. The German was uncomfortable, as he was to spend the next days and nights among the Czechs. He withdrew to a dark corner and kept to himself. He might have been a decent man who did not approve of German atrocities during the war, but he could also have been one of the brutal members of the dreaded Gestapo with innocent lives on his conscience.

The German did not exchange a word with the others. He was tolerated there, but it was an awkward situation. My leadership in the building assured him of safety while he remained with us. Whatever his past might have been, none of us ever found out. In any event, he must have been glad that he had found comparative safety in the basement while the exchange of gunfire in the streets above raged with increasing intensity. He could not know that a few days later his life would take a fatal turn, as I would witness.

I found that, aside from the two alcoves on the second floor, another strategic location existed on the third floor, which housed a corner office of a dentist. The dentist's swivel chair immediately appealed to me as an excellent base for my machine gun, should need be. Later it proved to be of great value in our defense.

One of the occupants of the building was an elderly Swiss citizen. Before moving to the basement he suggested that we display in one of the windows a Swiss flag, which he had been keeping for special occasions. He added that the Germans would respect the flag and would consider the structure and its occupants neutral. I rejected his offer, to his disappointment. I explained to him that we had an obligation to assist the Prague uprising and that we could not, and would not, hide behind a cover of false neutrality.

In the meantime, darkness settled over the city. The weather changed to the worse, and with it came more fear and uncertainty. Some bullets were hitting windows in nearby buildings. Another civilian with a rifle joined us in the early-evening hours. Later another partisan found his way to our station. He had been able to get hold of a German antitank bazooka, called a *Panzerfaust* in German, which, translated, means "tank fist." The reinforcement was most welcome.

Shortly before midnight a truck suddenly passed by in the direction of the tower. Its headlights were on. This was a fatal mistake. The Germans opened fire from the tower. It took only a few seconds to smash the headlights to pieces, stop the truck, and, we assumed, kill the driver. We gazed for hours into the darkness but could see only the rough silhouette of the disabled truck. There was no sign of life.

After spending a sleepless night amid the sound of bullets and not knowing what the next day might bring, we got a good look at the truck as soon as daylight broke. The driver was slumped across his seat, as we could observe through the window behind his back. Another man was spread over the truck's platform in a pool of blood. The sight saddened us. It also made us aware that we could not expect any mercy in any shootout with the SS men.

At this time the Germans had not yet discovered our position. We observed them carefully from behind the drapes, trying to assess their strength and intentions. There was considerable activity in the church. Soldiers were moving back and forth, past the windows of the various rooms and floors. It seemed that orders were being given and messages received and sent. From time to time an officer appeared from behind a curtain, thoroughly scanning the street with his binoculars. The activity increased further when a small tank carrying a Czechoslovakian flag appeared at the corner of the square and slowly moved toward the post office. It was an antique, probably utterly useless vehicle that had been discovered somewhere in the yards of military barracks. It might have been used purely for training purposes, but now, when it halted at the iron gate of the post office, it meant a great boost to the morale of the patriots, although not a single shot was fired from it during the uprising. But the Germans could not discount its possible effectiveness. They had to take any threat, even if it was only possible, seriously. From a military viewpoint it was unthinkable to ignore the situation. Their problem was, however, that the post office and the tank were on the same side of the street as the church. It was obvious that the tank could not be eliminated from the church windows. Even if this had been possible, the distance was too great for the use of bazookas or hand grenades. For us it was only natural to expect them to risk a direct assault.

Our guess proved to be right. Soon we observed several men getting ready for the attack. They had put on helmets that differentiated them from their comrades. They armed themselves with some gear, the nature of which we could not define at the moment. One officer even stretched out his hand through the window and, holding a pocket mirror, scanned the route of the coming attack. There was no longer any doubt that the assault would begin momentarily.

I telephoned Elias at the post office, telling him of my observations. He assured me that he would do everything possible to reinforce his defense. It was time for us at the Dutch Mill to make our final preparations. We pulled a large dining table close to the alcove facing the church. I placed the machine gun on the table and aimed at the corner of the church where the men who had been ordered to attack had gathered. Each of them in turn peeked from under his helmet to familiarize himself with the task. My friend attached a string to the window handle. He was to pull the window open at my command, at the moment I decided that the time was ripe to open fire. From my military training I was almost certain that the SS men would jump out from behind the church as a group and leap to the next available cover. This did not happen. Instead, one man at a time did so, and before I knew it five SS men had reached cover in short individual leaps. They were safe as far as possible shots from the post office were concerned, but not from the Dutch Mill. Their cover was almost opposite the alcove in which my gun had been placed on the table, though in the wrong direction.

Without drawing the SS commandos' attention I quickly corrected the position of the gun. I also had another man, who had come last night with a rifle, position himself at the second alcove and aim at the SS group. I stressed to him that he must not open fire until I did so myself.

The commandos were getting ready for their final leap toward the post office and the tank. Each man had several hand grenades on his belt, as well as fast-firing Tommy guns. Two of them were equipped with bazookas. As they stood up from their crouching positions, ready to jump forward, we opened fire from our second-floor alcove simultaneously with the machine gun and the rifle. The five men sank to the ground.

Only their leader turned swiftly around and fired a rapid burst at us. He must have been in many street fights during the war, for his reaction was incredibly fast. Then he slipped motionless down to the pavement to join his comrades.

The dreaded attack on the post office was over. It was a relief for its occupants and for Commander Elias. He expressed his gratitude on the telephone. We were both aware, however, that this was not the end of our problems.

About half an hour later the German Red Cross vehicle arrived to pick up the bodies. In charge was a muscular woman in a gray leather coat. She examined the bodies briefly before they were put in the van. She must have had considerable experience in what she was doing, as she lifted each body with just one hand and dropped it immediately thereafter, recognizing at once that there was no hope any longer. She spent much time looking in the direction of our position. She must have been aware without any doubt that the shots had been fired from the alcove windows, which in our excitement we had left ajar.

The van drove away and disappeared behind the church. Later we learned that the bodies were buried in its backyard. The street became quiet. We kept a close watch of the church windows but could not detect any more helmeted soldiers, although the general activity inside did not lessen. The officer with the binoculars now appeared more often behind the drapes. We had the distinct feeling that his attention was directed primarily at us.

Like almost all other city structures, our building had a spacious area under its roof where its occupants could store old furniture or small discarded items and where they could stretch their clothes lines and dry their linen. I went there to find out if one of the roof openings could serve us as an observation point. Indeed, I was able to look over a large part of the inner city. In the distance, at various locations, smoke was rising from burning buildings. In several streets, barricades made from cobblestones, pieces of wood, furniture, and-or overturned vehicles were visible. As I was busy scanning the surroundings, a shot suddenly rang out from the neighborhood. A bullet whistled past my ear. I was quick in descending from my position. Later, when I was back at the Dutch Mill on the second floor talking to my colleagues, another bullet came in. This time it was obvious that it came from the church. It penetrated a corner window pane, passed through the open door of the bar, and shattered one of the liquor bottles lined up on the shelves. We were in the room at the time, but no one was hurt.

We went to the dentist's office one floor up, placed the machine gun on the headrest of the dentist's chair, and fired several salvos into the parish windows in retaliation. Then we quickly returned downstairs.

There was no doubt in my mind that the SS men were well aware of our strategic position, as they watched our every move. We kept changing our location from floor to floor, which was easy, as all the occupants had been requested to leave all doors open. But our main gathering place was still the second floor, with its two alcoves.

About an hour later, as we were having a discussion on the second floor, a tremendous explosion threw us to the floor and blinded us for several minutes. Black smoke filled the room. When we recovered from our daze we realized how fortunate we had been. We suffered no injury aside from the tremendous shock. When the smoke and dust settled we found out that a powerful shell had been fired at us from the church. We did not know what weapon it had been fired from, but it tore a large hole in the concrete wall only inches from the frame of the left alcove. The glass panes of the alcove were shattered to pieces. Glass, chunks of concrete, and wood splinters were all over the floor. Had the shell gone through the window and exploded in the room, we could not have survived.

The second day of the uprising was coming to a close. We had had hardly any sleep or rest. During daylight we were able to keep a close watch on events. We could scan the street from our observation points and get ready to defend the building at any given moment. The entrance door and the windows on the street level afforded us some feeling of security, as we had reinforced them with whatever was at our disposal. When the night set in, however, uncertainty and fear crept into our minds. The SS men were aware of the danger we posed to them, but we could not speculate as to whether they would plan a major attack on us. Should this happen during darkness, we would have hardly any advance warning. So when we lay down on the hard floor, any burst of fire or suspicious noise coming from any direction alarmed us.

It started raining. Through the windows we could see only the silhouettes of the neighboring buildings. From time to time their roofs and walls lit up when bursts of tracer bullets passed over them. It was a long night. The uncertainty played on our nerves. Our faces were drawn and we were very tired as we faced the beginning of the third day.

The Prague radio kept calling for help, but none came. The only encouraging news was a message from the uprising headquarters that General Vlasov with some of his men might be moving toward the city to assist the patriots. Vlasov commanded several thousand Ukrainians who had been captured by the German armies. He had volunteered to the German command that he and his men would help liberate the Ukraine from the Bolsheviks. By doing so he was able to save many Soviets from starvation in German labor camps. During the last days of the war he saw this opportunity offering itself in Prague. He hoped not only to be able to help in the Prague uprising against the Nazis but also to take a step in the direction of securing a safe future for his men. He had never fought any Western power and was justified in hoping for their understanding after the war. We learned later to our regret that the West betrayed him, delivering him and his men to the Soviets, who mercilessly liquidated them. By heading toward Prague, Vlasov offered mainly a morale boost for the city defenders.

As a painful paradox, instead of U.S. or British aircraft coming to our help, several German planes flew over the inner city and dropped bombs. Damage was not excessive, although a few tall buildings on Wenceslas Square, close to the post office, were hit.

The toll on Prague civilians was mounting. We heard from our headquarters that several bridges held by the patriots were stormed by the Germans, causing heavy casualties. Some of the defenders lacked military training. They had built barricades on the inner end of the bridges, taking up posts behind them, instead of taking up positions in the surrounding buildings, from where they could have done a more effective job and saved lives.

Looking down from our corner window into Nekazanka Street, I witnessed another unnecessary killing. The building opposite, also a corner house, had large display windows on the street level. From the church the Germans could observe through the two corner display windows anyone trying to get closer to Jindrisska Street. I was too late to warn the Czech who slowly opened the door of the building and carefully inched his way to the corner. He had hardly covered ten steps when a single shot rang out from the church. The bullet penetrated both corner windowpanes and hit the man. He fell instantly to the ground. For a while no one dared go to his assistance. Then a man crawled on the ground to reach him. He turned the wounded man over. There was a red spot on his white shirt. Pinkish blood mixed with air bubbles was oozing from his chest wound. His face was ashen as his friend dragged him through the door. With the door closed, the building again became silent and almost mysterious.

Later that afternoon the radio announced that General Eisenhower had received an offer of surrender from the German Supreme Command in the West. This gave us renewed hope for an early termination of the fighting in the city. We had no idea how the surrender would affect our country, which had been declared as falling under the influence zone of the Soviet Union. We suspected, and were afraid, that the Nazis would not give up Prague as long as they had some hope to delay the arrival of the Soviet troops.

With the end of the war so near, we had fear in our hearts that we might become its victims during its last few hours even though we had survived the terror of the Nazi occupation for over six long years. We had now become accustomed to the unceasing shelling that had spread over the entire city.

The next day at sunrise the city faced another turbulent day, the fourth day of the uprising. Its citizens would pay a heavy toll in lives and damage in the coming hours. The morning was beautiful, turning into a warm and clear spring day. We learned from the radio that General Eisenhower had accepted the unconditional surrender in the west. The radio also kept us advised of the fast approach of the Soviet troops from the east and north. After all, we hoped, the day would end in joy and happiness, as the city would finally be free.

Our expectations faded with the hour. There was an ominous feeling in the air. It was not only the increasing sound of shelling but also the sight of numerous fires in the inner city. From the roof I looked around again to assess the situation. Smoke was rising from a number of buildings. Clouds of smoke also seemed to come from the direction of the old town square, with its historic structures and the town hall.

There was also a strange rumbling coming from the northeast side of Prague. It became louder by the minute. It seemed as if a great number of heavy vehicles were moving to the city center. Soon we recognized the sound of rolling tanks. German tanks of course. Our little obsolete Czech tank that had been positioned at the post office entrance withdrew that very morning. We could only guess that it had been assigned to another sector or that its crew did not dare face the onslaught of the German tanks.

I was trying to think of a way to locate the position and possible route of the tanks. From the roof I could clearly hear them from somewhere behind the tower but still several hundred meters away. In my judgment they were in the vicinity of the Masaryk railway station. I made an effort to get in touch with someone at the station. Several phone numbers were out of order, but I finally succeeded. Someone lifted the telephone on the other end. With a trembling voice he said he could not speak loudly because a soldier was standing in front of his office window with a machine gun in his hands. There was shooting all over the railway station. A number of Czech defenders had been summarily executed. Tanks guarded the action from the street corner outside. Before I could get additional information I heard some commotion at the office and the telephone became silent.

Opposite the railway station was a building with shops, passages, and a café. I found the telephone number of the latter and tried my luck. A feeble voice answered. It was that of the headwaiter. He could clearly watch the German actions through the windows. Again SS men were all over the street, he said, shooting and giving sharp orders. He added that everyone in the café had been ordered to stay away from the windows under penalty of death. He also described the ordeal the patriots in this area were undergoing. A number of them had been executed, among them two brothers, twins. They had been born together, and they died together on this tragic day. They were only about twenty years of age. The headwaiter then indicated that by staying on the telephone he was putting himself and all the people in the café in mortal danger. He was sorry, he added, that he had to put down the receiver. Before doing so, however, he noted that the tanks had begun moving from the railway station toward the tower, the church, and the post office.

It dawned on us that our final hour had arrived. How could we defend ourselves against powerful tanks? Our hearts pounded in expectation of the worst. Our only weapon that could perhaps incapacitate a tank was the German *Panzerfaust* bazooka. From its inscription we knew how to unplug the safety latch, but that was all. We could of course pull the trigger, but this could not be done from a small room in our building. Our bazooka would backfire a stream of hot gases that would work all right in an open field but not between four walls. I inquired by telephone as to what we could do with the weapon, without success. No one at the headquarters could give us any useful instructions.

The noise coming from the approaching tanks was increasing rapidly. As we looked toward the tower, two monstrous tanks came rolling slowly around it. The larger one was easy to recognize. It was the most powerful German tank, the Tiger. The other one was not as big, but it presented an equally deadly threat. Before we could decide on any action, the two tanks started maneuvering. While one of them moved several meters toward us, the other remained stationary but fired at our building with all the power available to it. Then the two exchanged roles. This went on for over an hour. Our building was hit with no fewer than seventy powerful shells. We recognized that this was surely in retaliation for our earlier action and in preparation for an SS assault.

The noise was deafening. At every round big chunks of concrete dropped off the Dutch Mill. We were scared to death, as we had never in our lives experienced anything like this. It was impossible to stay in any of the corner rooms on any floor. We withdrew to the staircase inside the building, where we pressed our heads and bodies against the stairs. Even so, pieces of concrete, dust, broken furniture, and glass were flying through the air. Dust and smoke beams of fire flashed through the building at every new explosion of a shell.

There was no doubt in my mind that this was the end. How long could we survive the terrifying shelling before the building collapsed? We would soon be buried, alive or dead. Even if the building somehow withstood the shelling, at the end of it there would most certainly come a concentrated SS attack on our position. No, we had no chance whatsoever. We were marked for annihilation, to be followed by an assault on the post office. We could not understand why we, a small group of badly equipped fighters, should be the target of such a massive attack. With this in mind I pondered what to do, if anything, after the men stormed the building. Should we put up a feeble but desperate resistance and face a certain death, or should we perhaps offer no resistance at all, hoping that we might somehow survive the last few hours of the war?

As we were contemplating what to do, we heard on the radio that peace had been declared and the war was over. Why, then, were we still exposed to the vicious attack by the elite SS men? Our minds wandered back to our families and friends, whom we might never see again. We looked at each other and understood. The shelling did not ease up.

Just then, when a frontal attack by the SS men seemed imminent, there was suddenly dead silence. Our ears and eyes had become so accustomed to the thunderous explosions and blinding flashes that the silence completely stupefied us. For several minutes we did not move. It seemed unreal that all this could end this way.

It took some more time before all the dust and smoke settled down and we could survey the extent of damage to our post. It was unbelievable that we had escaped the murderous shelling with our lives. I carefully approached one of the large gaping holes in the wall. What I saw was unreal. The two German tanks were slowly withdrawing in the same direction from which they had come earlier, leaving piles of empty shells on the street. There was not a single soldier in sight.

When the tanks disappeared behind the tower and their noise faded, we opened the door to our building. Then we rushed toward the tower and the church, still taking cover whenever possible. There were no movements anymore behind the church windows. Soon we found out that the SS men were gone. This was the explanation for the vicious tank attack on our position. The tanks had been used for the sole purpose of affording the soldiers at the church and other military men and German civilians in the vicinity to withdraw safely from the inner city.

This was confirmed to us shortly thereafter from the resistance headquarters. We were told that the German commandant of Prague had made an agreement with the Czech underground leaders. Accordingly, the fighting had stopped. The Germans were allowed to withdraw from the city carrying their small weapons for protection, but they were to leave all the heavy equipment and armaments behind.

Our joy was immense. It felt like being newly born. Doors and windows opened everywhere. We rushed to the tower. One of my men climbed on its old staircase to the top and hoisted a Czechoslovakian national flag. It was touching to see it flutter freely in the afternoon sun, for the first time after more than six years.

People streamed into the streets, jubilant. We now had the opportunity to survey the damage that had been caused to the Dutch Mill. Window frames and large chunks of concrete had been ripped out by the furious firing of the two tanks. What had remained of the structure was blackened and covered with dust and splinters of wood, bricks, and mortar. The dwellers of the building came out of the cellar and went back into their flats as far as the damaged walls permitted. Cleaning began throughout the structure. Soon heaps of rubble and dust started to grow in the corridors as the dwellers cleaned their rooms and removed whatever they could carry in their arms.

Later in the evening they decided to have a get-together in the rooms of the Dutch Mill. The Swiss citizen provided some fine cigarettes and cigars, as well as several cans of food and good coffee and a bottle of French cognac. The other dwellers brought whatever they could contribute from their meager resources. Thanks were expressed to my friends and me for the four days during which no harm came to the other inhabitants.

The German citizen who had spent four days in the basement with the others came to me in a state of shock. He was very frightened but managed to express his appreciation for the fair treatment he had received. He was at a complete loss as to what he should do next. It would have been suicidal for him to leave the building and expose himself to the Czechs, who at this moment found themselves in a lawless city. This was a time when they could let out the repressed hatred accumulated against the occupiers during the six years of war. Some of the Czechs had lost members of their families or friends; others had their sons and daughters sent to plants in Germany that had been heavily bombed during the conflict. Their fate was unknown, but it was hoped that most of them would return to their families. Again, some others in the streets did not have any special personal reason for revenge but were sucked into the stream of retaliation.

Under the circumstances I suggested to the lone German that I would have him escorted to the Czech police post that was only a few steps away, with the request that they protect him to the extent possible and have him join whatever German unit or group he might still be able to find. He agreed. I sent one of my men to accompany him to the police.

The modest celebration at the Dutch Mill went on until midnight. It was a quiet occasion. We were exhausted from our ordeal of the past days and could hardly keep our eyes open. We were offered comfortable beds by some of the inhabitants, but I decided that we should spend the last night together on the floor of the Dutch Mill as we had done on the previous three nights. This was the first time we did not have to fear a sudden attack on our position.

In the morning of the next day, May 9, 1945, Prague became alive. Streets were filled with happy citizens. No work was done. Separated families tried to unite. Those who had been fighting in the inner city, on the outskirts, on the bridges, in important buildings, and on barricades started on their way home.

I looked down from the second floor of the Dutch Mill. There was some unusual activity there. Shots were fired. This seemed strange to me at this time, when the war was over. Someone was pulling a man through the street, but not by his arms or shoulders. The man had a belt tied around one of his legs. He was being dragged over the pavement, which was littered with broken glass and rubble. He was being pulled by a young man who frequently stopped to fire another shot into the man's legs. It was a pitiful and shocking sight but only one among hundreds of similar cruelties happening all over the city. The victim's face was ashen. He was alive but did not cry or beg for mercy. Looking into his face, I recognized the lone German whom we had sheltered for the past few days. His business suit was torn and dirty. For some reason no blood was showing, as the now-increasing mob kept dragging him away, shouting obsenities. No one in the world could help him at this moment in this city where law had ceased to exist. Several minutes later I walked in the direction of the mob. There the picture was even more horrifying. By now the group, among it several women, had tied a wire around his feet and let him dangle from a lamppost. As he swung back and forth, his head almost touching the pavement, someone fetched a can of gasoline. Having been thoroughly soaked, he was set on fire. Several fanatics in the crowd cheered wildly as his head and body twisted in agony, but most onlookers stood silently or in shock, not daring to say a word. A rumor spread fast that he had been a brutal Gestapo official. It could have been true. He could also have been a harmless family man who happened to be at the wrong place at the wrong time. I shall never know, but the picture of his death would haunt me for years to come.

8

Soviet troops arrived in Prague on May 9, 1945, from east and north. Among them were a considerable number of women in uniform, who took over the regulation of city traffic. Circulation became confused with the constant arrival of new units. Prague was filled with soldiers and camions. They were covered with dust. The Czechs wanted to show their gratitude for the Soviets' part in the country's liberation, feeling an overwhelming relief that the Nazis had finally been decisively defeated and looked forward with almost childish expectations to the days ahead when the country would be free of any foreign troops. They hoped to install soon a freely chosen democratic government and take up the good work and achievements that had so abruptly been cut off six years earlier. The battle-worn soldiers seemed surprised at the warm welcome. Some of them waved back and smiled faintly; others stood motionless on their trucks and camions passing through the city.

The Soviet troops were a mixture of nationalities, races, and types. Among them were a great number of non-Russians, such as one had not seen in any previous descriptions or documents concerning the Soviet military establishment. One could see Mongols, Tatars, Uzbeks, Chinese, and other ethnic types. Some of them lay or slept on the ground covered with dust and dirt, in their long military coats, without any blankets or support under their heads. The Czechs who walked past them often did not feel comfortable seeing them motionless, with only their eyes shifting side to side. Soon some of the soldiers, not having had or even seen a watch in their entire lives, demanded them from passersby with a simple command in Russian: "Davay chassey!" meaning, "Hand over your watch!" They were fascinated with any type of watch, working or not. Then they strapped the watches on their wrists. Some of them had "acquired" several watches and had neatly adorned their forearms with them. It became dangerous not to surrender a watch. It was equally dangerous to carry a camera or fountain pen.

Soldiers who drove camions did not have the opportunity to acquire watches or other valuables. To compensate for this, they decided to cut up Persian rugs or draperies at the places of their lodging. Cut into small pieces, they adorned the camion windows, seats, and platforms.

It was difficult, if not impossible, for the soldiers to differentiate between the people who had been hostile to them in other countries and the Czechs who had the intention of greeting them as liberators. The initial enthusiasm of the citizens cooled off after a while.

With the arrival of Soviet troops in Prague I was hoping that Georgine and our two children would also be able to return from the countryside. I was aware, however, that with the unending movements of Soviet troops the whole transportation system was in shambles. Furthermore, all the trains that were still in operation were overfilled with those returning from detention camps and forced labor camps, anxious to rejoin their families scattered all over Europe. Many of the travelers were in rags, sick, and undernourished, sleeping on the floors or benches with pitiful bundles of belongings under their heads. It was doubtful that Georgine would be able to get on a train. At the moment I could not find out whether or not she had been able to return to our apartment, as we had been deprived of our telephone during the occupation.

It was late in the afternoon when I decided to see Bruno on the other side of the river. There was still enough daylight to cross the bridge in comparative safety. To my relief, Bruno and his wife had not suffered any harm during the last few days. Their flat remained intact except for a hole in one of the windowpanes from a rifle bullet. Bruno surprised me by advising me that Georgine had indeed returned to Prague and no doubt had already reached our apartment, on the other side of town. By now the darkness had set in. Nevertheless, I decided I immediately had to get back home, to be with Georgine, hear about her and the children's experiences and tell her about my own adventure.

Only a few isolated street lamps shone in the otherwise-total darkness. The bridge I had to cross was guarded by Czech patriots who had taken part in the uprising and had fought the Germans in the city. My heart was pounding when I sneaked through the dark streets and took my first step across the bridge. Somewhere in the darkness of the bridge was the Czech sentry still on duty, armed with a rapid-firing gun and a flashlight. I hoped desperately that the young man who during the past few days had often used his weapon with pride and precision, and without hesitation, would give me a chance. At his sharp command I stopped a respectable distance from him. He approached me carefully, coming out of nowhere, his light beam directed at my face. Fortunately, I was unarmed. He demanded an explanation for my being out at this late hour, then asked for my identification papers. It would have been foolish to reach in haste into my pocket, and so I indicated to him the pocket in which I carried the documents. After looking carefully through the papers he nodded his approval for me to continue crossing the bridge. His flashlight beam accompanied me until I reached the other side. There I continued walking through narrow streets and around corners and passages, among gray houses and little plazas. In several open spaces I had to pass Soviet trucks and camions, with soldiers lying on them or on the bare ground nearby. I was aware that I would be risking my life if I tried to sneak by them in silence or in haste. There was no other way than to walk as noisily as I could. This was not difficult on the cobblestones with which many streets in Prague are paved. Whenever I passed a group of camions and saw a figure or two rise against the dark sky, I held my breath and walked as carelessly as I could manage while my heart pounded with great anxiety. The darkness made my night walk the more daring, as the Soviet sentries were not equipped with flashlights to identify me.

After two hours I was happy to reach the suburbs and the apartment building where my home was. I walked slowly up to the fifth floor and opened the front door. It was a great joy to find Georgine there unharmed. She assured me that the children were comparatively safe back in the village, where only a few soldiers had been stationed. We talked for hours about our experiences and the great fortune that our family had managed to survive during the war, during which thousands of other families had been destroyed through deportation or executions or perished in concentration or forced labor camps.

Georgine told me how she managed and survived her travel to Prague. With the waves of Soviet soldiers and equipment moving toward the city she had hoped to get a lift on one of the military vehicles. Standing on the side of the road, she was fortunate that a camion stopped nearby. On it was a young, intelligent officer to whom she was able to explain partly in Czech and partly in sign language that her husband was in Prague and she desperately needed to reach the city. The young officer took pity on her. As she found out during the ride to the city, he came from Moscow and was married and looking forward with great expectations and impatience to rejoin his family, whom he had not seen in four years. Georgine was fortunate indeed. As we found out later, some of the women who got close to convoys simply disappeared and were never again accounted for, having run into some ruthless soldiers or officers.

In turn I told Georgine about my days, during which I had participated in the Prague uprising. Georgine was pleased to note that our neighbors in the apartment building were aware of my role in the uprising and that they appreciated what I had done in the center of the city.

We could hardly believe that our troubles were now over, that we would no longer hear the Nazi camions drive by in the early-morning hours with political prisoners or the sunrise salvos of their execution squads. We discussed plans for the future, for ourselves and our children, for our friends and relatives. After more than six years of terror it was hard to realize that this was a reality. Our joy would be complete when, after a short while, we retrieved our two little boys from the countryside.

Life in the country began to take on a normal appearance, slowly but steadily. Pres. Edvara Beneš, who had been the head of the Czechoslovakian government in exile and whose ministers had been with them in London during the war, returned to Prague. This was considered a good omen, considering the fact that none of the leaders of other previously occupied countries were allowed by the Soviets to return from forced exile as victors. Beneš's success was costly, however. Stalin had insisted, and Beneš's London exile government could not but agree, on his returning to Prague via Moscow. There several adjustments demanded by the Soviets had to be made. While the country had many political parties before the war, the system had to be considered simplified to suit the Soviets before Beneš and his ministers were permitted to return to Prague. Four political parties were permitted. Beneš was determined to ensure through them the return to democracy. Stalin, on the other hand, used them to set the course toward converting the country into a formidable communist stronghold.

It must be understood that the Yalta and Potsdam conferences left Czechoslovakia no choice. It was decided there and accepted by the world leaders that the country would fall under the Soviet sphere of influence. History has proven since that this was a grave error, although at that time it might have been a reward for undeniably great sacrifices of the Soviet population during their struggle against the Nazis. Even recognizing the latter fact, the world's conscience can never forget or forgive the sacrifice of millions upon millions of families that had been thrown into the Soviet lap. Stalin never felt any friendship or compassion for the Western people and their leaders. Even while he smiled when pictures were taken during the conferences, he detested them in his heart. He had been determined at the outset to reap the greatest possible advantages from the Western trust, goodwill, and general naïveté.

The Czechoslovakian government arrived in Prague in May of 1945. It consisted of four approved political parties: the Communists, the Social Democrats, the Socialists, and the Christians. This story is not an endeavor to describe in detail the historical events caused by this arrangement. The ensuing Communist actions, motives, intrigues, manipulations, pressure and terror, political goals, military implications, and personalities involved would require a great deal of explaining.

These political developments completely upset any plans in factories and various other industrial and business enterprises to restore to management positions the prewar leadership. With the announced nationalization of everything that had been held in private hands, radical changes were ordered. In many companies the Communists quickly installed their sympathizers in leading positions. This could not very well be opposed. It left only limited options to others. Workers were skillfully manipulated by the Communists, who insisted that the assets now belonged to the "people," meaning the radical workers.

Personnel changes were being effected everywhere. Previous managers, even if they had been persecuted by the Nazis, had no chance to be reinstated. In Prague, a so-called Revolutionary Union Movement (ROH) was formed in haste and sanctioned by the government. It supervised and approved, or rejected, nominations to leading positions. They had to be presented by committees formed of employees. As a rule, citizens hardly ever belonged to any political party. The four parties that had been sanctioned were basically unknown to them. Their actions would have to be watched before people could make up their minds. Later it was unceasing pressure by the Communists that dictated the choice.

In our company it was out of the question to propose the reinstatement of the former managing director, although he had spent several years in a Nazi detention camp. The ROH would have rejected it out of hand, notwithstanding the fact that our oil refinery workers in Moravia would have considered this contrary to their wishes.

A small employee committee of our Prague office established contact with ROH and with our refinery people. The intent was to select someone who had no prewar managerial position, who had been anti-Nazi and helped to sabotage production during the war, and who had not behaved in a cowardly manner during the uprising. With the support of my many friends in the refinery and with the approval of the ROH, the choice fell upon me. Thus I became the official "national administrator" of our new nationalized company.

It must be noted that at the time I did not belong to any party, although the pressure to express sympathy for the Communists had been increasing. I was unable to do so when I observed their actions and intentions to destroy the last vestige of democracy in the country.

The Prague Association of the oil industry continued its meetings in order to regulate oil supplies for the benefit of the recovering economy. It was difficult to secure sufficient crude oil supplies from abroad. During the war crude oil came from Romania via the river Danube. It had to be transferred to trains to reach our refineries. Some of the crude oil originated in newly opened Austrian fields. Individual oil companies made great effort to secure the largest possible share of oil imports for themselves. I had a difficult time convincing the association that our refinery, being the only one with full operational capacity, deserved a good portion of the imports. My efforts failed. Our allocation was entirely unsatisfactory.

I instructed the supply manager, who spoke Russian, to establish contact with the Soviet bureau in charge of crude oil and general transportation. Two officers whom we treated with courtesy, respect, and excellent French liqueur listened to our story with understanding. As a result they directed all the trains carrying crude oil from Austria to head to our Moravian refinery. The association was furious, but the actions helped us to become an important link in the Ministry of Industry's efforts to speed up the economic recovery.

The Communists with their clandestine accomplices, the Social Democrat leaders, brought with them Stalin's secred orders for a gradual takeover. In the past it had been well known that social democrats in the various countries had always been considered adversaries of the communists. In this case, however, their leader, Fierlinger, later proved himself to be a traitor to the Social Democratic Party. It was Stalin's clever trick to disguise Fierlinger as a defender of democracy while from the beginning he had been an obedient servant of the Communist chief, Gottwald.

The Socialists were middle-of-the-roaders and the Christians more or less conservatives, but both were strongly anti-Communist. It goes without saying that soon important ministries ended up in strong Communist hands. These were: the Interior, supervising the police and militia, the Secret Service, and Education. The minister of defense, who later openly supported the Soviets, had previously declared himself as belonging to no party, again a clever move instigated by Moscow. The Social Democrats were allocated to the Ministry of Industry and Commerce. The Socialists and Christians were left with hardly any political clout but managed to keep their press, in which they continued to express their own democratic ideals and criticism of the other parties' misdeeds.

President Beneš made all possible efforts to ensure, at least to some extent, the survival of the democratic system. In the beginning he succeeded to a considerable degree, but the anchor to which the country had been tied inevitably pulled it deeper into the abyss in a hopeless struggle. Even if democratic forces were fighting for everything good that was worth preserving, progress was being obstructed and made unworkable. It went so far that the Communist minister of the interior sanctioned terrorist attacks on non-Communist members of the government. Among the attackers Gottwald's son-in-law figured prominently. The minister also ordered the creation of units of so-called factory guards, whose members were issued rifles and ammunition to guard against alleged "foreign saboteurs" but who, in fact, were to occupy the factories by force when the proper time came.

The two anti-Communist parties realized that on their shoulders now rested the fate of democracy in their country. The Christian Party was led by Monsignor Sramek, a man of pleasant and mild manners but of a strong character and convictions. He was a worthy leader of his followers. Even with these qualities he could not overcome the growing domination of the country by forces of evil.

Dr. Peter Zenkl became the chairman of the Socialist Party, which was highly visible in its anti-Communist teachings. He was also one of the deputy prime ministers, as was his right as a leader of one of the four sanctioned parties. On two former occasions Zenkl had been Lord Mayor of Prague. He was a well-known personality at home and abroad. His social achievements and wisdom, as well as his sense of justice and truth, were undeniable. The Nazis had sent him to a concentration camp, together with thousands of other prominent personalities. Fortunately he survived the ordeal. Only three years later, in 1948, he was arrested again, this time by the Soviet-guided secret police. President Gottwald could not tolerate such a respected and honorable man in the political arena. A few months later Zenkl was clandestinely smuggled out of the country by a handful of loyal patriots, to the dismay and embarrassment of his jailers. He and his wife spent their remaining years in the United States, where he continued his tireless work helping his native land become free again, unfortunately without success.

I joined Dr. Zenkl's party with pride, as an active member. This meant a binding and bold commitment on my part and an open expression of my anti-Communist feelings. I became a member of the party's central committee, dealing with industrial and economic problems. Some of my articles were published in the party's weekly, *Svobodny Zitrek* (Freedom Tomorrow), which dared to criticize the ever-growing misdeeds of the Communists.

During the second year that followed liberation it became obvious that democracy would have a hard time surviving. The Communist minister of the interior, to whom the police and secret services reported and who was responsible for law and order, methodically placed his confidants in powerful positions throughout the country. Together with placing his party's watchdogs in every company, office, factory, shop, and building, he collected information on those still dreaming of preserving some civil rights and ideals. Under flimsy accusations of "antipeople" activities, arrest became common. Unrest was created, and fear similar to that prevailing under the Nazis was implanted among the population. Promises were made to the rural population, and land, in fact, was distributed to former farmers and workers. Ceremonies to this effect were held under the red banner in the villages. The new owners were not told, naturally, that this was a cruel trick and that, not much later, after the Communists took over all power in the land, the new landowners would have to surrender their recent acquisitions "voluntarily" to form state kolkhozes (cooperatives).

Under these conditions elections were held. Frightened citizens were openly urged in the polling rooms to vote for the Communist ticket. Upon entering the room they were given two lists, one for and the other against the Communists. A guide then took them to the box collecting the Communist votes. Above, on a platform, sat a member of the Communist Party taking note of the voters' names and choices. The voters were "free" to reject the Communist slate and to exercise their democratic right. Only a few had the courage to do so, as their names and choices were registered and marked for future retaliation. The election result was predictable. It gave the Communists a legal majority. This further strengthened their determination to recklessly impose their will upon the nation. A complete takeover by them could not effectively be prevented much longer.

No private ownership existed any longer. Everyone earning a living was working for one giant employer—the government. The changes occurring in the system affected every family. Only the strong ones kept resisting the domination of the Communists. The majority of the population were forced to consider how their open behavior would be viewed by the strongmen in the local and central committees. They were understandably afraid for their livelihood and the well-being of their families; although in their minds and hearts they detested the developments, they could not afford to refuse to go along. The twisting of minds, accompanied by pretense and lies, became a matter of survival.

The minister of industry and commerce, Bohumil Lausman, was a true social democrat. He openly defied, and actually succeeded at one point in replacing, Fierlinger as party chairman. When all the Czech oil companies, already nationalized, were fused into a single entity under the name Czechoslovak Oil Refineries, National Enterprise, he was able to nominate its top management. He chose one central and three deputy directors. This slate reflected to some extent the national front of political parties. A nonaffiliated man with a doctorate in chemistry became the central director in charge of production. A Social Democrat was appointed deputy responsible for supply and distribution matters. As expected, a Communist was put in charge of employee and social matters. This left me, a Socialist and staunch antiCommunist, with the financial sector, under the title of Deputy Central Director. I was charged with handling all the financial and budgetary affairs of the entire nationalized Czech oil industry. In my case it was a daring move by the minister, who at that time still wielded some power in his field of responsibility. My credentials of having headed one of the important oil companies were in support of his choice. And my being a member of the Socialist Party, which was a legitimate political entity, even if it did not have much power, could not be objected to.

My rapport with the about two hundred financial and accounting personnel was cordial and warm. They respected me for the democratic and fair ways in which I treated them and the matters we had to deal with. The Communists in the company put up a cooperative front, but everyone was aware that they were patiently working toward radical change, in our industry as well as nationwide. Even so I enjoyed two years of constructive work in my function.

The end of the quasi-democracy came on February 24, 1948, less than three years after the despised brown and black Nazi colors were firmly ousted. They had been replaced by red.

President Beneš had been under savage pressure from Gottwald, the prime minister, and his party. He was a sick and tired president who finally could not resist the pressure and constant threats any longer. Gottwald took full advantage of the situation. He proceeded with the installation of the most brutal and loyal Communist Party members in every position of power in the country. The minister in charge of armed forces had already been on his side from the beginning, although he had kept stressing his nonpolitical alignment. Factory workers now openly declared that they would defend themselves with weapons against any "antipeople" actions and the plants and factories against "saboteurs."

On that fateful day in February all Prague workers and employees were ordered to assemble at the large Wenceslas Square in the heart of the city. They were marched collectively from their working places. There was no escape. In fact, everyone had been told to sign a list prepared by the Communists stating that he or she would participate in a rally designated to be of the highest national interest. I did not sign up and instead went home. Georgine and I listened to the speeches culminating with Gottwald's personal proclamation. President Beneš had given in. Gottwald had become the new head of state. Our heads and eyes were burning. This was the end of the once-renowned Czechoslovakian democracy and of a dream of all honest and patriotic citizens that a free and fair future could ever be built for them and their children.

The next morning as I walked through the inner city, I was aware that the worst had come as the result of yesterday's rally. Every strategically important building that I passed on my way to the office was guarded by militants in civilian clothes, armed with machine guns and rifles. Non-Communist newspapers were banned and their printing presses smashed. No one could get in touch with non-Communist representatives or political headquarters. Their respective telephone ties had been disconnected. Arrests were widespread. Overnight the nation had been rendered utterly helpless.

The atmosphere in the office was gloomy. Employees found on their desks urgent invitations to join the Communist Party for their own good. Aside from the shock of what was happening to the country, everyone was faced with an urgent requirement to make a hasty decision: should he or she sign up or at least denounce his former belief in decent political procedures, thus proclaiming loyalty to the ruthless new masters, or find the courage and honesty to refuse? Being passive meant disagreement and a clear proof of resistance.

No work was being done. At this point many of the men and women in the company who had always been loyal to me came to my office. Some of them cried openly. They were torn between their allegiance to decency and their desire, or almost duty, to survive in the coming years and be able to support their families.

It is impossible for those who have never experienced a fascist or communist takeover or an occupation of one's country by ruthless foreigners or by fanatics from one's own nation to appreciate these heartbreaking times. To the Czechs this happened barely ten years after the Nazis invaded the country. For the Czechs, communism and Nazism represented the same evil, brutality, and disregard for human rights. It was sad to realize that people born since 1939 had not had one single day of freedom in their own country! What a tragedy for the human race! Animals would not be treated this way in any civilized country The various societies for the prevention of cruelty to animals would not tolerate it.

On that sad day in February of 1948 I could not with good conscience encourage my friends and coworkers to openly resist the brutal new regime. I stressed to them that the government, the sole employer in the land, would proceed ruthlessly against those opposing it. They would be labeled enemies of the people. I urged them to carefully weigh, in their minds and hearts, their obligations to their families and friends, and to consider seriously ways and means of survival. I added that in my prominent position the least I felt obliged to do was not sign up but remain passive, for the moment.

They all felt saddened with the distinct feeling that everything was collapsing around them. I had a terrible feeling of guilt that I had let them down. On the other hand, it would have been utterly impossible on my part had I urged them to actively and openly resist in a situation that was entirely beyond hope. As I learned later, only the most courageous ones kept showing their opposition more or less openly. They were badly outnumbered. The majority accepted the new situation in a resigned manner to save their families from hardship and separation. A few survived well and even improved their lot by pretending they had, in fact, for some time in the past supported events leading to the Communist takeover in 1948. And a very few of the latter, who became new Communist Party members, overdid themselves to prove their dedication to the red cause.

Shortly afterward the Communists formed our company's "action committee," as the revolutionary rules established in Moscow dictate for such occasions. A meeting at the nearby Smichov Brewery was ordered, to be attended by about eight hundred Prague employees of the company. Streams of employees were marched to the large assembly hall, in front of which was an elevated stage sometimes used for theater performances or speeches. There was only standing room in the hall. My friends around me covertly pressed my arm. Suddenly there was absolute silence. The act began. The curtain opened. On the stage there was a simple desk and a few chairs resembling a scene from a simple play. The men around the table were not actors.

The chairman of the small group, an engineer and a longtime loyal communist in his thirties, stood up and addressed the frightened employees. He notified them that he was the people's choice as the head of the action committee, whose members he then proceeded to introduce. Among them was one of the company's drivers, a janitor, a clerk, a laborer, and two other men whose identity I no longer remember. "We are here," the chairman said, "to bring to your notice that this committee represents, based on the will of the people, the company's political leadership, whose task is to temporarily manage its affairs and to cleanse it of undesirable elements. The purpose is to shape the future in complete accord with communist revolutionary principles. Those in opposition will suffer dearly under the people's fist."

A deadly silence filled the hall. After a tactical pause, the chairman announced that as a first demonstration of their determination, three of the most prominent enemies of the people would be dismissed from their positions. From this day on no compensation at all would be paid for either past, present, and possibly future claims. The crowd stiffened, awaiting the verdict, against which there was absolutely no recourse. No lawyer would dare or be permitted to take up a case against the "people's will" in order to protect an enemy of the "people."

After another dramatic pause the chairman pointed the finger at me, announcing my name and position. Two other high-ranking employees were named. We were informed that as of tomorrow morning we were forbidden to enter any of the company's premises.

The chairman then stressed that the decision was fully valid and in line with the newly established revolutionary order and that absolutely no question or remark would be tolerated. The assembled employees were then ordered to return to their working places without delay and to continue performing their duties efficiently and with dedication to the cause.

At that point I raised my hand in an effort to say a few words that I hoped might perhaps give some comfort to the majority present. I observed tears in many eyes, not for those condemned alone, but also for the abyss into which the nation had been thrown. I was not permitted to say a word but could only observe with great sadness the despair on the faces of all the decent and honest friends leaving the hall. It was comforting, however, to observe that in their sadness they were not divided into any political groups but acted as simple human beings. Finally even the stage remained empty, the same table and chairs to be used in some theater play in the future.

Back in the office I collected my few belongings. My closest friends came to shake hands. I parted with a heavy heart. The situation brought about by the revolution to the nation as a whole, to my friends, and to my wife, Georgine, and our two little boys, Peter and John, had become a disaster. I found myself suddenly without a job and practically without any financial means. I would not even receive that part of my salary due me for the actual work performed up to that fateful day.

In order to survive and support my family I had to accept a minor job at a small nationalized service station outfit. It was only a temporary arrangement, lasting a few months. I was not allowed to continue because of my status as an enemy of the people. We were forced to sell various personal items and our living room furniture, which we had purchased proudly only two years earlier. This was the only way we could meet our rent payments and pay for the bare necessities and food.

We felt like outcasts. No one in the country would protect us. Fear as to what might happen to us gripped us. One day the secret police arrived at our apartment, apparently tipped off by the janitor living on the ground floor. As a dedicated Communist party member she had been entrusted with reporting every movement of our family. She had dutifully reported that our furniture had been moved out of the building and that there might be good cause for an investigation. There were countless people throughout the country who felt that denouncing enemies of the people was their duty to the Party, notwithstanding the political and material gains they hoped would be showered upon them.

Two members of the secret service searched thoroughly through our belongings and personal documents, asking not only for invoices covering the purchase of the furniture in question but also for a great deal of nonrelated information. They made a great effort to discover any incriminating financial, political, or other evidence. Nothing of the sort was found. At my request they confirmed this in writing.

Several weeks later the Employment Office, having been advised by the action committee of my dismissal, directed me to come to their offices so that a work assignment might be given to me. As a classified "enemy of the people" I had no illusions as to the type of work I would be assigned to: a dangerous job in the huge uranium mines in northern Bohemia that were supplying vital atomic raw materials to the Soviets or heavy labor somewhere in the country. This would have meant to us, and to numerous other families in similar situations, a separation and probability that we would not see each other for a long time, if ever again.

I decided to temporarily ignore the order to report to the employment authorities, relying on bureaucratic delays. This was serious disobedience on my part, but I felt I should try to gain some time to delay the inevitable. In the end, I knew a small delay would not make any difference to my fate any way.

Several weeks later a second reminder arrived from the office. I decided to ignore it, too.

All the time Georgine and I were thinking of a way out of this situation, which not only deprived us of any personal rights and dignity but also shattered our hopes for the future. It was sad for me to realize that my love for the country expressed by my actions during the uprising meant nothing to the Communists. I had been on the list of patriots to be awarded medals for bravery, but I could not accept my medal because a strict condition had been included in the military section's notification that any recipient of the award must sign a declaration that he or she approved and supported the new communist regime. The document is still in my possession, unsigned.

Among our secret thoughts was leaving the country one way or another. Soon Georgine and I began talking about such a possibility. The need to escape became more urgent with each passing month. It would have to be done in deepest secrecy. It would be, of course, unthinkable to apply for a permit to travel abroad. This would have been considered open rebellion against the government and would result in severe punishment, particularly in my case.

Then one day at six o'clock in the morning we were dealt another serious blow, and our hopes and dreams were shattered again. Two plainclothesmen knocked at our door and demanded of Georgine, who opened the door, that I immediately come with them. On her questioning them as to the reason, they rudely pushed her out of the way and ordered her to "shut up." When I came into the entrance hall I was instructed to dress in haste and, unshaven, accompany them to their headquarters. The building, called the Petchka Palace, in the center of town near the Central Post Office, had been previously occupied for six years by the dreaded Gestapo until May of 1945. It was indeed ironic that not long ago I had fought the Nazi SS men in the same vicinity during the Prague uprising and that like other citizens I had been looking forward in anticipation and joy to the arrival of the Soviet "liberators."

The two plainclothesmen wore long gray overcoats of the Soviet military cut. They spoke Czech well but were no doubt, trained by—and subservient to—the Soviet secret services. We traveled by streetcar. The other passengers had no idea as to the reason for our trip. When the gate of the former Gestapo headquarters closed behind me, I trembled at the thought that this was an even more catastrophic setback for me and my family than when I lost my job and income or when the secret police searched our apartment.

I was taken to the third floor and seated behind a small desk. Soon three characters in their twenties sat around me. A girl with a typewriter was taking notes. None of them impressed me as having any education or intelligence, but then again, these were times when the Party favored people who absorbed the communist philosophy with crude determination and dedication, regardless of background.

Their leader looked at me sharply and said "Tell us all about yourself, and don't manipulate your memory to fool us, or you will most certainly regret it!" I was taken by surprise, for I had no idea at all what they expected me to talk about, and so I dared to ask why I had been detained and what I was supposed to talk about. This for them was a signal to show their authority. With the words "you dirty bastard" they shouted at me to begin talking without further delay, ordering me to tell them "everything" about myself. From that I understood that this was the proven way the secret police in the Soviet Union and now also in the occupied countries would hope for a slip of the tongue that might lead to the discovery of antigovernment plots, rebellions, crimes against the "people," and possible accomplices.

In the coming hours, with only short and irregular interruptions, I was forced to keep talking. I became tired but was offered no food or drink. This went on from the early morning, when I had been taken to their headquarters, until three o'clock the next morning. I strained my brain and memories to recollect anything about my youth, studies, employment, marriage, children, parents, and relatives, in order to fill the time. It was dangerous to stop, as I was constantly urged in strong words to keep talking. I was completely exhausted when their leader in the early hours of the next morning informed me of my crime. He was not tired, for he and his men had taken turns leaving the room frequently for rest, refreshment, and consultation with their superiors. I was accused that while a director of the national oil industry I tried to prop up the book values of the plants in order to award to their former owners abroad higher-than-justifiable compensation for their nationalized properties. The leader warned me that the penalty for such serious action against the people's republic was fifteen years in prison or forced labor.

The accusation that I had manipulated the property assessments was a bitter and painful blow to me. I had always been proud of my honest dealings and behavior during all phases of my life. I realized, however, that the new regime would not hesitate in the least to fabricate false accusations. This was often initiated by individuals in some companies who aspired to certain assignments and who were determined to climb the ladder leading to favored positions at any cost.

The interrogators now fired at me in rapid succession questions in connection with the alleged crime I had been accused of. I had no problem whatsoever answering them, for my conscience was absolutely clear. My position before the war was too insignificant to put me in any position to deal with any of the foreign owners, directly or indirectly. I had never been aware of their whereabouts or addresses. This was particularly true during the Nazi occupation, as well as thereafter under the Soviet domination of my country. I had been in no position even to exchange a single word with them directly or through an intermediary. I had no other than a professional interest in the evaluation of the nationalized company's assets. Being the financial director of the company, I was aware that we could not produce any valid financial statement and balance sheet without assessing in greatest detail the actual physical state of every single piece of machinery, pipeline, tank, building and other construction, and equipment of every refinery and distribution facility. This was our duty.

Since the plants and all the other assets had been damaged to a higher or lesser degree by Allied forces toward the end of the war, our engineers and auditors had to be dispatched to these places. Their assignment was clear: to establish the actual degree of damage and usability of each and every item. There were thousands and thousands of objects to be scrutinized: motors, lines, buildings, refining stills and other treatment facilities, oil stored in tanks, transportation means, furniture, roads, tanks, and many others. The engineers and accountants were instructed by me to take great care in their evaluation, taking into account the depreciated values of the objects prior to the bombings, the percentage of possible damage caused, and the remaining useful life. My engineers and auditors had spent long weeks and months in each plant. They had been assisted by local employees, many of whom had mainly their revolutionary ideas in mind. It would have been absolutely impossible for me to manipulate the work and final results of the assessors. A possible compensation to foreign owners did not even cross our minds. If any compensation were to be considered at all by the new regime, which under the prevailing circumstances seemed out of the question, any negotiation or determination of the policy would have been handled at the highest level of government.

An amusing thing occurred while I was being interrogated. A plainclothesman stuck his head through the open door and motioned to those around me to come into the next room. They left the door slightly ajar. I could hear every word. The newcomer boasted that he had "busted" a small shopkeeper and had succeeded in appropriating several pairs of high boots. At that time goods were extremely rare and scarce, after six years of war and plundering by the Nazis. The group went on deciding who should get the prized boots based on their shoe sizes. For me it was a welcome break in the interrogation, but also a confirmation as to the moral level of the new leaders and their followers.

It was a relief when the leader announced that I could go home, because the jails were fully "booked" at the moment. I was warned in a most stern manner not to leave my apartment and to be ready to reappear at their headquarters at their pleasure at a moment's notice in the coming weeks.

It was delightful to get a breath of fresh and crisp air when the gate of the former Gestapo building closed behind me. At three o'clock that morning I started walking home through the dark, deserted streets.

The following days were nerve-racking. Whenever the telephone rang my heart began to pound. The suspense lasted several days, during which I stayed close to the telephone. Whenever the call came from the secret service, day or night, I had to take the first available streetcar and present myself again for subsequent interrogations. Being innocent, I could not be lured into admitting any guilt, but my nerves began to be affected by the ordeal. On my way to and from the secret service headquarters I had to pass by the post office where I had almost lost my life fighting the Nazis. All others like myself and those persecuted during the war were now classified as enemies of the people unless they had joined the Communists. This included the brave Czechs who had joined the Royal Air Force and other military units in Great Britain to effectively assist in defeating the Nazis.

To make my situation worse, the third and final notice arrived from the Employment Office at the end of 1948. We could not delay our escape from the country any longer. Our plans had to be firmed up at the earliest possible time. Even if my family survived, Georgine and I could not take upon our conscience to let our children grow up in a country dominated by the Soviets, where everyone, in order to survive, had to resort to lies and pretenses. We could not let our children be taught in school that Marxism and Leninism, teachings that had done so much harm to human decency, moral values, and freedom, must replace the teachings of the Scriptures.

It seemed too risky to get in touch with any person or underground organization assisting people to cross the borders clandestinely, as it was no longer safe to assume that some of these "helpers" were doing so out of patriotism. Several cases came to light where the secret service had penetrated and split families, confiscated their assets, and sent the breadwinners to jail or forced labor camps, rendering it impossible for their wives and children to survive in a decent manner. On other occasions traps had been set. There were usually no survivors among those trying to cross the border when they were guided by traitors.

9

Georgine and I discussed the subject of our escape for days and nights. We could not mention the thought of leaving the country to anyone, not even our closest relatives and friends. This would have endangered not only the possible success of our plans but also our lives and those of our dear ones. It was relatively late in time to try escaping, almost a year after the communist takeover. Most of those wanting to escape did so shortly after February 1948, when there was still confusion at the borders. At that time one could still find sections where guards were either absent or not so numerous. In January of 1949 the situation was entirely different. On the western and southwestern parts of the border leading to the American Zone of Germany, precautions against possible escape efforts were extremely efficient and refined. Barbed wire, watchtowers, many guards with or without dogs, rapid-fire weapons, and stringent security checks now sealed the border almost hermetically.

In spite of all the precautions, people still managed to sneak to the other side every week, but only with the assistance of dependable and loyal Czechs familiar with every feature of the terrain and the schedule of the guards. The authorities tried to prevent escape right from the start. People not living in the particular border region were obliged to carry with them special certifications authorizing them to travel toward the border section or to conduct business within it. It goes without saying that such certificates could only be issued by party offices or the management of nationalized enterprises.

In spite of what I knew about the grim escape possibilities across the border leading to the American Zone of Western Germany, I felt that I had no alternative but to make sure myself. With the help of my best friend, who did not ask any questions but certainly must have been aware of the reason, I armed myself with a faked letter from a nationalized company certifying that I was to travel to a town in western Bohemia, which was right next to the border, to "inspect an oil depot." Without the document I would have been caught on the train long before I arrived at the small town early in the morning. The next train back to Prague was not scheduled until later that afternoon. The town had only a few small places where I could sit down and order something to eat or drink. The one I entered to have breakfast was empty. I could not stay long without arousing suspicion. The streets were covered with snow. It was freezing. I walked through the town several times from one end to the other. Every time I felt less comfortable and more conspicuous under the eyes of those whom I met repeatedly. The hours seemed endless. I felt cold and tired. I decided to knock at the door of a small house where I hoped to find a man whose name I had memorized some time ago and who I understood probably could be of some help. By doing so I took a calculated risk, hoping for the best. A woman cautiously opened the door. She did not ask about the purpose of my visit but told me, almost routinely, that her husband was out of town. I decided not to press further, realizing that there must have been a good reason for her attitude. Under the circumstances I could not blame her.

During the long hours I spent walking through the streets the picture became clear to me. There was no longer any doubt in my mind about the stringent precautions and activities along the border, which was clearly visible in part through the spaces in between buildings. It was frightening. Numerous gendarmes patrolled the road from one end to the other, some of them accompanied by trained police dogs, watching out for suspects. From the distance I saw the heavily guarded border station. Along the border were observation towers, and as I had been warned earlier, mines had probably been placed in strategic places. From time to time a group of soldiers on military vehicles passed by, forcing me to stand in deep snow until they were gone.

In this state of mind I began to feel that everyone I met on my walk eyed me with suspicion. I feared meeting more guards, dogs, gendarmes, soldiers, and even civilians. Some of the latter probably would have sympathized with me or given useful advice, but I couldn't risk approaching them for fear that they might have been loyal party members.

Discouraged and tired, I walked slowly to the railway station and sat there on a dirty bench to wait for my train. I told myself that no one in his right mind would risk his life and those of his family members in an attempt to break through these parts of the border.

My journey home on the train was depressing. Georgine was eagerly waiting for my description of the situation, but I was in no condition to give her any hope or encouragement. We agreed after hours of analyzing the facts that we simply had to discard any attempt to flee into the American Zone of Germany. This we had to do in spite of the fact that once anyone succeeded in reaching that zone he found himself immediately in a free world.

The days dragged on. Each one seemed more hopeless and gray. The radio and the official newspaper were filled with lies promising a red paradise as soon as all the enemies of the people had been uncovered. This wore us down in body and spirit. Former owners of businesses, the so-called capitalists and exploiters, suffered the most. Some of the prominent ones were detained and placed in display windows of the now-nationalized shops. They had to carry signs informing the passing citizens that they had committed serious crimes in amassing fortunes through the sweat and toil of the masses.

We were constantly under observation. In our building it was the woman janitor who watched our every step. When we looked down from our windows, any person in the busy street could have been a plainclothesman watching exits from our building in the area assigned to him. We tried avoiding visits to our relatives and friends and telephone calls. In any event, we could only talk in generalities, as otherwise we might have given away our secret thoughts and intentions to the authorities, who, we were convinced, were listening to our conversations.

The final order from the Employment Office to appear before it had been received only a few weeks ago. My reaction must certainly have been expected without further delay. Consequently we had to act now or never.

After a thorough discussion and without mentioning a word to anyone, Georgine and I worked out a plan that we swore to each other we would try to put into effect no matter what. We knew that otherwise we would never gather the courage to do so. It was obvious to us that the government precautions on the southern border of Bohemia were somewhat less perfect than those put into effect on the line bordering the American Zone in the west. We looked at the map and realized with despair that the southern part was bordering on the Soviet occupation zone of Austria. Vienna, its capital, was at that time divided into four sectors of interest, namely, the Soviet, British, French, and American zones.

Despite this terrifying act, we decided not to change our decision. We would take the risk of crossing the southern border into and through the Soviet Zone, trying to arrive somewhere in Vienna, in a suburb of which Georgine had an aunt whom she had never seen before. We only knew that she and her husband lived a modest life in this small suburb.

The town in the south of Bohemia, about a kilometer of the Austrian border, was familiar to me. I had lived there as a young boy. The river formed the border. All the boys from the neighborhood used to gather there in my younger days to swim and frolic. The water was ice cold, but that did not deter us from diving in and splashing around as only youngsters with boundless energy and joy of living can do. During school vacations we spent the long summer days around the river. When we got tired of swimming we chased each other, playing hide-and-seek in the dense bushes on the riverbank, on both sides of the border. This got us into trouble sometimes with youngsters on the Austrian side, who considered it a serious offense whenever we entered their territory. The animosity between our two nations, dating back to 1918, when Bohemia and Moravia ceased to be a part of the Austrian empire, had not easily been forgotten. One morning about fifty young boys gathered on either side of the river. Everyone, including myself, was armed with rocks and homemade shields. We succeeded for a while in occupying a small territory on the Austrian side but had to withdraw in haste when reinforcements arrived from a nearby Austrian village. The war was abruptly ended when gendarmes from both sides, attracted by the noise of the battle, chased the wary warriors away.

In spite of occasional setbacks, these were happy times in my younger years. But Bruno did not enjoy our games. He did not seem to like sports. His hearing impairment was another factor that kept him isolated from the rest of the youngsters. For me the river had a special fascination. Sometimes I sat on the elevated embankment for hours watching the twisted course of the clear water and following it until it disappeared behind the last bend. It did not occur to me that one day, years later, the river would play a strange role in my life.

Now, in January of 1949, it had been nineteen years since I had lived in this border town. It was necessary to survey the area anew and to visually reacquaint myself with the terrain and landmarks that would either lead us to freedom or make us victims of a terrible disaster. Armed again with a bogus certificate, I took the train to the town. From my earlier days I had a loyal friend there. Although we had not been in touch for some time, he proved to be a real friend. First we talked in generalities only. I did not tell him clearly the purpose of my visit, but he must have understood. Without asking questions that would have incriminated both of us later, he walked with me patiently down the snow-and-ice-covered main thoroughfare. From there I could ascertain that not many changes had taken place in the area. The main difference was the silence and desolation hanging over the stretch of fields separating the town from my beloved river. The barrenness also extended far beyond the river to the Soviet-occupied zone of Austria. I felt a shiver down my spine when I realized the vastness of that space and the possible perils that lurked there for four desperate figures who would soon plod like shadows through the deep snow.

My friend walked back to the station with me. On our way we passed several men in uniforms. I wondered if I would face any one of them when the die was cast. Before I departed, my friend whispered to me the name of a reliable man in the village across the river. I was grateful for his kindness.

The days that followed back in the city were filled with feverish preparations. Heavy doubts were lingering in our minds: were we making the right decision, considering the immense danger? We could not mention our intentions to a soul, not even our closest relatives and friends. Bruno and his wife, who lived in the same modern apartment building as we did, did not have the slightest idea of our plans. It required great restraint and willpower on our part not to ask for their moral support in those trying times. We had good reason for that. Whenever someone was caught in an attempt to leave the country, people around him or her were detained and accused of assisting the "enemies of the people." This would have notably been the case in my situation as a marked man. During interrogations that were conducted by the police without mercy, the accused often, understandably, lacked the stamina to withhold politically damaging actions or conversations with the would-be escapees. Thus, as a result of a single escape attempt, a number of people would suffer for a long time.

It is difficult to express in words our mental anguish. There are things in one's life that cannot be related to anyone else, even by the greatest writer or narrator. No one can make another feel what it is to be afraid, thirsty, hungry, cold, hot, depressed, hopeless, or desperate. Any description consists of words only.

We were outlaws in the true sense of the word. Innocent of any wrongdoing or crime, our passive resistance toward the brutal regime had deprived us of any protection whatsoever against accusations, searches, interrogations, threats of forced labor and jail, dislocation from our comfortable apartment, and dismemberment of our family. We had to be watchful of every word we spoke and every move we made so as not to give the secret police reason to interfere physically, in addition to their usual harassment. Seeking legal protection was utterly out of the question. There was no authority in the land that would have listened to a complaint. On the contrary, had we submitted even the slightest protest, this would have been interpreted as treason and would have accelerated our fate. A protest would have been looked upon as an attempt to discredit the regime that—after all—was representing and expressing the "will of the people."

The expression *people* had been used by the Communists on every imaginable occasion since the end of the war to justify their terror against the general population. Workers were asked by "the people" to arm themselves against foreign agents sabotaging their plants; "the people" demanded confiscation of properties of the smallest business holders; "the people" asked for severe punishment of "enemies of the people." After the war I was contributing on various subjects to the democratically oriented paper printed under the auspices of Dr. Zenkl's party. The paper had been abruptly stopped by the revolutionary Communists in February of 1948. In one of my articles I had asked a bold question, to the dismay of the Communists. I demanded to know whom the Communists defined as "people" and whether those not belonging to the party did not belong to the human race. The article, naturally, had become a black spot on my personal record.

It did not make any difference that both Georgine and I came from modest middle-class families who certainly could not be accused of being exploiters of the working class. Our fathers had been low-ranking government employees who had performed their duties honorably and with dedication and who supported their families with incomes only covering the modest necessities of life. They had behaved honorably during the Nazi occupation, as Georgine and I had. Why, then, had we been accused of being enemies of the people? Simply because we had not joined the Communist Party and had not given the brutal masters an assurance of unlimited loyalty and support, because we were unwilling to change our revulsion toward spineless and corrupt dictatorships, whether of the left or the right.

The third of February 1949 was our ninth wedding anniversary. We were hardly able to think of it. Our minds were occupied with one thought only. Tomorrow would be the day. We still had the opportunity to abort our escape plans or delay them, but would that solve anything? As the daylight dimmed and the city streets lit up, we looked once more over the roofs of our beloved Prague as we stood silently at the window. In a handbag, a small bundle of our belongings was ready to take with us the next morning. Although we had disposed of the living room furniture earlier in order to meet our expenses, there was still the remaining furniture, rugs, pictures, personal effects and family mementos. It was particularly painful to leave behind a record made of Peter's voice when he was two years old. The gramophone record was too big to be hidden in our bag. It was also heartbreaking to leave behind the hundreds of valuable books that Georgine had accumulated with love during our marriage.

Naturally, we could not carry a suitcase. Georgine would carry the small bag such as one carries on an inconspicuous day visit perhaps to relatives or to the countryside. Therein she put an extra pair of underwear and socks for each of us. The clothing we were to wear had to be carefully chosen. Anything that we and our boys could put on without creating undue suspicion was neatly laid out on the sofa. It was in the middle of a hard winter. It was gratifying to know that our winter coats had been lined with fur at an earlier time, in preparation for our plans.

In spite of the careful planning and precautions, Georgine and I could not rid ourselves of a deep fear and uncertainty. It was heartbreaking to watch our two small boys go to warm beds with clean linen after saying their daily prayers. We reminded ourselves that this might be the last night of comfort for them for a long, long time. They had no notion what was going on.

The night before us became endless. We could hardly close our eyes. The darkness made our situation look truly hopeless. Any outside noise made us listen with fear until everything quieted down again. When dawn finally arrived we felt like condemned people being taken to their ominous destiny. It was sad that we could not say a few last words to my brother, Bruno, or to mine and Georgine's fathers, who all loved us very much. We recalled how often Bruno and Georgine's father played with our children, making them laugh and happy.

We got up and had a simple breakfast. Then we dressed the children and ourselves, carefully going over every single piece of clothing. The small bag together with our overall appearance fitted the picture of a family leaving for a short visit. We said our prayers and embraced and kissed each other. Then Georgine and I nodded, giving the signal to put our carefully conceived plan into effect.

Georgine left the apartment with the children first. Had the janitor downstairs inquired about the reason for leaving the building, Georgine was to explain to her that she was taking the boys to her father for a short visit. She then took the streetcar to the main railway station, where she purchased tickets for herself and the two boys on a fast train to a city about fifty kilometers from the southern border of Bohemia. Without waiting or looking around for me, she boarded the train. As a precaution, as we had agreed in advance, she was careful not to buy direct tickets all the way to the border town.

About an hour after Georgine's departure from the apartment I left, too, carrying nothing whatsoever except for a few personal documents. The janitor did not seem suspicious when I passed her window before entering the street. Once out of the building I turned in the opposite direction to the one Georgine had taken. Arriving at the same railway station, I bought my ticket and boarded the same train. As previously agreed, I stayed in a different carriage until the train moved out of the station. Then I walked slowly through several carriages until I found my family. The children behaved well, asking no embarrassing questions. They believed that we were taking them to visit Grandmother, my stepmother. They were not aware that she had died years ago and, in fact, was buried in the very border town where we were heading. In any event, our journey was confirmed by a false travel authorization on the letterhead of a nationalized company. Even so, my heart pounded whenever someone in uniform passed by our compartment. If there was any plainclothesman on the train we could not have been able to recognize him. We were fortunate not to encounter any control points. A slip of the tongue would have resulted in disaster for us.

We carried nothing on us that would have compromised us. At any given moment we were ready to argue that our journey was approved by the authorities and that it was to be a short one. We could not dare to carry any foreign currency that would be used after crossing the border openly with us. First of all, it was most difficult to acquire any foreign money, and second, there were heavy penalties for being in possession of it. The Czech currency was, of course, utterly useless beyond the border. I was hoping that if we seemed suspicious during an inspection and search the absence of hard currency would give us an additional margin of safety. I took, however, a calculated risk insofar I had acquired a very few single dollar bills to enable us to reach Vienna after crossing the border. This pitifully small amount, which today would hardly cover a tip in a restaurant, was carefully hidden in one of my shoes, inside a slot in the leather. Even if discovered, I hoped this would not be considered as being in connection with any escape attempt, in view of the small amount.

On arrival at the city from which we would have to travel for another hour to reach the border town, we went for a short walk to stretch our legs and prepare ourselves morally for the ordeal that awaited us in the coming hours. Then we purchased the train tickets for our final ride into the unknown. It was already late in the afternoon. The children became restless. Georgine and I were tired and depressed. The naked reality dawned on us with full force. We sat down on the bench of a large open compartment that was mostly occupied by workers returning home from their labor. The children behaved well but kept asking questions about our destination and the time it would take us to get there. We tried to keep them as calm and reassured as we could. We could not help overhearing parts of the conversations between our fellow travelers. At one point our hearts sank when someone mentioned in a subdued voice that some people had been caught recently trying to cross the border. Looking at the faces of the passengers, we could not make out who was friend or foe and whether the remark was casual or intentionally offering a subtle warning. We would have liked to hear more about the incident or the location where it actually happened, but we had to keep a neutral and disinterested front while we forced ourselves to bite our tongues. The overheard news added considerably to our worry.

The train crawled through the countryside, stopping at numerous small stations. The fields were covered with fresh, glittering snow. It was freezing. The train passed through long stretches of woods. The treetops were bathed in bright moonlight while the forest itself looked dark and impenetrable. The sight disturbed us, as we had not expected such a clear night, which could complicate our plans and increase the peril we would be facing soon.

When the train rolled into the border town station, everyone began rushing toward the exits. We passed several men in uniforms. Customs officers, gendarmes, guards, and a few soldiers watched as the passengers went by them. The hall was only dimly lit. We were able to mingle with the homeward-bound workers and general passengers without arousing any suspicion. Once out of the station building we slowed down and let all the other people pass by. We could not very well walk ahead of them, as our plan called for turning off the main street and heading toward the border.

At first it seemed that our strategy worked well. But then we encountered a serious problem. A border patrolman in a gray uniform appeared a short distance behind us. He carried a rifle and slowed down every time we did so ourselves. At that point he did not seem to suspect anything. It was apparently his duty to follow and watch the crowd coming from the station upon every train arrival. In this way he could observe any unusual action or movement. The awful truth crept into our minds that there could be no way out of our predicament. We could not turn back nor could we continue walking in front of him much longer, having no place to stay. Our plan had hit an obstacle not provided for in our preparations, which was now about to end our dreams for freedom.

Without saying a word to me, Georgine suddenly stopped. She grabbed little John, who at the time was only four years old, dragged him to the roadside between the trees, and energetically pulled down his small pants. The guard with the rifle reached us. He hesitated for a moment, which seemed endless to us. In the meantime Georgine scolded John for not announcing his need to relieve himself earlier at the station. He protested vigorously, but Georgine covered his little mouth with one hand, holding his pants down with the other.

The guard weighed his next move but then decided to continue on his way. He must have realized that by waiting for Johnny to attend to whatever was pressing he might neglect his duty to follow the rest of the crowd, which by now was already some distance away. Georgine and I sighed with great relief. This obstacle had been overcome by her presence of mind, but other ones lay ahead.

The road pointed directly south toward the river and the border. About a kilometer farther down it merged into the main street, stretching left and right parallel to the river. We turned right on the last leg of our journey, as we had planned. We passed the drab houses on both sides until we reached a strategic point. We stopped in the shadow of a building to get a little rest and take courage. Opposite was the old house with the large wooden gate through which I had passed many times on my way to school in my younger years. We made sure that we were out of sight of anyone who might have walked by at this late, dark hour. We were facing a small lane to the left between a shack and a garden fence. We sneaked silently to the far corner of the fence, where we squatted down in the dark shadows. A dog barked in one of the nearby yards, some voices sounded in the neighborhood, and a dim light went on and off somewhere in a backyard. It was freezing cold. We were now entirely on our own. No one could help us. We prayed to the Almighty to hold a merciful hand over our heads.

I waited for a considerable time, observing the moonlit stretch of fields separating us from the border river. It was important to detect any noise or movement. A few times I almost gave the signal to move, but something told me to hold out a little longer. In times like this a few minutes could make the difference between life and death. Making this decision was solely my responsibility.

Suddenly I felt that the moment had come. Something inside urged me to go. I took Johnny on my shoulders, and with eight-year-old Peter behind me and Georgine at the end we began to move cautiously across the frozen fields, trying to avoid the brightly lit areas. A low ridge along which we proceeded gave us some shelter. Soon we began increasing our pace through the deep snow, and finally, with the river line approaching, we began running for our lives. We realized that every second counted. The deep snow made it difficult, and we fell every few steps. The run took all our strength, but we managed to get up again and again and continue on. Although we were almost out of breath, we could not afford to stop. Georgine began to despair in her anxiety for the safety of her family. Although I felt great compassion for her, I was forced to reprimand her sharply, reminding her that we must continue at any cost or pain. She nodded in agreement, realizing that this was the only way.

Now we had to cover the final two hundred meters to the river. In our determination we ran and fell and ran and fell. Little Johnny on my shoulders was hitting the ground with me. Peter and Georgine hobbled behind, to the best of their ability. Almost all of our strength was consumed. If God was watching us, he must have had pity on us. If the Devil was looking at us, he must have laughed at our misery.

The river suddenly lay before us. I looked for the spot where I used to wade barefoot when I was a young boy. Aiming at the same place, I hoped that we would not fall through the frozen surface. During the day the sun had partially melted the ice. A thin crust had formed in the afternoon, but fortunately, a solid tier of ice remained underneath. We could not hesitate. Determined, we dashed across, crushing the surface under our feet. In the silent moonlit night this sounded like explosions, which must have been heard all around us. It must have also been heard by the border patrols to the left and right of us, who, no doubt, had been assigned to this important sector. That we had not run into them and that they had not been at this particular spot at the time of our crossing is one of the mysteries of fate, perhaps even a small miracle.

Little strength was left in us, and we could hardly breathe. But this was not the time to relax. The area beyond the river in front of us was open, not allowing any cover. We forced ourselves to stumble for a few more minutes until we reached some bushes between fields. Then we stopped, looking back across the river at our beloved country, which we, decent humans and devout patriots, had to abandon. The country had forsaken us. Tears were in our eyes when we urged the boys to have a last look at their homeland and the little town where only a few lights were burning. Peter understood later when we explained the reasons for our leaving. When we stressed that we did not want our children to grow up amid lies and brutality, he only nodded. After a while he noted that, in fact, he was happy to leave his communist teacher behind. Peter could not forget that at one time the teacher had let the class play soldiers between the Soviets and Americans. Only a few boys dared to represent America in that cruel game. The woman did not stop the "Soviets" from abusing and mistreating Peter and his pals. Peter is now over forty. Since our escape he has not seen his homeland or the city of Prague, where he was born. At the time of leaving his birthplace, John was too small to understand the situation, but as long as we were together he stoically accepted it.

Standing in a foreign land, Georgine and I felt the full impact of the seriousness of our action. We could no longer reverse our decision and try to sneak back. It would have meant exposing ourselves to the same perils. Even if we had managed to crawl undetected over the river and the wide field, reached the small railway station safely around midnight, and returned to Prague and our apartment, agony would engulf us anew. We would turn time back to the point at which he had already realized without doubt that by staying in our country we would be exposed to a constant life of lies, twisted characters, and brutal oppression.

Of course, it was utterly out of the question to try to return. The thought of such a possibility crossed our minds only for a second. We must go on! There must be no hesitation! Even if a flicker of doubt lingered in mine and Georgine's hearts we did not share it, being afraid that it might weaken our determination.

As we crouched in the bushes we were still perspiring, although our gasping for air became easier. The night was bitterly cold. The temperature reached a good number of degrees below zero. We could rest no longer without exposure to frostbite. Turning our backs to our homeland, we resumed our walk, slowly and carefully, heading toward the small Austrian town that still lay some distance away. Our trail took us mostly over frozen snow, but from time to time we could not avoid sinking deeply into spots that had stayed shaded during the day and consequently had not formed a hard surface. Occasionally we stopped briefly so that I could determine our course from one group of shaded bushes or trees to the next. At no time could we ignore the fact that we were intruders into the Soviet Zone. Nothing in the world would have frightened us more than being stopped by men in gray uniforms.

Upon reaching the outskirts of the town we behaved as if we belonged there. Our steps led us through the main street in order to be less conspicuous. Had we chosen to walk behind the buildings or through back or side alleys, we would have drawn a lot of attention in this small community.

After a while we located the bus station, which at this late hour appeared lifeless. The schedule on the wall indicated that there were only two bus departures each day going to Vienna. The afternoon bus had left many hours prior to our arrival. The other one was leaving at four o'clock in the morning to arrive in the city in the early-morning hours.

It was almost midnight and still several hours until departure time. Georgine and I could not sit with the children in the cold waiting hall for such a long time. Also, sooner or later, someone might confront us, perhaps an Austrian gendarme or, heaven help us, a Soviet soldier or guard to inquire as to the reason for our being there at this late hour and demand to see our papers (called *boumashka* in Russian). This would have immediately revealed that we were foreigners who had come without Soviet authorization. Although we spoke fluent German, we knew that if we fell into the hands of a gendarme there would be some chance he might take us to the local Soviet headquarters, as was his duty. On the other hand, the majority of Austrian officials were strongly anti-Soviet and despised the occupation forces, as would people of any country having a similar experience. Even so, we could not risk meeting any Austrian guard or trying to contact any unknown civilian for fear that he might be a member of the Austrian Communist Party.

We had no recourse but to fall back on a name I had been holding in reserve for an emergency. It was the address whispered to me several weeks earlier on the other side of the border by my friend who had joined the Party out of sheer necessity, to preserve his job and feed his family.

It was ironic that his pretense and lie would be to our advantage at this critical hour.

In the darkness we found the modest home surrounded by a small garden and wooden fence. I knocked at the door not knowing what the next moments would bring. After initial hesitation, an elderly man opened the door and scrutinized the visitors. When he saw our little boys and heard us uttering a few Czech words to them, he understood without asking questions. It was dangerous to stay outside. He ushered us inside and shut the door quickly. By that time his wife had also awakened. We all stood in the entrance hall viewing each other. Georgine and I were grateful to find the old couple kind and understanding. While the lady talked with us, her husband went to the back of the house and drew the curtains. Then he ushered us to a room that had one large and one smaller bed. He urged us to try to get some rest before our morning bus trip to the south. None of us mentioned the name of our mutual friend at whose risk and on whose advise we had come. The old lady went to the kitchen and prepared hot tea. It was most welcome. When the door closed behind her and her husband we sipped the hot beverage. A pleasant warmth spread through our tired bodies. A feeling of deep gratitude toward our hosts filled our hearts. Georgine and I could not help reviewing the adventure we had just been through and the difficulties we might still encounter in the future. The children fell asleep instantly. Their innocent minds did not grasp the magnitude of our undertaking. We prayed in silence for a long time, until we were overcome by a deep sleep.

When the door opened again and our host whispered that it was time to get up we felt like we had slept only minutes. In the cold and unfriendly morning hour, shivering, we dressed. The two old people saw to it that we had some hot coffee and bread before they opened the door in total darkness. They pressed our hands warmly and bid us a good journey and even put a small amount of local currency in my pocket. We will never forget the kindness and concern reflected in their eyes.

It did not take us long to reach the bus terminal. Some people were already seated on the benches in the waiting room. They looked like manual workers or tradesmen waiting for the bus to take them on their daily journey south, perhaps to Vienna. Georgine and I bought our tickets and whispered to our children that we should avoid speaking Czech, as then the local people would immediately know that we were foreigners. We were concerned that some of passengers might be party members who would not hesitate to denounce us. All the men looked grim in the cold morning darkness.

The waiting seemed endless while we were trying to penetrate the facades of those around us. Finally, shortly after four o'clock, a signal was given to board the bus. We had been well prepared for this moment. We rushed to the entrance and succeeded in moving hastily to the rear of the vehicle before anyone else did so. There we thought we would be safer, not being exposed to so many eyes. We huddled together in the dark corner. The bus was only half-full. Some of the passengers tried to sleep during the bumpy trip; a few of them talked in subdued voices, sometimes glancing at us. No one, however, approached us with any question, for which we were thankful. We could not sleep with the danger of our situation running through our minds. Occasionally the boys inadvertently blurted out a question in Czech, the only language they knew. Georgine and I managed to cover up with our German, signaling to them that they must remain quiet.

With the arrival of dawn we could watch the countryside. We no longer saw the mysterious frightening shadows or strange silhouettes that we had imagined while it was still dark. At each bus stop, however, our anxiety was aroused again. New passengers brought with them a renewed uncertainty for us. We could not know who among them might have been a policeman disguised in civilian clothes or a party member. The Soviets were well known for their mania for identification papers and for permits covering travel from one place to another. Even in their own country their citizens were required to carry special permits merely to travel from one town to another to visit relatives. Had we observed a uniformed man heading for the bus entrance at any stop, we were determined to try to leave immediately through the rear exit and then make efforts to continue on our journey at a later time through whatever means might become available. Fortunately, such a dire situation did not occur.

As we neared Vienna, the bus was almost filled to capacity. Some of the travelers were probably going to work, others to look up relatives or friends or to shop for the items that had begun to appear in the markets for the first time after the long and devastating war. When, near the city, some women with children boarded the bus Georgine and I were relieved because we now fitted better into the pattern.

Through the window we observed the drab and poor outskirts of Vienna as the bus headed for its destination. This was no longer a picture of the clean and friendly city of the past. Here and there we observed a few Soviet soldiers with stern looks on their faces. If any civilians were in the open they walked like shadows, without any spirit. This was the Soviet Sector. A crucial point in our adventure had arrived. Should we get off at one of the next stops or stay on the bus as long as we could? Once again our decision had to be guided by sheer instinct. Soon we were approaching the inner part of the city. The surroundings seemed somewhat friendlier, and there were more people in the streets. It was that time of the morning when most of them would be rushing off to their places of work. There was a certain purpose in their faces, contrary to what we had seen earlier. This, we decided, was the right time to get off. Just as we were getting ready, all the others were preparing to do so. They stretched, yawned, and gathered their belongings. The driver announced that we had reached the bus depot.

Our children hung onto us as we stepped down and touched Austrian soil. It occurred to us here, at this important bus terminal, there surely would be some kind of control. We feared the worst. When nothing of this sort happened it dawned on us that we must not have landed in the Soviet Sector. The other passengers walked off in different directions, and we, too, began walking. The sun was up in the clear air, but it was still very cold. It did not matter to us. Fate had been kind to us once more. It had been only twenty-four hours since we had left our Prague apartment. It was like a dream. Happiness filled our tired bodies as we thanked the Almighty for letting us stay together as a family, to overcome the initial obstacles in our quest for freedom. Except for the clothes on our back we had no worldly possessions, but this was of little importance to us.

Our joy increased further when we learned from an elderly woman that we had landed in the British Sector. Now we were certain for the first time that for the moment we were safe. In our own country we had to live under fear and terror while here, on foreign soil, the very first few minutes permitted us to breathe the air of protection and liberty. No one here would be allowed to accuse us unjustly of any wrongdoing or punish us for simply expressing our thoughts and opinions, we believed. If indeed this was true, our physical and legal protection would be guaranteed.

Although free, we had no money except small change. Our situation was still a desperate one. Our immediate need was for shelter and food. We were unaware of any international assistance group established to aid people like us. In fact, we learned only a few months later of the existence of the IRO (International Refuge Organization) which maintained a small office in the city. Ultimately we turned to the IRO for help in May of that year, but its Vienna office turned out to be of little help to us.

We had a friend in the city who was the owner of an export business. He used to travel to Prague, where he had been a guest in our apartment on several occasions. He had enjoyed our hospitality and friendship in addition to the excellent meals that Georgine used to prepare. During his visits he used to stress that he would be happy to reciprocate in some way should we ever call on him in Vienna. I was determined to get in touch with him in the near future, but in our present situation it seemed advisable to first see Georgine's Aunt Anna, who lived in one of the suburbs. It would have been difficult to remember exactly, and dangerous to write down, her complicated address. To overcome this problem we had embodied the name of the suburb, the street with its house number and the particular section of town, in Peter's storybook that he carried with him. We devised a code system applying individual letters and digits throughout the book and marking them with a barely visible dot where applicable. Even had we been caught we believed that the address could not have been deciphered by a stranger.

The few shillings left in my pocket bought us tickets on the streetcar to her suburb, which fortunately was also in the British Sector. From the stop we had to walk through a long snow-covered lane. Several small dwellings were situated around a church and a school. Not far from there we found the clean little house with a garden. An iron fence surrounded the small lot. We took courage and sounded the bell. For a long time there was no answer. A shepherd dog kept running excitedly up and down the garden path leading to the house entrance. At one point there was some movement behind a curtain. But silence followed.

After a long while that seemed endless, the door slowly opened and an elderly woman with a scarf around her head came to the gate. She was bewildered at the sight of us, as we had never before met. In an apologetic manner Georgine introduced us and explained the reason for our coming. We desperately needed a temporary shelter, she added. Aunt Anna looked at us and our children with understanding eyes. After some hesitation she opened the gate and let us in. We walked eagerly through the path covered with snow. The house had been built by her and her husband with sweat and toil, using up all the resources they had been able to scrape together from his meager income as a carpenter in a distant plant. He was not at home because his workplace was in a town that was miles away from Vienna. His only relaxation was during the weekends when he returned home. Then he would walk slowly around the house and through the small garden where he grew a few fruit trees and flowers. When he got tired he returned to the bright corner of the kitchen, sat on a chair, and enjoyed the peace and quiet surrounding him there. Anna always did all she could to please him and made his weekend stay as comfortable as possible. Uncle Rudolf was not a man easy to get along with. He had serious health problems, to which he drew Anna's attention by frequent sighing and grumbling.

Anna sympathized with us. She was a deeply religious person. Her faith demanded of her that she be a Good Samaritan. She could not, however, hide her fear as to what her husband would think of the situation. She was afraid that he would consider our stay a serious intrusion into his well-deserved rest during weekends, when he had to gather new strength for his heavy work in the coming week.

Her fear was justified. When Uncle Rudolf arrived on Saturday afternoon, Georgine and I sensed at once that our arrival was unwelcome and that it was causing a disturbance to his routine. For us, who fully appreciated the reason for his attitude, it was a painful stress. We felt guilty of causing his discomfort and unhappiness. When Uncle was home we did our best to be out of the house for as long as possible. This entailed taking the children for long walks despite the freezing weather. We usually went to the city and walked through parks or visited museums until we could stand on our feet no longer.

Anna allotted us a small room with a spare bed and a dilapidated garden chair. The little house was not equipped for visitors. The room was cold, as was the whole house, quite different from our comfortably warm Prague apartment. There were moments when we asked ourselves whether it was really fair to burden our relatives with the discomfort resulting from our venture. But then we had to admit that at the moment there was no easy solution to Uncle's justified resentment and our suffering from the cold, inadequate nutrition, and continuous depression.

It was one of the most severe winters in a decade. Georgine and the children slept on the bed in the cold room. I had no choice but to settle as comfortably as I could on the old garden chair, in which I tried to rest in a semi-seated position. The chair would not unfold completely. There was no mattress there, just an old blanket over the canvas. The cold nights and my position prevented me from falling into a deep sleep. Because of the chilly nights Georgine and the boys did not get a good rest either. One night while trying to turn I tore a big hole in the decayed canvas.

The next morning Anna was badly shocked, not so much for herself, but because she knew that Rudolf would blame her and us bitterly for it. No matter in what condition their possessions were, they were precious to him, as he had to work hard all his life to acquire them. And during the war material possessions had become even more valuable.

Being an old Austrian citizen, Rudolf could not help disliking the Czechs. At that time, past history still had a considerable influence upon the various European nationals. To make matters worse, he was exposed to communist propaganda in the plant in which he worked. Some of his coworkers naturally praised the Soviet victory and loathed political refugees, a considerable number of whom had sought shelter in the country. They hoped that Austria one day would become a communist-dominated state, too, contrary to the aspirations of a great majority of Austrians.

It became absolutely necessary for Georgine and me to make efforts to be less dependent on Uncle Rudolf and Aunt Anna's charity. I was determined to earn some money so that we could contribute to the food and shelter. Our friend whom we had known from his visits to our Prague apartment came to my mind. His export business had considerable opportunities during the postwar period. He was not surprised when I called him on the telephone and told him about our adventures during the past weeks. He offered immediate help. In view of the dire employment situation he could not offer a regular job to a foreigner. He suggested, however, that I perform some special work for him as a consultant. For this he paid me a nominal monthly amount, from which I could give Anna a portion and use the rest for small necessities for my family. For some time I was assigned to assist in developing a certain patent on which he and his scientist associate had been working on. It concerned an electronic de-rusting process that promised to become successful in the war-devastated cities, where heaps of rusting metals were everywhere. We made good progress, but the going was slow, as research money was not readily available at the time.

Our stay in Austria required that we register at the police headquarters, where a tight record of foreigners, refugees, and other unwanted elements in general was kept. The government had to exercise prudence in granting permanent residence permits or political asylum to strangers. This was particularly true with regard to those who had come here because of oppression by the Soviets, who now, together with the Allies, controlled Austria and its people's lives. After four months in Vienna I was called to the police, who explained to me that as a foreigner I could not stay in the country. They forcefully suggested that I leave shortly. They were not in a position, they stated, to extend our temporary permit.

My friend did not want to see us leave, as he had grown fond of us. He offered to intervene with the highest Austrian authorities. He also offered to speed up a possible petition for Austrian citizenship and to vouch for us personally and financially. We expressed our deep gratitude for his efforts and his true friendship to us. After careful consideration we felt that we had to decline politely, as we had misgivings as to our security in the country. We were not far enough away from Czechoslovakia, and parts of Austria were under Soviet occupation, the end of which or its consequences no one could foresee at the time.

We were reminded of the Soviet power every day. Their sector could be seen from the windows of the house where we were staying. Only a stretch of land not wider than several hundred meters separated us. The Soviet guards patrolled along the dividing line. They were too close for comfort. The city streets themselves were far from safe. From time to time some people suddenly disappeared in broad daylight and were never seen again. In some cases eyewitnesses watched helplessly as a person was dragged by the Soviet secret police into a civilian car. No one dared to interfere. Later, at one point, this happened to the former Czech minister of industry under whom I had been appointed deputy director of the Czech oil industry. He subsequently perished at the hands of his enemies back home.

Reasons for our leaving Vienna became urgent. Having no savings and only a few meager personal belongings, we needed outside help. After some inquiries and searching we found out that the IRO might be of assistance. We located its Vienna office. The first step was to obtain from them a special identification card authorizing us to seek help from its branch somewhere outside the Soviet Sector. Before such cards were issued we were required to tell the IRO officials and investigators our life stories and the reasons for leaving our country. They were not friendly, having been deluged with a stream of people of many nationalities. The refugees were coming from all corners of Europe, trying to find new homes in various parts of the world. Many of them were coming in without personal identification papers; some were even former concentration camp inmates or escaping political refugees. Some lied about their real identity to cover up their sometimes-shady past. Others decided to burn all bridges behind, severing all ties with their families and friends.

If any of them had had close ties with the Nazis, they would not brag about it, as it would be held against him.

Our life story was put on record in the IRO files. We will never know how reliable its employees were and how many infiltrators succeeded in working for the organization. One cannot help wondering if and how much information filtered back to the places of origin, ending up on blacklists in the carefully kept Soviet records on a worldwide scale. Aside from processing us and issuing identification papers, the Vienna office of the IRO could not assist us any further. The Austrian refugee camp of the organization was located at Trofaiach, near Leoben, in the British Zone. To get there, we were told, we must cross the soviet Zone, in which the IRO had no jurisdiction at all. If caught when crossing it, a political refugee would face dire consequences. If successful in crossing and reaching the camp at Trofaiach, anyone armed with IRO identification would be taken care of there.

The Soviet danger zone lay ahead of us once more. We had earlier overcome its perils on our journey to Vienna. Would our good fortune stay with us when we made our way through red territory once more?

After a few days of feverish preparations, we thanked Anna and Rudolf for their hospitality and said good-bye. By that time Uncle seemed to have gotten somewhat used to our being around the house, but our departure must have meant a welcome return to his old routine. Anna, who had been so good to us during the past months, was visibly moved. The night before we left we heard her praying in a room adjacent to ours. She used to pray out loud frequently, but this time her voice sounded strange through the wall. She had told us on previous occasions that she had vivid visions of saints in the dark corners of her room while she prayed to them. She had often called out to them in a strange, crying voice. Her faith was so profound that during these rituals her spirit almost parted from her tormented body. This time her suffering must have been immense. Her screams sounded like those of a wounded animal. Her voice kept changing from a high pitch to the lowest depths. Her words were blurred, making no sense. The ritual kept us awake and frightened for long hours. It ceased as suddenly as it started. The house was dark and quiet again when we fell asleep, amid worries as to tomorrow.

Anna's face looked haggard the next morning. We did not mention a word about the previous night. There was also no sign on her part that would have indicated what happened. We did not doubt that she had been praying emotionally for us to reach a safe harbor in these troubled waters.

Her own life had not been an easy one. Her concern for us showed that there was much generosity and kindness in her heart despite her own suffering.

Our Austrian friend also showed great understanding for us. He was concerned as to our safety while we were attempting the journey across the Soviet Zone south of Vienna to reach the refugee camp in the British Zone. He offered to provide his car for the trip to Semmering Mountain, which formed the demarcation line between the two zones. By accepting his offer we were able to take along a small suitcase that we filled with modest items we had bought with my meager income during our stay. He sent his driver to meet us at the house and personally wished us a safe journey.

We stopped about ten kilometers from the border dividing the British and Soviet zones. We got out of the car, but the driver continued with our suitcase across the line. As instructed by his employer, he deposited the luggage in a small town in the British Zone. As he was an Austrian citizen, it was not difficult for him to move from one zone to the other. For us, his assistance was a great help.

Here we were now, again in enemy territory. Before us was a deep stretch of land spiked with green meadows and brown fields, with a few villages in between. The terrain gradually rose until it merged with the mountain covered with trees. Somewhere high up was the end of the Soviet Zone. The forest looked mysterious and forbidding. In places unknown to us it sheltered men charged with the protection of the line.

We did our best to behave like any Austrian family on an outing. First we sat for a while in the open at a table of a tourist inn that was not far from the highway. There we carefully observed what was going on around us. Several cars turned off the highway and stopped at the inn. A number of passengers sat down and ordered refreshments. Others walked leisurely around the grounds. When we felt that we did not look much different we stood up and began walking away from the inn at a slow pace.

It was a beautiful May day. Flowers were in bloom in the peaceful countryside. Upon arrival at the first village we looked up a shopkeeper, a reliable man recommended to us by our Vienna friend. He invited us inside while he himself left to make some inquiries. After a while he came back and assured us that it was safe to proceed to the next village. It was a long walk on a narrow tree-lined road between fields and meadows. At the end of the village we stopped to rest. Not far away, at the foot of the mountain, lay the forest. The next few hundred meters over the last open space would require the utmost caution and timing.

The afternoon shadow of the mountain was reaching the village when we started on our way. We reached the first trees safely and hid in the darkness for a while. Although there was a path leading over the mountain, we could not take it for fear of being discovered. Our decision was to painstakingly wind our way between trees and bushes, climbing ever higher and higher. Every time we heard a strange noise, we stopped and held our breath. Gradually we got tired and had to slow down considerably. We made headway with great effort. This was particularly harsh on John, who at the age of four had to struggle to keep up with the rest of us. I could not carry him for long stretches, as I was tired myself. It was not only the physical exhaustion but also the mental anguish. We were still exposed to perils that would not lessen until we reached the British Zone.

Although we had rested frequently, we were utterly exhausted when we reached the summit. It had been a constant struggle with low branches, sharp, thorny thickets, and large boulders. We were breathing hard and perspiring profusely, but we sensed that the worse was over. The borderline ran along the summit, but we did not know where the actual division was, so it was not yet time to abandon our caution. With our last strength we forced our bodies downhill, as far away from the top as possible.

When we felt that we had, without a doubt, left the enemy zone at a reasonably safe distance, we sat down in a secluded and dark spot protected by thick shrubs. There we rested for a long time to afford some reprieve to our trembling bodies.

At first Georgine and I did not fully realize our situation. Only after we had rested for some time and regained some strength did it strike us with great force that we had indeed overcome the major dangers that had been blocking our race for freedom. When we looked at our children, who had so faithfully and patiently shared our fate and who had survived the ordeals of the previous months and those of this day with us, our hearts filled with warmth and pride. We knew at that point that our love and concern for them would stay with us throughout our lives.

For the first time in many months we were absolutely certain that we had made the right decision, no matter what the future might bring from then on. Peter and John must have sensed the peace that had entered our hearts. Their faces lit up. Their faint smiles rewarded us more than anything else could have done.

In the distance down below a dog barked. It came from the village that was our next destination. Descending was almost as difficult as climbing. We tripped over roots and rocks and hit low branches. At the bottom we came upon a country lane that led us to a nearby inn. Before we entered it, we assured ourselves that we were indeed in the British Zone. A public notice on the wall of the inn confirmed it. It was not difficult to rent a small room. After eating a modest meal, we dropped into clean beds and fell asleep almost instantly.

The next morning, after a good rest, we got up in high spirits. It had been a long time since we had awakened with relatively few worries. This was the first day of our new freedom. Our feeling was indescribable. Georgine and I were sailing on clouds. It felt like we had stepped out of a dark, cold cellar or prison into the open, filled with warmth and clean sunshine. Our boys must also have observed the change in our behavior. Their little bodies seemed suddenly filled with happiness and a new vitality.

The next town was not far away. There we looked up a small merchant who had received our little suitcase for safekeeping. At first he pretended not to understand. Apparently he had to exercise caution even here. In a little while, however, when no one else was in the shop, he took us to a small room in the back. There was our suitcase containing the treasures we had acquired in Vienna. In normal times they would not have amounted to much, but now these modest belongings would help us start a new life somewhere in a faraway country. They included a small typewriter courtesy of our friend.

With the suitcase recovered, we headed to the railway station and boarded a train that took us to the Trofaiach refugee camp. Having reported to the camp commandant, we were allotted a small room in one of the dirty wooden huts that had served as quarters for various prisoners of war. The camp operations were financed with funds mostly originating in the United States. Several hard weeks awaited us. Either the money was utterly inadequate or there was a large-scale misuse of funds, but the lack of basic food to sustain life was appalling. We became weaker by the day. Georgine and I tried to share some of our food with the children, but our portions were very small and had hardly any nutritional value. Not a drop of real milk was given us during our stay. Instead we were given a whitish liquid that must have contained more than three-quarters water. Our main dish was a maize porridge that tasted and smelled musty. Although we were constantly hungry, our bodies were too weak to eat much of the meal. We forced ourselves as much as we could, but soon John could not stand the look and musty smell of the gray gruel any longer. He threw up every time he tried to swallow a spoonful. From malnutrition and complete lack of fruit and vegetables he developed badly infected boils on his head.

The mattresses on our bunk beds were filled with straw. The covers were filthy, as they had been used by weak and dirty prisoners of war for several years. The straw had pulverized, most of it becoming fine straw dust, with which the room was filled with our slightest movement. Breathing became difficult. We all developed some kind of asthma that forced us to stay outside whenever weather permitted.

We complained to one of the administrators of the camp, who, as we found out later, had been an SS officer during the war. He was known to have often complained bitterly as to the treatment the Nazi soldiers received during their stay in a Texas prisoner-of-war camp during the latter part of the war. It was ironic that he, a member of the former SS forces, with which I had been involved in a deadly shootout at the end of the war, was now attached to the camp management in charge of political refugees, many of whom had suffered from the Nazis as well as from the communists. He could not help us. Food supplies to the camp were poor both in volume and quality. The funds allocated for this purpose by management must have been quite limited. We had to accept it as a fact, although in the back of our minds there was as strong suspicion that an audit might have determined otherwise.

Something had to be done. It was important for our survival to supplement the dreadful, inadequate meals we had been receiving from the camp kitchen with at least some amount of nutritious food from the outside. One day we ventured into the village and spent a good part of the money we had left on an electric cooker, a few pounds of potatoes, and some butter. It was forbidden to use any electrical utensils in the camp. There was danger of fire in the wooden huts from the straw-filled mattresses. The main reason, however, was the weak electrical current that hardly permitted decent lighting. It was even impossible to read at night under the dim light. We did not care any longer for safety. Observing us, an outsider would have thought we were attending some kind of strange ritual when, after having plugged in the newly acquired cooker, we placed several potatoes in an empty tin can filled with water and stood around with our heads bowed over this pot. After a long while, the water began to boil. In the dim light, with the steam rising slowly toward the ceiling, the four figures appeared to be performing a mystical ceremony.

The smell of boiling potatoes promised us a delicious meal. With melted butter this was a real feast. The boys ate as much as they could digest. Georgine and I finished the rest. From then on we arranged for potato feasts on several occasions. It was pleasing to see the children gain a little weight and be more content with camp life. Georgine and I also felt better while waiting day after day for a sign of relief.

The camp was not to become a permanent home for us or the other refugees. The refugees were of many nationalities. Some of them were people like us fleeing from countries behind the Iron Curtain who had found themselves under Soviet occupation. Their dreams of a happy and free future had been shattered. Others tried to hide their wartime activities, seeking a fast way out of Europe and possible prosecution by their angry countrymen. Some Germans who had been born in Bohemia but had been loyal to the Nazis and their cause during the war suddenly claimed to be Czechs. They succeeded in being registered as such in view of their birthplace. There were also Russians and Ukrainians who had been forced into hard labor in Germany or who had been prisoners of war there. They despised the idea of returning to their homeland in fear of reprisals from their government. Surrendering to the Germans or working for them was by itself a crime in the eyes of the Communists. In the confusion that had lasted several years after the war, hundreds of thousands of people deprived of their homes for political or other reasons found themselves under the wings of the IRO, to be transferred free of charge to strange faraway lands.

The camp served only as a base for resettlement. The length of stay depended not only on the individual's background but also on immigration restrictions imposed by the various free-world governments that were prepared to accept these unfortunate ones.

Georgine and I had always dreamed of living in America, the land of freedom and opportunities. The United States had a reputation for being generous, good-hearted, unselfish, understanding, and willing to assist those who suffered under any form of tyranny. But to be transferred to America would have meant a long waiting period, as we knew no one who could sponsor us there. The main stream of refugees from Czechoslovakia had already resettled in the United States under a simplified and accelerated procedure shortly after the war, in the spring of 1948, at the time of the Communist takeover. There was no longer a special quota available to us more than fifteen months later.

The next possibility was either Canada or Australia. The Canadian representative let it be known that his country was looking for strong men capable of strenuous labor rather than people not used to heavy manual work. This condition virtually eliminated us as prospects for Canada. Australia was now our best chance for a speedy departure from Europe, where we had experienced so many troubles and which appeared headed for many more political and economic problems in the years to come.

We learned that it was not too difficult to immigrate to Australia. The land seemed exotic and tempting. The brochures we were shown displayed many pictures and statistics that fascinated us. The wide open spaces, exotic vegetation, and strange animals appealed to us. We felt we could contribute to the progress there, which seemed to be in full swing. Our great enthusiasm for starting a new life and working hard to make up for all the lost years in Europe should be beneficial to this young country. When the Australian commission arrived at the camp in the next few weeks we decided to apply. The two conditions were good health and a two-year labor commitment to compensate the government for the free passage and for the initial shelter, food, and clothing. One of the commission members stressed that though I had been one of the leaders of the Czech oil industry, I would have to spend the first two years in any laboring job that would be allocated to me in any part of the country. This did not frighten us.

The physical examination went well. The examining doctor did not discover Johnny's boils under his hair. We were given Australian temporary identification papers indicating my profession as "laborer."

The official camp notice board displayed from time to time lists of names of people assigned to departure whenever a new transport was to be assembled. Weeks passed without any action. Then one day we jumped with joy. Our names were among those selected for transport leaving by train for Naples, Italy, from where we would be shipped to Australia.

The miserable camp life had become almost unbearable. The waiting, uncertainty, hunger, and bleak atmosphere had left deep marks on our spirits and bodies. But the moment we embarked on the train at the small Austrian railway station to be taken to Italy, all suffering was forgotten. We were on our way to a new future, on the next leg of our odyssey.

The trip to Naples took four days and nights. Our compartment space was restricted to a pair of short benches opposite each other. The benches were hard, but we did not mind. Most of the time we watched the countryside going by. Often we were shifted to sidetracks or obscure little railway stations to wait for hours for a signal to proceed farther south. At one station we watched a group of refugees waiting for their train on the opposite side of the platform. A young man was carrying his violin case and a small bundle of other belongings that he placed at the edge, in front of the oncoming train. It took only a split second for the engine to catch his head. With a terrifying impact his body was lifted into the air and thrown back onto the platform.

We were shaken by the sight of the slumped body and his ashen face covered with blood on one side. He was taken away on a stretcher, with his violin lying on the blanket that covered him. We envisaged in our minds a lonely man without a homeland who probably had great hopes and expectations for the future, now shattered. As we pondered this with sadness, we could not help speculating what might still lie ahead for us.

There was only little room in our compartment to get any meaningful rest. Our boys had priority when it came to stretching out on the seats, while Georgine and I crouched in a sitting position on the dirty floor. The nights were endless. While the train sped through the blackness and we could hardly close our eyes for any length of time, our thoughts returned to our homeland and our relatives and friends who had stayed behind. Would their fate be more merciful than ours? Would they somehow manage to survive? Had we done the right thing? Answers to our questions would not come.

During the day our spirits lifted again. We watched the countryside with great interest, the little villages of Italy, the many olive and citrus trees that reminded us strongly that we were indeed going through a foreign country. There had been no rain for a long time, so the earth was parched and dusty, but this did not affect us at the moment. We tried to absorb as much of the warm sunshine as we could through the window of our small compartment. At one point the train approached the coast of Italy. The Mediterranean Sea appeared before us in all its splendor. Its blue waters basked in the bright sunshine stretching from the coast to the far horizon. The beauty of the sight was indescribable. We had never seen such a wonder in all our lives. It was a time to rejoice.

The train arrived at Naples late in the afternoon on the fourth day. That year was one of the driest in the history of Southern Italy. Strict water restrictions were in effect. After our long journey on the dusty train we had been looking forward to a good refreshing shower. From the station we were taken by camions to the Bagnoli refugee camp near Naples. It was a modern complex of casernlike buildings that had served the Luftwaffe during the war. Bagnoli lies on a hill high above the sea. From the camp we could see the blue water and the ships moving majestically by, to unknown destinations. To our disappointment, we learned that water indeed was very scarce. The disappointment turned into shock when we found that aside from a trickle of drinking water there was no running water, neither in the showers nor in the toilets. We could not even wash our dusty hands and faces.

With the arrival of thousands of refugees adding to those who had already arrived before us, the hygienic conditions were deplorable. Without water, the toilets could not be flushed. Human waste accumulated fast. The floors in and around the toilets were soon covered with it. The hot summer temperature added to the stench and spread of disease.

During the three weeks in the camp our health and strength again suffered heavy blows. We all contracted severe diarrhea, like hundreds of others in the camp. The food served to us made things worse. Milk, soup, and other dishes were all diluted with great volumes of water despite shortage of the latter. Our stomachs could not take it. As it was impossible for the children to wade through the human waste to reach the toilets, we got hold of a large tin container that now had to serve that purpose. Any time they got up from the tin there was a deep red circle imprinted on their bottoms. Hot tea was urgently needed to halt the progress of our diarrhea. We had with us a small packet of tea, but it was useless without hot water. The camp cooks I approached for a cup of boiling water rejected my request outright, but one of them took me aside and indicated that anything could be had in the camp for American cigarettes, dollars, or other valuables. When one is in distress as we were, health takes preference over anything else. We traded Georgine's gold watch and, as time went by, other valuables for boiling water from the kitchen and for some solid food from the camp's private shop, where unscrupulous dealers skinned the desperate refugee families sometimes of their last modest belongings.

Only a week before our departure, when our health had reached a low point, did we discover a cure for our diarrhea. We had befriended an old Ukrainian doctor, also a refugee. He advised us of a remedy we would never have dreamed could work. He urged us to acquire a few eggs in exchange for our last valuables, then discard the yolks and swallow the raw egg whites. Our stomachs almost revolted at the thought, but we followed his advice out of desperation. A miracle happened. Almost instantly we felt better, and within a day we were on our feet again. Our good feelings were topped by advice from the camp administration that our ship for Australia would leave in a few days.

10

The *Anna Salen* was a ship that accommodated about two thousand people. During the war it had served as a military transport boat. Its equipment and facilities were simple, designed for soldiers. Each cabin held sixty people. Families had to be split. Women and girls were segregated in one set of cabins, men and boys in others. Our two boys and I were placed together in a men's compartment with some sixty other refugees. I was not used to taking care of them, as this had always been done by Georgine or a helper back home. I did my best to protect and assist them. Johnny called out for me several times during the night from his elevated bunk bed to help him get to the toilet. The ship's engines made a constant noise, and the iron doors leading into our cabin swayed and banged throughout the voyage.

A Yugoslavian refugee in his thirties had been appointed our cabin leader before we sailed from Naples. At that time he had acted firmly, like a soldier used to giving orders. We had to keep our cots neatly arranged and the floor clean while still in port. He did not divulge the reason for leaving his homeland. We did not ask. I could only speculate that he may have been persecuted by the new Communist regime for either loving freedom and democracy or having cooperated with the Nazis. Also, he may have been simply running away from his family and friends. With so many different characters, faces, and nationalities among the two thousand people aboard, what difference did it make to us? Some of them probably had found their families exterminated after they themselves returned from forced labor or concentration camps. Who will ever know? When registering at the refugee organization a number of them wisely denied their past, including marriages, in order to avoid complications and delays.

Shortly after leaving Naples the boat began swaying. Although the waves at that time were relatively gentle, the first signs of seasickness appeared. The Mediterranean was actually quite calm at that time of year, but as only a few passengers had ever sailed before, it was an entirely new experience for most of us. Our cabin leader who acted so businesslike while we were in port was now hopelessly confined to his bunk bed. He did not care anymore about the cleanliness of our cabin. In fact, he kept throwing up throughout the almost-four-week-long voyage to Australia, messing up the floor and creating a nasty sweet odor throughout the cabin.

The temperature aboard kept rising. From Port Said through the Suez Canal and the Red Sea the atmosphere became hardly bearable, particularly to us Europeans who had never been in the tropics. During the day we stayed inside. Only after sunset did we dare climb up on the deck. There Georgine and I spread our blankets or bedsheets, trying to get some rest. The air was still oppressively hot and humid. We managed to snatch three or four hours of light sleep during these nights. The many children aboard, including our boys, suffered the most. To make matters worse, the ship's cooling system broke down and could not be repaired. The food stored in the lockers soon began to deteriorate due to the oppressive heat. Our diet became restricted to staples that did not need refrigeration. The perishables were thrown overboard.

We found ourselves in a situation comparable to that of the sailors in the Middle Ages who, after a few weeks on the open sea, were deprived of fresh fruit and vegetables and meat. To make matters even worse, drinking water, although plentiful, could no longer be cooled and had to be drunk warm. In the beginning this was a mere inconvenience, which somehow was tolerated. As the days went on, however, we had to force ourselves to consume at least some of the ever more repugnant and smelly warm water.

The only water that was cool and available in any volume was seawater. We took every opportunity to take showers. This was the only means of refreshing ourselves. The sores on Johnny's head burned terribly whenever he took a shower, but in the end the salt water proved beneficial to the healing process.

The temperature under as well as above deck became particularly critical when we reached the mouth of the Red Sea. From there we sailed nonstop for twenty-one days to our destiny. When we passed close to Somalia, the hot wind from Africa felt like heat coming out of an open furnace. Our breathing became heavy, our eyes bloodshot, and our bodies limp. We dragged ourselves like leaden shadows. Our thoughts and hopes for the future somehow dimmed at that point. All we wanted now was to survive. The ship carried us farther from our homeland and Europe every day. We could not help considering the cost to our spirit and body that our determination to escape from tyranny had already inflicted upon us.

The Indian Ocean now lay before us. It should have offered us some relief from the oppressive heat that we had experienced in the Red Sea, but it disappointed us.

Although the sun was burning hot at the outset, the skies gradually clouded over and a big storm began brewing. The sea got restless and threatening. With only a few exceptions the refugees became hopelessly seasick. The decks became a pond of vomit. Some parents lost all interest in life and just wished to die. In their state of health and spirit they did not care any longer for their own children, who, also sick and constantly throwing up, were left to roam through the cabins and corridors without supervision. Georgine and I were not hit with the worst of the sickness. We managed to stay with our boys during the day while retreating to our respective cabins at night.

The worst was yet to come. The *Anna Salen* was heading directly into a frightening storm. In our homeland we used to have heavy rains and thunderstorms combined with blinding lightning. They could not, however, stand comparison with what we faced now. The ship was being tossed from side to side and stern to bow, like a matchbox. At times it seemed as if this might be the end of us all. At one point the ship was lifted upon the crest of a gigantic wave, and in the next minute we felt like we had been swallowed by the sea in a deep, churning, monstrous crevasse. The air inside the hull smelled rotten and sweet in the hot and humid atmosphere. Those who dared tried to climb to the upper deck. This was most difficult, as the staircases and ladders moved with the ship. I had to hold on firmly so I would not be swept away. At times the staircase on which I intended to climb onto the deck suddenly pointed downward due to the ship's erratic movements.

The air on the deck was somewhat lighter, but the danger of being swept overboard was a real one. I left my family downstairs while I tried to hold onto the rail with all my strength as the sea raged furiously in the black night. I could not stay long, but even so with the vast blackness all around me and only lightning interrupting it—I realized how alone and insignificant a single human being was in the huge and endless universe. I asked myself why it was that some individuals or whole nations could become obsessed with power, permitting them to kill, torture, oppress, and terrorize just to maintain and further increase such awesome power over millions of ordinary people whose only desire was to live out their comparatively short life span in peace, decency, and freedom. It occurred to me that the world would be a good place to live if it had not been for the Nazi or Communist hunger for world domination. The billions of dollars that have to be spent to preserve liberty by peace-loving nations are staggering. The millions of lives lost in the battles for power on the one side and to preserve freedom on the other can never be brought to life again. The tragedies caused by a few power-hungry dictators upon several generations of decent human beings cannot be repaired. And still new followers keep joining them and listening to their gospels that incite the simple minds with cheap slogans in the name of peace, a false peace that would become a reality only after all the opponents of tyranny had been forced to their knees.

Perhaps, I tried to assure myself, the situation was not totally hopeless. Perhaps the world would sooner or later realize that it is preferable to suffer or die for freedom than to live in permanent slavery.

In the distance I suddenly saw a flicker of light. It must have been another ship fighting its way through the broiling waves. It disappeared from time to time as the huge waves obstructed my view, but I kept staring in its direction. I could not help but compare the lone light on the endless horizon to the flicker of freedom that one day must reach its safe port.

To our relief, the storm and heavy downpour subsided in a few days. The sky brightened, and the sun came out again. The air was not so hot anymore after we had crossed the equator and continued on our southeastern journey. Gradually we recovered from our seasickness as the *Anna Salen* steadied herself in the calmer waters. At night we were intrigued by the gradual change in the sky. Strange new stars and constellations appeared in the firmament. Among them was the Southern Cross, which we had heard so much about while still in Europe.

One early morning a general signal was given that within twenty-four hours the *Anna Salen* would dock at Western Australia's port of Fremantle. We were taken by surprise because our family's destination initially was to be Melbourne in the state of Victoria, with only a short stop in Fremantle. We could only hope that our small crate containing our modest belongings would be unloaded there. We were wrong. The crate either continued to travel eastbound without us or had been loaded in Naples on a different, Melbourne-bound ship.

From Fremantle we were taken on a local train to a former military camp at Northam. This was in August of 1949. After frantic efforts to locate our missing luggage, we almost gave up hope. It was a most welcome present when it was delivered to us on Christmas Day four months later. When we opened the box we expected to find the treasures that we had thought to bring with us. We suddenly realized the difference in values one places on worldly goods under different circumstances. In refugee camps in Europe even small pieces of soap, string, pencils, scraps of paper, or empty coffee cans had been considered valuable and useful items after years of deprivation. Several months later in Australia these items reminded us of the poverty and economic disruptions the old continent had suffered because of the war.

Refugees brought with them sometimes pitiful and even grotesque items. In one case one of them opened his crate for the customs officers' inspection. The sight of it was comical but also had a tinge of sadness. The box was filled with black coal. To us this was understandable. Every refugee was aware that starting anew in an adopted country would not be easy. Every little bit would help. To the customs officers it seemed unreal. They searched thoroughly through the coal, not believing it to be the true cargo brought into their country.

The Australian officials were generous and helpful. The new arrivals at the Northam camp were placed in tin huts formerly occupied by the military. Our transport was the first one sent to this rehabilitated camp in Western Australia. Summer was approaching, but the nights were bitterly cold. In the beginning, the exhausted men, women, and children could not match the endurance and stamina of the soldiers for whom the barracks had been built. With solid nourishment their strength increased. They enjoyed the generous servings of bread, butter, jam, milk, and meat of which they had been deprived for a long time. After each meal one could see some of them sneaking around the mess hall tables collecting bits and pieces of food that had not been consumed. The instinct for survival remained with all of us for months to come.

The immigration authorities fitted us out with sets of underwear, boots, and clothing. This meant a great improvement in the appearance of the camp occupants. Their spirit was rising from day to day. Naturally, the general desire was to be released from the camp in the shortest possible time and earn a living in their newly adopted country. In the evenings people sat on the steps of their tin barracks, watching the strange sky and speculating on what the future might bring. Those who were called to the office and given travel instructions for settling somewhere in the vast countryside felt very fortunate. No one minded if the place was hundreds of miles away in some desolate location in the middle of sand, bushes, and hostile environments. At that time Western Australia, a territory as large as about half the United States, had a population of only a half a million, of whom two-thirds lived in its capital city of Perth. One could describe the situation as similar to that existing in the 1800s when North Australia's lifestyle and eating and drinking habits, with isolated progress based on local domestic conditions, reminded us strongly of what we had read about the early American era. However, Australia had suffered from additional disadvantage insofar as it had been in a long, almost total isolation from the rest of the world.

The immigrants brought with them a burning desire to work hard and to accumulate enough means to build their own dwellings. Everywhere they worked they stood out by their keen approach to hard work and saving. This did not go well with some Australian workers, whose powerful unions had established much more relaxed working conditions. They disliked seeing these "disturbing elements" penetrate their ranks. It was not unusual when on occasion the owner of a workshop or factory called the European worker aside to remind him to slow down and stop disturbing the peaceful conditions in his work group. It was difficult to change working habits of the newcomers even though by working harder in their assigned jobs they could not earn much more than their counterparts. The so-called basic wage was the same for everyone in any particular job. However, the newcomers did not hesitate to work harder in their own free time, clearing their newly purchased pieces of land, preparing building material for their future homes, or helping each other with construction.

The waiting time of those who had to remain temporarily in the camp was a burden for them. The administration worked diligently to speed up their departure, but it was a slow process due to lack of suitable employment opportunities and accommodation. The newcomers were restless and dissatisfied and the camp administrators frustrated. The delays deprived the "New Australians" as they were called, of an early opportunity to get on with it, that is, to start energetically building up their future. The waiting time was partly filled with camp entertainment such as dances and "pictures," or movies, as we now call them. To improve the immigrants' English, several teachers were employed by the administration. They tried hard to impart to the newcomers a basic knowledge of the language. This was a superhuman task, as the refugees represented a dozen or more European languages and only a few of them could speak or understand some English. Georgine, a teacher herself, volunteered to assist the Australian teachers in their task. Her knowledge of European languages and customs and her passable knowledge of English were very much appreciated.

Our first Christmas in Australia, or "down under," as the country is sometimes described, was depressing. We were still in the camp. This was a serious religious holiday for us. It fell at the height of the Australian summer. Except for the passage through the Red Sea we had not experienced so much heat in our lives. Rather than winter's snow and ice we were now surrounded by a sea of sand, bushes, and strange trees. Instead of a festive religious family celebration we saw around us Australians and newcomers engaged in wild drinking and country fair–like celebrations. We could hardly blame them. For the Australians this was an occasion to cool off from the oppressive heat, which even for them was excessive. And for the immigrants, with their minds still on Europe and their thoughts drifting back to the time they were amid their relatives and friends, this was an occasion to force themselves to forget.

Georgine and I were still waiting for our labor assignments, as was half the camp population. We were not idle, though. Our initially modest knowledge of basic English kept improving. The camp administrators sought our assistance in dealing with the various chores involving the New Australians. Georgine was soon involved in social work sponsored by the YWCA, which had a local representative here. Several months later she was invited to take charge of programming of food preparation for about five hundred children living in the camp. This was not a small task. With the dozen or so nationalities, it was most difficult to satisfy them. Every group naturally longed for and demanded the meals to which they had been accustomed in their native lands. On the other hand, a majority of such meals simply would not have qualified as balanced and nutritious for the children who had been deprived for so long of the necessary basic food. Georgine, having had considerable experience with our children and having read and studied for a number of years the latest advancements in nutrition, was the only one who could put together food programs that were satisfactory in terms of both taste and nutrition requirements. She had to take into account the limitation of fresh food supplies to the camp and the peculiarities of the Australian ideas concerning food preparation. Often she ran into opposition from some of the mothers, who usually had not the slightest notion about real food values. But she overcame all the initial difficulties and the children's kitchens became a showplace that attracted a number of outside officials from the government, who kept expressing their admiration and thanks to her.

Under my own contract as a laborer I was assigned to the camp store, which stocked supplies of linen, tools, clothing, and sanitation materials. I officially became a storeman and had to join the Storemen's Union. In addition to my other manual duties, once every week I collected badly soiled bedsheets from the whole camp. I had to count and sort them and replace them with clean linen. On occasion, the newcomers switched the dilapidated sheets and pillowcases they had brought with them from Europe for those from the camp stock, in expectation of leaving the camp ultimately with good linen. The administration officers took such misdeeds with a considerable amount of tolerance and even understanding.

There were also a few instances of tragedies. One must understand that before arriving in Australia the majority of the immigrants had experienced shocking events such as political persecutions, bombings, escape attempts, life in concentration or labor camps, loss of family and personal property, mental anguish, and other crushing personal tragedies. The scars from these experiences healed slowly but in several cases ended in new disasters upon arrival in the new country that had granted them freedom and a better opportunity.

One night I was assigned as an officer on duty staying overnight in the small guard room close to the camp's entrance. At that time I had advanced from storeman to assistant to the administration in handling the affairs of one of the camp areas. A driver with a small camion was assigned to me for emergencies and to enable me to patrol the camp. Early in the morning hours he knocked frantically at my door. He drove me to the outskirts of the large camp grounds, and we walked through the thick underbrush until we reached a large tree. Several people had already assembled there. On the ground was a small body that had been removed from a rope attached to the tree shortly before we arrived. We put the limp body on the platform of the camion and rushed to the camp hospital. The doctor on duty examined the body but could do nothing to help. As I had a close look at the body, now covered to the neck with a white sheet, I was shocked. It was a boy not older than fifteen or sixteen, with blond hair and a face that appeared very peaceful and content in his death. His parents were Ukrainian and could not, or would not, disclose any possible reason for the tragedy.

Several suicides occurred during our stay in the camp. There were also other tragedies, such as serious illnesses, which the doctor on duty tried to treat to the best of his ability, sometimes unsuccessfully, with the limited means at his disposal. In one case a young German emigrant had been complaining for weeks about his high temperature and pain in his abdomen. His wife tried to comfort him as much as she could, but his condition kept deteriorating. The examining doctor recommended that he stay in his hut under complete rest while taking aspirin tablets regularly. After a few weeks the patient's fever suddenly shot up and he was finally sent to the nearby Northam hospital. There it was found that he was suffering from acute appendicitis. An operation should have been performed much earlier. The young man died on the operating table, where his and his wife's dreams of a happy new future ended.

Some camp occupants suffered great anguish when their marriages broke up, at a time when mutual understanding and help were crucial in a foreign land.

The unusual climate and sudden switch of seasons had a damaging impact on health. This was particularly true of women, who had the hardest time adjusting. Georgine, although very active, suffered from swelling and deep depressions. We felt it was absolutely necessary to get out of the camp, which did not give us any opportunity to start building our future in Australia. We were very thankful for the chance given us in the camp, where both Georgine and I had earned some income with which we could acquire some better clothing, a bicycle for the boys, and a radio. But we knew that we must try harder for an assignment outside the fence. A job closer to the city would have been welcome. One day, reading advertisements in the local paper, I noticed an opening for a clerical worker at a small import-export firm in Perth. There was only a little chance that my status as a laborer could be changed, as I had performed manual tasks for less than one year while my labor contract was to last two years. But my efforts, supported by the camp administration officers and the Immigration Department, finally succeeded.

11

It was a big day for us when we moved to Perth. We found two small rooms in a nice suburban residence where we had the use of the kitchen. We shared the house with another immigrant family, as neither family could possibly afford the full rent. Even half the rent took a great part of my income. We did not mind so much, as we were finally on our own and out of the camp.

The business firm in which I started working belonged to an unpleasant but capable and shrewd man who had come to Australia years ago from Singapore. He was originally from the Middle East but had to leave when his religious status began causing him and his family serious problems. Soon I learned that the man was most difficult to work with. No one before me had stayed in his employ for more than a few months. I clenched my teeth and stuck it out for over five years. He paid slightly more than I could have earned elsewhere. Thus I considered staying worthwhile and necessary, to give my family a little more than the bare necessities.

The office consisted of a small room in a dirty backyard of a building that faced one of the main streets of Perth. Adjacent to it was an even smaller room where some stores were kept. It was a fire sale of shipwrecked small goods, such as tobacco and canned goods, which my boss sold in small parcels at reduced prices. The customers often complained as to their quality. It usually took a great deal of haggling before my boss reluctantly agreed to exchange the goods or refund the money. The business consisted of exports of canned fruits and vegetables, potatoes, and flour to neighboring countries such as Malaya, Singapore, India, Indonesia, Hong Kong, and other destinations. The major portion of our export shipments consisted of various grades of the excellent Australian flour to the Middle East. Destinations included Kuwait, Saudi Arabia, Bahrain, Muscat, Dubai, Sharjah, and Aden.

Working under the constant watch of the owner was exhausting, but I learned a great deal about international trade and the character of the overseas importers of the various nationalities. Among the Arabs, Chinese, Indians, Indonesians, and Malayans I found the Chinese to be scrupulously honest in their business dealings. Once they had accepted a price for a commodity, they never backed down from their word, even if the market had in the meantime dropped to their disadvantage. I could not say the same about the others, who sometimes found hundreds of excuses for not adhering to their initial agreement, although many of them, too, held up their good business honor and reputation.

In my heart I sometimes resented the methods applied by my boss, too. He used every trick, method of persuasion, and even underhanded method to achieve his goals. In due time he became the largest flour exporter in the state. This did not, however, induce him to improve the working conditions in our shabby office. The furniture was dilapidated, lighting was inadequate, and the place smelled. There were rats under the floor and in the adjacent storage room. The owners of the building complex used poison to reduce the rats' numbers. The persistent stench was unbearable and caused me many headaches. My only break in my work occurred for a short lunch hour and twice a day when I had to take our teapot and walk with it across the yard to a small eating place managed by two Greek brothers who could hardly speak English. They would have liked me to fill the pot with their tea and pay for it, but this was against my boss's orders. Instead, I had to wait in the little shop for a break in the service to regular and paying customers, whereupon I had to politely request that they fill my teapot with boiling water, to which I then added some tea leaves in our office. The Greeks, too, are businessmen, of course, so the boiling water was not entirely free. They sometimes required of my boss that he explain to them and fill in some government forms and tax questions, as they had little education and had not mastered, after years in Australia, the language beyond the few words they needed in their shop.

In my work I had to apply a great deal of concentration and precision. In the beginning this caused me considerable tension and anxiety. I was responsible for calculating and typing up the entire export documentation for shipments to the various destinations. This included bills of lading, invoices, bank drafts, insurance documentation, and customs papers. The metric system that I had been used to in Europe was of no use. Not having any calculator in the poorly equipped office, I had to work out all the figures on a piece of paper manually. It was difficult to get used to long tons instead of metric tons, to hundredweights, quarters, and pounds rather than kilograms. This was further complicated by the English currency system of pounds sterling, shillings, and pence. There were hundreds of individual shipments that had to be documented and invoiced. At times I thought I was losing my mind, but I persevered.

Gradually I acquired great skill and proficiency in my work and found ways and shortcuts facilitating the complicated and cumbersome calculations. My boss became very dependent on my reliable work. On occasion he realized that the volume of work grew beyond our combined capacity and tried to hire office help for typing and errands, but no one could take the pressure for more than a few weeks or months, although some of them needed the income badly.

Our family made all possible efforts to assimilate the Australian way of life and environment. Georgine had always been an active woman. Here she worked with women's clubs, gave talks on the local radio, and made good friends of a number of pleasant Australians who then loved to come to our home for talks or dinners. They enjoyed the European cuisine and we often shared our experiences late into the night. Georgine and I were grateful for their friendship and attention. In recounting our adventures, we always made a point to stress the political reasons for our escape, hoping they would understand and learn from them.

In time we managed to move into a small house that was badly in need of repairs. I did not mind doing some work toward improvement, being happy that we did not need to share our quarters and the kitchen with another family any longer. But the first time we lit a fire in the wood-burning water heater to take a bath, we had a sad disappointment. We were standing around the heater in expectation of instant hot water, almost hypnotized by the gadget. Without warning, the warm water started spurting from hundreds of tiny holes in the rusted heater. Apparently it had not been in use for an appreciable length of time. Its repair was one of our first priorities.

Peter and John did well in school. Soon they spoke English (or rather Australian) as if they had been born there. Peter had his share of misfortunes that, luckily, ended well. One time he was hit with a hard cricket ball on his forehead while playing with his friends on the school grounds. His face swelled so badly that we could not recognize him. Another time his friends were playing under a tree and one of them decided to throw a short steel pipe into the branches. It happened that Peter was standing under the tree where the pipe came down. It hit him on top of the head with terrifying impact, causing a deep and bloody cut.

We took him to the nearest doctor, who repaired the damage. At that time doctors' offices in Australia did not look as clean and reassuring as they do now. The doctor himself did not wear a smock, his pants were held up by old-fashioned suspenders, and the sleeves of his shirt were rolled up. The furniture was of an old vintage, with its dark brown paint peeling off at the corners. We did not complain, being happy that Peter's injury would, except for a permanent scar, leave no other damage. At that moment I could not help but recall the scar on my brother Bruno's skull that I had inflicted on him in our youth when he urged me to crack open a melon he had held in his arms.

Four years after our arrival in Western Australia our third son, Thomas, was born. My new responsibility for a larger family forced me to do more than just spend my good years working for a rude and unpleasant man whose goal was to make money at any cost and who had no regard for the feelings of his employees.

I was determined that my family should live in a home of our own. In the auction I acquired a small piece of land in an underdeveloped area in the suburbs, designated for family dwellings. The problem was not only money but building material shortages as well. At that time most of the immigrants were busy building their own homes. Where there were more men in the family, the construction progressed fairly fast. My sons Peter and John, not to mention Thomas, were still too small to be of any help in my plans to build a house. Whenever I could, I spent time admiring our lot and working on clearing it in preparation for the future. Although its area was rather small, the removal of bushes and deep and long underground roots represented tedious and time-consuming work.

We faithfully met the monthly installment payments for the land from our modest income. Considering the unavailability of bricks, for which there was a long waiting list at the time, I decided to make my own concrete blocks. They had to comply with the stringent Australian building code required for double walls by law. For the next eighteen months I spent every evening and weekend mixing sand and cement, pressing by hand the mixture into proper block forms, then carefully removing them and stacking them on wood boards for slow drying. From time to time they had to be sprayed to keep them moist and prevent undesirable cracks.

It was most annoying whenever a cat sat down on the still-wet bricks. Cats seemed to love the moist feel of wet cement. I tried to persuade the cat gently to abandon his comfortable seat. It always meant the loss of several hours of hard work when a cat jumped right into the fresh batch of new building blocks. It was heartbreaking to see so many crumble under the animal's weight.

In the end, I had manufactured with my own hands, and without any help, twelve truckloads of concrete blocks, a sufficient quantity for our dream house. We admired and studied the plans in every detail at every opportunity.

After a few years in Australia, and having some experience of the life in the country, we began having second thoughts as to our future prospects. On the one hand, we realized that we were indebted to Australia for offering us shelter, safety, and freedom after years of suffering and oppression on the old continent. On the other hand, we felt that Australia, isolated from the rest of the world for a very long time, could not offer us the opportunities that we, with our skills and determination, could apply toward the advancement and faster progress of the country. At the same time, we tried to be fair in judging those Australians whose attitude toward newcomers was somewhat lukewarm or even hostile, considering the endless stream of immigrants of many backgrounds, races, and characters. The public naturally reacted negatively whenever a crime was committed by the foreigners. Among the thousands of newcomers from Europe who were decent and honest people it was unavoidable that a few were accustomed to disregarding the law. These were usually young people who had to lie, cheat, and rob in order to survive while assigned to forced labor groups in the European war zones. Upon arrival in their newly adopted country they were unable to change their habits abruptly. The unusual climatic conditions in Western Australia also played a big role in their behavior. Small crimes did not disturb the public unduly, but when in a span of two years three murders were committed by immigrants, the normally lenient authorities decided that capital punishment was in order.

In one case two young men in their twenties got stranded in the Northern Territory, in an area where for hundreds of miles they saw nothing but sand, occasional bushes, and strange animals. The heat was unbearable and the water scarce. They managed to drag themselves to a poor settlement that was far away from the nearest town. The owners had a two-way radio and agreed to call a taxi that was to take the two men to that town. On the way they killed the driver and took over the vehicle. They were caught and subsequently hanged. It was a sad day for us immigrants, who were, albeit indirectly, associated with the guilty ones. We also thought of their parents and friends somewhere in Central Europe thousands of miles away who must have felt a tremendous grief for the tragic ending of two young lives.

Western Australia had been relatively safe from violent crimes for many years. In fact, the execution of the two men followed more than fifty years of tranquillity in this part of Australia. It was unfortunate that another execution had to be performed several months later. In this case it concerned a man from our own country, a thirty-year-old farmhand. The police could not find out exactly what happened. They could only speculate that the murder of an Australian farmer was due to a heated argument between him and his foreign helper, who killed the farmer with a large rock. A rumor was going around that the farmer had demanded a sexual favor of the murderer and was drunk at the time. These were only speculations; the fact remained that both men lost their lives, one by murder, the other by hanging.

The government had realized for years that the country's population must increase drastically if it were to survive the rigors of tense international relations and make rapid progress in worldwide trade and industrialization. True, the country was in dire need of fresh ideas and trends, but progress was rather slow. Labor, trade, business, and professional organizations and other groups strongly opposed the intrusion of foreigners into their established and protected circles. The newcomers recognized and agreed that they had an obligation to work for two years as laborers. But even after that period of time, highly skilled tradesmen and professionals with prestigious European diplomas were restricted to manual occupations. When this was the case with medical specialists and members of other highly skilled professions who had won fame in Europe, it was undeniably cruel to these people and at the same time meant a considerable loss of talent to Australia.

It was not uncommon that the fine skilled hands of physicians and musicians were forced to perform rough manual work. One of our friends, an excellent surgeon, considered himself fortunate that he was permitted to work in Melbourne Hospital, though only as a medical orderly moving beds, washing floors, cleaning up operating rooms. and carrying supplies. Only when the government needed a physician to accompany a scientific expedition to Antarctica and no Australian volunteered was he offered a temporary position as the expedition's physician. During his time as a member of the group, his talents as a skilled surgeon saved the life of a crew member who had to undergo an emergency appendectomy aboard the ship. Upon return to Australia he had to resume his manual duties. Later, he succeeded in being assigned to the jungles of Papua, where he could at least treat the natives who welcomed him with open arms. There was no native medical association there. He enjoyed his good work for the natives very much, but being under the supervision of Australian authorities back in Melbourne, he was specifically forbidden to treat any white people.

It was not only the professional people who complained as to the fairness of these restrictions. Tradesmen and manual workers in general also felt that they could contribute to the progress to a much larger extent than they were permitted. No wonder a larger number of immigrants, including Georgine and myself, began making inquiries about possibilities offered in other countries, even though it was recognized that it was Australia that had accepted us in the first place without any questions and given us a chance to recover from past wounds.

We were also concerned about another problem. We had opened our hearts and minds trying to convey to the nations the horrors of both Nazi and communist cruelties, oppression, and terror. We could not understand that every time we tried to do so we were met only with polite nods. Why, we asked ourselves, having risked our lives in leaving our homeland, couldn't we convince our Australian friends and acquaintances of the alarming dangers that were threatening the free world? We were truly shocked by the political ignorance and naïveté of the otherwise intelligent, honest, and pleasant people. It was not unusual that after we had made great efforts to describe events in Europe during and after the war and the absolute loss of personal freedom someone in the audience asked innocently, "Why did you not change the government?" In other instances we could read behind the smiles that our stories were not considered credible and that they believed we had probably violated some law and as a consequence had to flee our country. Communist propaganda directed from the Soviet Union did its best to discredit refugees and to paint the totalitarian governments behind the Iron Curtain as freedom-loving and desiring to promote peace. Collaborating clergymen from Czechoslovakia and other communist-dominated countries flocked overseas under the auspices of their oppressive governments to influence the naive people of the Western world while thousands of honest and dedicated priests suffered in communist jails.

Some of our friends who had friends and-or relatives in the USA decided that they would move there, too. The Czech immigration quota was a small one, causing a long waiting list for entrance and working visas. From what we had heard of America's dedication to freedom and the great opportunities it offered to immigrants of so many nationalities, we became convinced that we would also fit into its mainstream. Upon presenting our application to the American consulate in Perth we were told that we would have to wait several years for approval. Although we had no one who would sponsor us, we relied on our friends who had left Australia earlier, hoping they would make suitable arrangements on our behalf.

As time went on and we had not heard about any progress in our visa application, I made efforts to find less nerve-racking employment. I was hired as a minor clerk in a British oil company that had recently completed the construction of an oil refinery at Kwinana, near the seaport of Fremantle. They were looking for someone skilled in administrative work associated with the oil business. My credentials, showing that I was one of the four managing directors of the entire Czech oil industry, together with a recommendation from a friend's brother, a Western Australian senator, helped.

When I advised my boss in the export firm of my decision he was shocked. He had depended so much on my work that he refused to accept my resignation. He realized that it would be difficult to replace me with someone so loyal and patient and willing to tolerate his abuses. At first he threatened and screamed at me in the hope that I would change my mind. He was a born actor who could change his role from one minute to the next. This was, in fact, part of his business success. When his loud abuses and threats brought no results he began to appeal to my sense of honor and loyalty, reminding me that he had "taken me out of the gutters" when he helped me get out of the Northam camp. Finally he almost begged me on his knees to stay, promising me a small partnership in his firm. It was all too late.

Working in the oil company I soon established a reputation as a reliable worker. It was my job to prepare invoices for various oil shipments based on complicated international price formulas that changed daily. I enjoyed my assignment and the decent working conditions and atmosphere, which were in sharp contrast to those that prevailed in my previous job. It seemed that this was now the place for me to build a permanent career in Australia, our adopted country. To demonstrate our commitment Georgine and I applied for and received our Australian citizenship, for which a minimum of five years of residence was required.

At that time we had lived in the country for six years. The local town council made efforts to make the ceremony as festive as possible, and we appreciated it. The heat was oppressive and speeches were somewhat slurred after the officials had been refreshing themselves generously with cool Australian beer.

Our new citizenship made a good impression on the oil company management. Some of the staff had only recently arrived from Abadan in Iran after Mossadeque had seized the huge British oil installations. In the beginning, the English staff members occupied all the important positions in their new Western Australian plant. It was up to the Australians to undergo rigorous training in order to be able to gradually replace the Englishmen in some of the highest jobs. I appreciated it very much when only after a few months I was assigned a so-called staff position with additional challenging work opportunities, although my new position was not one of too great importance in the overall administration.

The salary was somewhat higher than the one I had been earning in Perth but not sufficient to accumulate any meaningful savings. I was still thinking of building my own home from the bricks I had made in the glaring Australian sunshine. They were lying idly on the building lot in the Perth suburb. The only way of making progress concerning my dream house was earning some extra income. The opportunity to do so was given to me by an Australian businessman whose wife was of noble Indian origin. He had befriended us while we lived in the city. He offered me a night-and-weekend job in his Perth company, which was also engaged in exports of various commodities. I accepted gladly but could not see how I could get to the city on a regular basis, as the assignment required traveling about one hundred kilometers on each round-trip. He solved the problem by lending me one of his cars.

For the next twelve months, after my work at the oil company I drove to the city every evening after five o'clock. After midnight, tired from the long day's work, I drove home again. The next morning I was again behind my desk at the oil company. On Saturdays I spent most of the day in the Perth office of my exporter friend.

One night when I came home, Georgine showed great excitement. She had gone that morning to the city and visited the American consulate just to find out where we stood. She had been encouraged by our friends who, one by one, had received the necessary visas and begun leaving Australia. With my new job at the Kwinana refinery I was no longer seriously contemplating leaving the country. I had been told that the name

Kwinana had been derived from the language of the Australian aborigines, meaning "Fair Maiden." Kwinana had indeed been fair and generous to me, but at the same time I had been much concerned about Georgine's health. She had been suffering for some time with exhaustion, general weakness, and swelling of the joints. The Australian climate was obviously damaging her health, as was the case with many women who had come from Europe, where climatic conditions were entirely different.

That day our fate took a new turn. Georgine had found out that nothing stood in the way of our leaving Australia any longer if we so desired. It was a difficult decision in view of my safe and promising employment in Australia. Also, I was not young anymore, to start all over again. At forty-four, with a wife and three children to take care of, I had to weigh all the contingencies with the utmost care. Our friends who had moved before us had been quite enthusiastic about the opportunities in the USA. They raved in every letter about the working and earnings situation and had been proudly reporting their successes. When they heard about our possible move, they began to cool their enthusiasm and hinted at the worsening economic conditions there. As friends they felt a great deal of responsibility for us and wanted to spare us any possible disappointment. On the other hand, they all were willing to look for a suitable sponsor to support our immigration request. I was warned that it might not be easy for me to secure a suitable job.

A difficult decision had to be made. In addition to Georgine's health, we had to be concerned about our financial situation, my employment, and our children's well-being. Peter and John were well settled in their Fremantle church school. Their teachers were rather strict. Physical punishment was not considered unusual, but we knew that our boys were getting a good education and appreciation of excellent moral values. They were also given the opportunity to participate in various school festivities, including plays. At one time John, who was about eleven years old, was assigned the role of a Dutch girl in one of the staged plays. He wore a blond wig with long braids. Rosy cheeks and lipstick completed his disguise. We liked his appearance, since secretly we had always wanted to have a girl in the family, but he was quite embarrassed.

Both Peter and John loved the Australian outdoors. Our home in Kwinana was next to wild bush country where Peter could chase the many wild horses. The authorities did not like it when he and his friend caught a young foal and tried to tame it. Our lovable Tommy usually played around the house, but sometimes he also ventured into the bush with his two brothers. They took good care of him.

Having considered all the angles, the advantages and possible disadvantages, of moving to the USA, Georgine and I made up our minds. It was important, we thought, to secure for our three boys the best opportunities for their future. This, we felt, was offered more in America, despite the hectic life and competition there. We were not afraid of it.

Our preparations had to be begun without delay. Our building lot and bricks were sold at the best price attainable. With this and our savings from the night job, we were able to book passage from Fremantle to San Francisco. After we had sold off our modest furniture and some surplus items, we had about five hundred dollars left for the start of a new life in America.

My parting from the oil company was not without regrets. Its officials were gracious. They understood our reasons, which were serious health considerations. They wished us a "Bon voyage" and a good start across the ocean.

The day arrived when we stood on the deck of the *Orsova* to wave good-bye to our friends and acquaintances whom we left behind. Among them were Tom's godparents, who had been living in Australia for several years after resettling there from Austria. They were good people whose friendship had influenced our life in Western Australia to a great extent.

As the *Orsova* moved away from the port we could not help reminiscing about our previous passage from Naples to Australia on the *Anna Salen* seven years earlier. Then we traveled as people without a country, at the expense of the Australian government, with physically weak bodies and broken spirits. Now we were sailing as free Australian citizens and had paid for our own tickets. We enjoyed comfortable accommodations, excellent food, and the many recreational facilities aboard. As to the future, we armed ourselves with optimism and determination. We knew that no one would offer us charity and that we would have to fend for ourselves. Our children's happiness, the ship's relaxing atmosphere, and the clear ocean air filled us with confidence.

What a difference it was from the years in the humid climate of Western Australia, where the heat during the long summer months was so oppressive that we often had to leave our bedrooms at night to stretch out on the lawn, where mosquitoes attacked us mercilessly, not allowing any rest.

The voyage took us to Melbourne and Sydney, then Auckland in New Zealand, the Fiji Islands, Hawaii, and up to Vancouver and finally down along the North American coast. After the dry and hot climate in Western Australia we loved every minute of our journey. The *Orsova* was a comfortable liner. Food was plentiful. Various activities kept us busy throughout the voyage. The swimming pool was a great attraction for us and the children. Peter, already an accomplished swimmer, won the competition for the fastest underwater recovery of all the teaspoons that had been thrown into the pool by the ship's recreation officer. Everyone roamed freely about the ship's various decks. One day Thomas, who was then only three years old, lost his way in the maze of corridors and cabins. He was grateful to his big brother John, who was able to locate him wandering aimlessly around one of the lower decks.

When we neared the North American continent we were speechless watching the beauty of the blue skies and the white snows of the high mountain ranges. We had experienced an unbelievably beautiful vacation as a family. With new strength in body and spirit we landed in San Francisco in June 1956.

A fresh leaf in the book of our lives had been turned.

Part II
To Rebuild Life under Freedom

12

Our limited funds had to be carefully budgeted when Georgine and I considered our new living quarters. We appreciated the help of one of our good friends who previously also had lived in Australia. He had found a modestly furnished apartment for us before we arrived. It was in the older parts of San Francisco's Nob Hill. The streets were narrow and noisy. The hustle and bustle gave us a taste of the lifestyle we were to expect in our newly adopted country.

Our arrival during the summer months coincided with the school summer holidays. Being confined indoors most of the time, the boys became somewhat restless. We tried to walk as often as we could through the city, particularly the lovely center and the picturesque area along the piers. They enjoyed it, but at home it was not easy to keep them occupied and happy. I was unemployed, and this added to the general restlessness of all of us.

To bring about a change for the better, we took a rather adventurous step. Spending a greater part of the cash we had left, we bought a television set. For us this was a novelty and incredible invention, not being available in Australia, but also, and in fact mainly, a valuable source of entertainment and learning. To our boys the scenes of the Mickey Mouse Club will remind them all their lives of our beginnings in America.

Only about thirty years earlier I had witnessed a demonstration of the first radio set in the small border town of our home country. A local enthusiast had been working on the contraption for months before he was confident enough to invite the townspeople for a demonstration. The stage of the large theater hall was crisscrossed with wires hanging from the walls and the ceiling. They led to a large mysterious black box equipped with primitive knobs and homemade switches. The audience was utterly silent as if watching some famous magician's performance. From time to time the silence was broken by strange noises and screeches, replaced momentarily by distant music and even some faint voices. The spellbound audience, including myself, responded enthusiastically, recognizing that the world had just entered an age of unbelievable progress and daring changes. Hardly anyone could comprehend how the sound waves coming through the air permitted themselves to be harnessed by that unwieldy box surrounded on all sides by brick walls.

Now, three decades later, we had the privilege of living in a country recognized as the world leader in technical and scientific progress and achievements. Even now it was difficult for me to comprehend how the beautiful colors, voices, and music could have been transformed from the incoming air waves into the numerous programs on our black-and-white television screen.

Before leaving Australia I had been cautioned by my friends in America that it would not be easy for me, a man in his early forties, to find a suitable job that would allow me to take care of my family not only momentarily, but for many years to come. On the other hand, I had been told that hard work, knowledge, and devotion to any company's goals were absolutely required for success in this free-enterprise society. It was my firm determination not to fail in this respect and also never to become a public burden.

For several weeks I had been unsuccessfully knocking on the doors of oil and other companies in search of employment. Then one day fortune smiled on me. I was hired as a ship scheduling clerk by the Tidewater Oil Company, one of the entities of the Getty Group. Their inquiries addressed to the British Petroleum Company in Western Australia, my previous employer, had been answered satisfactorily. At that point the limited cash we had brought with us to San Francisco had almost run out. This, however, did not dampen my enthusiasm. I had already been at the point of accepting a job with a small entrepreneur distributing ready-made sandwiches to shops around the city. This I would not have minded, but the job that came up in the oil sector was something I could only dream of, being a newcomer to the country. It was heartwarming to realize that Americans treated foreigners with respect, and often also with admiration and warm curiosity. After years under Nazi and communist domination of our own homeland and living in a number of foreign countries, this was a tremendous boost for us.

I was almost forty-four years old. Again fate played an important role in the determination of my future. Had I been only a few months older, the company could not have hired me. Its firm policy was mandatory retirement at sixty-five, after a twenty-year participation in its pension plan preceded by a one-year waiting period. Had I been slightly older, my family's future would have taken a different route.

My starting salary was $500 per month. After deductions this left just enough for rent, modest food, and small necessities. We had no furniture of our own and not much clothing either. Many new things had to be acquired. We lived modestly, but Georgine always saw to it that we had adequate nourishment and that we were clean and healthy, in spite of her limited household money. She went to great lengths shopping for low-priced vegetables, meat, and fruit in order to provide us with adequate calories and vitamins. She prepared nourishing sandwiches for me to take to work. She in her role as wife and mother was probably more valuable to the family than I in my work. To save money I walked to the office every working day. The bus fare was ten cents at the time.

In my work I was given the task of scheduling the company's fleet of owned and leased tankers. The ships' loading ports in the Middle East, their various cargoes, and sailing and arrival times at the various discharge ports in the USA and elsewhere had to be correlated to the finest degree. The needs of the company's refineries on the U.S. east and west coasts, the changing types of crude oil, and storage capacities had to be taken into account.

To facilitate my work I devised a large magnetic board covering half of the office wall next to me. There I listed the oil tankers in the left column, while the rest of the board was cross-divided into days, weeks, and months for a full year. Individual tanker miniatures cut out of cardboard were attached by magnets and were moved along the dates in accordance with the radio messages received by the company's marine department. Various-colored stickers depicted the types of cargoes and destinations. The length of the cardboard tanker represented the departure date from the loading port and the estimated time of arrival at the receiving port. With the telephone in my hand and without leaving my chair I was at all times able and ready to oversee the entire scheduling operation.

George Getty II, the eldest son of J. Paul Getty, used to frequently stroll to my office to look at the magnetic board and let me acquaint him with the up-to-date picture. George was the president of Tidewater Oil at that time. He liked my system so much that he even called in a professional photographer and then sent my picture with the magnetic board to his father in England. Paul Getty was quite fond of oil tankers. He was known as having thoroughly studied all aspects of ship construction and was considered an expert on technical matters in this particular as well as other diverse fields.

Later my job was transferred to my successor whom I had been training for several months. He was a college graduate, but the English language was not his forte. He needed help when writing business letters.

I soon had a new assignment as that of assistant in the company's central crude oil department, with responsibility in the operations connected with the company's membership in the so-called Iricon Agency. This was a U.S. group jointly operating 5 percent of the huge Iranian oil output. This arrangement had been put into effect after the nationalization of the Iranian oil industry by former prime minister Mosadeq was reversed, and international oil companies were again permitted to enter the picture. My previous experience in the oil business was of considerable help in my assignment. It also provided an opportunity to meet executives of other participating oil companies in meetings throughout the USA. Often their wives were invited to travel along and to enjoy the various social activities. Georgine came along on a few such occasions. One of the more memorable was the meeting aboard the yacht *Argo* sailing from Los Angeles to Catalina Island. After a few drinks on a rather rough sea the members assembled around a large table in the ship's salon to listen to the chairman's report. When he got up to present his eloquent speech it was obvious that seasickness had gotten hold of him. With great effort he managed to say, "Gentlemen," after which he rushed to the exit door to seek relief.

On another occasion I had the opportunity to fly with my boss, the headquarters' crude oil manager, to New York. We traveled on one of the recently introduced jet planes. This was a great experience at that time. The flight was marred only by an alarm on our return flight to California. The pilot announced that a red warning light was indicating a fire in the luggage section of the jet. At the highest possible speed he aimed his plane for the nearest airport, in Denver, Colorado. As the dark clouds were whizzing past the windows we realized the incredible velocity of the aircraft. It was a scary situation. One passenger suffered a heart attack. We were relieved when we reached Denver, hoping that everything would turn out well. Fire engines and ambulances were waiting for us on the ground. Fortunately, it was only a false alarm that had been caused by a defective wire, but I could not help wondering what would have happened to my family had we crashed.

To learn more about California, we made a down payment on a brand-new car. It was a daring move because the price was almost two thousand dollars. For us this seemed a fortune. Our monthly payments put further restraints on other necessities, but the car afforded us a tremendous amount of pleasure when we drove south or across the Golden Gate Bridge to explore the beautiful countryside. We did not venture far, at least not in the beginning. All we could spend on gasoline over the weekend was not more than two or three dollars. Gas cost about twenty-three cents a gallon at the time.

A salary increase after a few months helped us. We started to breathe more easily, and we gained more confidence in our future. After summer vacation we were able to send Peter and John to a reputable parish school, thus continuing their education with relatively strict discipline and high standards. At one point I had to write to the school authorities that I was unable to meet the modest school fees. It was heartwarming to receive their letter of understanding. Both boys and later the youngest, Thomas, attended good schools, and they grew up to be honest, straightforward, and intelligent men. Georgine and I are very proud of them and their families and love them deeply.

Two years after our arrival in San Francisco the company moved to its new headquarters in Los Angeles. I had been hired with the understanding that I would not object to moving there, too.

My boss was a bright man who had earned his law degree in Texas when he was under twenty years of age. He was a half-blooded American Indian, though for some reason he did not like to talk about it. Apparently, he was concerned about the racial prejudices still prevailing in the South. In my view he should have been proud of his ancestry. In my home country I had read a lot of Indian stories. I admired their bravery and their customs. My boss was an imposing figure, with pitch-black hair and wide, high shoulders. When I saw him the first time, I could not help visualize Sitting Bull with a crown of eagle feathers. My boss was a hard worker and a driver, always preparing drafts for his secretary to type. As a lawyer, he apparently did not want to make any errors in his communications that could perhaps occur when dictating the words. He held his pencil, which he hardly ever sharpened, with his fingers in a peculiar way, pressing hard. His forefinger was missing, so he had to hold the pencil between his thumb and middle finger. Some people presumed that he had been wounded during the war. But there was a different explanation. He was reputed to have been a "macho" man. One evening in his younger years he had attended a reception given at a fine hotel. A group of people were assembled in the entrance hall awaiting the signal to proceed to the reception room when one pretty woman complained about a cold draft coming from a large electric fan. George—this was his name—did not hesitate for a moment. To please the lady, he decided to stop the fan once and for all. Rather than pull the switch, he took a shortcut and stuck his right forefinger into the rotating blades. He did not stop the fan, but his finger was instantly severed at the middle joint. Blood spurted into the room, over the ladies' party dresses and his dark suit.

The event strongly influenced his habits and lifestyle for the rest of his life. In lieu of alcoholic beverages he began consuming dozens of cups of coffee every day and smoking packs of cigarettes. In my job at Tidewater I traveled with him to various places, but I never saw him touch alcohol, although there were always tempting opportunities. When toasts were announced at special meetings or celebrations he had his glass readily filled with plain club soda and ice, giving the impression that he was drinking vodka or gin.

George was a strong-willed man. He demanded hard work from his staff and often accused them of preparing erroneous reports, without admitting his own mistakes. He would get angry if the reports did not turn out exactly the way he had planned. In the eyes of his staff he frequently acted like a prosecutor in court. After a while, recognizing his own problem, he would try to make up with unusually kind words.

He and his wife showed great kindness to our family. They often brought gifts for the children. At Christmas one year they came to our modest home again, bearing presents. This time our youngest son, Tom, got a baseball bat. While we were having coffee inside we suddenly heard a loud bang across the street. Tom's new baseball had just gone crashing through a neighbor's window. It all ended up in a true Christmas spirit.

In the spring of 1959 a cable from George Getty in Europe arrived at the headquarters in Los Angeles. He had been talking to his father, J. Paul Getty. They had been discussing the possibility of constructing an oil refinery somewhere in Europe. The plant was to be able to process the high-sulfur-content crude oil coming from Getty's concession in the neutral zone located between Saudi Arabia and Kuwait. Paul Getty had been granted the concession through personal presence in the Middle East and friendship and negotiations with the respected rulers of both of these countries. He was anxious to increase production, because crude oil sales had been causing considerable problems. This was in spite of the fact that its price at that time was relatively low, around $1.20 a barrel.

George Getty's cable directed me to travel to Denmark without delay. I was to join two other members of a committee that was to recommend the site of an oil refinery and thereafter present to the Tidewater board of directors a feasibility report including legal, technical, financial, and economic aspects. I was given the task to prepare the financial and profitability section of such a report.

Flying to Europe took much longer then than today. Including our Canadian stopover I spent about twenty-four hours in the four-propeller plane, arriving at the Copenhagen airport in the early-morning hours. A strange feeling gripped me when I stepped on European soil again, after ten years abroad. I realized that in the last decade I had almost completed a trip around the world from Prague to Vienna, Naples, Western Australia, Hawaii, and California.

The chairman of our committee was John Gendron, a charming and knowledgeable man with a wonderful disposition. He was a great asset to Tidewater Oil. While we were still in Copenhagen, I was the first to learn from him that he was accepting a challenging job with a much larger oil company in California. I was told that Paul Getty himself had tried in vain to keep John in his group of companies.

After a few hours' rest at a quaint hotel in the suburbs of the city, I joined the chairman and the other member of the committee. Daily meetings with government officials, real estate people, tax experts, local business leaders, mayors, and other important people took place. This went on for four weeks. We learned a great deal about Denmark and its pleasant people. The countryside looked clean, almost groomed. Our final plans centered on the city of Kalundborg, a charming town with good access to the sea. Our recommendation to management was to erect a sizable plant in that town. As an additional incentive we stressed that Denmark was a country that had no oil refining facilities whatsoever and that it had to import all its required finished products from abroad.

Back in Los Angeles we prepared a written report. I contributed my ideas about the economic aspects connected with various crude qualities, the prices for products to be obtained, the transportation, refining, and marketing costs, the taxation problems, and associated matters. According to my estimates, the refinery had to run at almost full capacity to make a small profit. After reading the report, J. Paul Getty and George Getty favored the idea. It was generally assumed that the most important aspect of the project would be the fact that the lesser quality of the neutral zone crude would be processed at Kalundborg.

The plan had to be formally adopted by the board of directors of Tidewater Oil in Los Angeles. I was asked by George Getty to make a presentation at their board meeting. This was a great privilege, coming ten years after I had lost a position of considerable importance in my home country. The board approved the plan. Following the meeting I was invited to join its members at the usual luncheon. It happened at the time when the USA was crippled by a powerful steel strike. At the end of the luncheon George Getty suggested that the members of the board, as well as I, make a guess as to when the steelworkers' strike would be settled. Everyone would contribute five dollars, and the total amount of about fifty dollars would then be given to the one whose estimate was closest to the actual strike end. It happened that every director was more or less optimistic about the strike outcome. I—on the contrary—predicted a long strike duration. My date was the last of all the predicted ones. As time went by, one after the other the dates were eliminated while the strike continued in full force. Finally my estimate stood alone, passing those of all the board members. It made me proud but also aware that my victory, a guess of a newcomer to this country and a relatively low-ranking employee, would hardly be pleasing to George Getty and the board, consisting of financiers, bankers, and other experienced business and industry leaders. I was disappointed and tried to understand, however, when George wrote to all of us competitors that since no one guessed the exact date of the strike end, no one was entitled to collect the bets.

In December 1961, in a moving ceremony at the Los Angeles District Court, Georgine and I became proud American citizens.

My salary improved further. Georgine and I had set our sights on a new three-bedroom house in a suburb near the Pacific Ocean. We were prepared to meet the monthly mortgage payments covering the purchase price of some $24,000 but we were not yet in a position to make the minimum required down payment of $500. My boss, George, and his lovely wife, Andrene, who had been so good and generous to us in the past, again demonstrated their friendship and understanding. They offered us an interest-free loan, which we gratefully accepted and later repaid when our situation permitted us to do so.

13

It was a great day for Georgine and me when we moved into our newly purchased brand-new home in Los Angeles in May of 1962, thirteen years after we had left our own country as poor refugees. We now owned a real piece of land and a house in our newly adopted country. We filled the home with practical and simple but functional furniture and decorative items. It made us proud.

After the first three days in our new home, a surprise awaited me in the office. I was instructed to depart promptly for Denmark, to stay there on a temporary assignment for three months, and to assist in handling the considerable difficulties that had arisen in the management of our Dansk Veedol oil refinery and its marketing and administrative operations. The three months eventually became nine full years of my working for the Getty Group in Europe. I had slept in our new home a mere three nights!

The name Veedol was a brand name for excellent lubrication oils manufactured by the Getty Group. It is interesting to note that Admiral Byrd used Veedol oil on his flight over the South Pole. One of Getty's oil tankers was also named Veedol.

The Kalundborg refinery had been built in 1959 following the recommendation of the previously described committee of which I had been a member. The other major oil companies operating in Denmark had not been enthusiastic about our project. Rather than drawing their needs at least partially from our refinery, they preferred to import their marketing products from their own resources abroad. We could hardly blame them for their attitude. In order to keep our operations alive, our general manager, Everette Skarda, having little business experience, felt obliged to sell our products at cut rates. Otherwise he would have been forced to reduce the plant throughput, resulting in even higher production costs. The losses were compounded by the fact that not even halfway decent prices had been negotiated with buyers. Skarda had been Getty's excellent geologist in the neutral zone. It was not a good choice to bring him to

Copenhagen to handle complicated oil business deals. A new general manager was appointed. He was J. Fletcher Chase. His lean, muscular physique was impressive. Rumors of his daring underwater war exploits always accompanied him, but he never talked about them himself. His self-discipline was amazing. Eleven years after I met Chase he figured prominently in his daring contact with the Italian kidnappers of Getty's grandson Paul III. Fletcher and I got along extremely well.

I was to make radical changes in the marketing department. I was told that Paul Getty himself wished that most of the marketing staff be fired on the spot. It was a painful introduction to the Danish operations for me. I called the marketing people, including their manager, into my office. The manager was the son of a very prominent Danish citizen, which made the event even more painful. The atmosphere was tense. It was a gray and gloomy day, with heavy clouds hanging over the city. The room looked dark and sinister. When I told the affected employees of their fate, there was complete silence for a while. The shock was enormous. Never in the history of Denmark, where employees had always had a feeling of a certain degree of security, had this happened. That the great Getty company could do such a thing was unbelievable. Getty had come to Denmark with the reputation of being a solid corporation on which employees could bank their future and progress. The newspaper immediately got hold of the event. Their headlines could not have been more dramatic if the whole nation had suffered a catastrophe. Suddenly I found myself in the middle of big corporation politics, where I was now a soldier performing orders given to me.

In a press conference, Fletcher Chase made a statement intended to reassure the Danish public as to the stability of Dansk Veedol. He said to the reporters that the company's Danish losses hardly made a dent in Getty's resources. This did not go well with Getty. To appease him, Chase resigned.

Eventually our Danish subsidiary began to recover from the shock. A Danish manager was hired. Vaughn Jorgensen had retired after working as an executive in one of the largest international oil companies. He proved to be a valuable asset. I was asked to stay to become deputy general manager and board member. My family, except for my son Peter, who continued his university studies in California, finally joined me after months of separation. We found a charming residence with a large garden in a lovely Copenhagen suburb. We spent three years there before moving on to another country.

The Kalundborg refinery director, a pleasant and knowledgeable American, together with his entirely Danish staff of several hundred, reported directly to me. The Danish general manager was in charge of administration, with a special responsibility for marketing operations. I helped in straightening out some of the damaging former sales contracts on which the company had been losing a good deal of money. Among other actions, I succeeded in renegotiating an agreement with a tough West German businessman. George Getty was pleased with my accomplishment that resulted in an improvement of $195,000 for the company.

George's friendship with me grew strong as time went by. It was pleasing to me when, several months later, he expressed his friendly thoughts toward me while vacationing with his family in a pleasantly relaxed atmosphere at the company's Acapulco hotel.

As mentioned earlier, our Danish refinery had been built with an eye on the crude oil coming from Paul Getty's concession in the neutral zone. The heavy oil had a high sulfur content. This made it less desirable because it required use of costly de-sulphurization equipment in order to convert it into salable finished products. It gradually became obvious that even with the best refining and marketing efforts it would hardly be possible to successfully compete with products imported by others into Denmark. The situation worsened further when the Suez Canal was closed and oil tankers had to travel the long route around South Africa past the Cape of Good Hope.

One day the senior vice president from Los Angeles arrived in Copenhagen. After formal talks with the Danish general manager, the vice president invited me to a private conversation at his hotel room. There he advised me of the executive management's intention to sell the refinery to Esso-Denmark, a subsidiary of Standard Oil, headquartered at Rockefeller Plaza in New York. I was instructed to secretly negotiate the sale with a high official of Standard Oil without letting my Danish general manager, or any of the other employees, know about it. I was the only American in Dansk Veedol in Copenhagen and was relied upon to not let word of my actions leak out and cause great harm to the group's interests. My task was not an easy one, as I had to refrain from requesting all the needed financial and other information required by the prospective buyer. Instead I had to scan technical and financial data myself from the available records. It was a nerve-racking time for me, but I was proud that after weeks of secret negotiations I was able to provide the solid basis needed for the conclusion of the transaction. During all that time I was writing my progress reports to Los Angeles under the code name "Operation Parker." This was the name of the New York executive of Standard Oil with whom I had many meetings.

Only at the finalization of the basic agreement did the transaction become public knowledge. A signing ceremony was held at the Esso (now Exxon) offices in Copenhagen with the Veedol board members, including myself, officiating.

The sale included only the refinery at Kalundborg and the transfer of its staff. The Copenhagen marketing operations remained intact. However, the agreement called for Dansk Veedol to have certain crude oil processing rights that assured us of a secure supply of finished products for our marketing. Our Los Angeles technical experts together with the Esso representatives worked out the processing fees to be paid to Esso for individual products. In lieu of firm rates they, unfortunately, accepted fluctuating increments applicable to every slight deviation from the standard refinery products. This, in the end, amounted to total prices that were much higher than the market could afford.

When a provisional understanding that was based on the purely technical calculations had been reached in this respect at the Rockefeller Plaza Center in New York, a formal letter of proposal was handed to the chief technical negotiator from Los Angeles. The proposal also stipulated that certain surplus processing rights of Dansk Veedol, which it had been unable to utilize anyway, would revert to Esso without any payment whatsoever. I was also present in New York at the Standard Oil discussions handled by the refinery experts from Los Angeles. Their draft terms left me generally unimpressed.

The formal written proposal was presented to Tidewater's executive management, who in turn recommended it to J. Paul Getty, who, as I learned later, approved it.

On my return flight to Denmark I reviewed in my mind the consequences of Esso's proposal. It did not seem to me to be fair, particularly as far as the free transfer of the surplus processing rights was concerned. I knew that if Esso had to build such extra refining capacity it would have to expend high capital investment.

After a few days in my office, and not being aware that J. Paul Getty had already approved the deal, I got in touch with Dansk Esso's management and told them that I could not imagine that our group would favor the proposal in its present form and that I thought some improvement would be called for. As I hoped, Esso did not reject my idea out of hand. On the contrary, they inquired as to what improvement I might have in mind. I threw in a figure that had just come to mind: $500,000. After some lengthy discussion on the telephone they came up with a final figure that included a compensation for our surplus processing rights and a small adjustment to the processing fees for finished products, for a total improvement of $350,000.

The result made me proud and happy. It was late in the afternoon in Copenhagen. My telephone call reached Los Angeles in their morning hours on the same day. My recommendation that they immediately accept Esso's new offer met with an awkward silence. No words of praise for my achievement. Their reaction would come, they said, within a day or two. When they called back the next day, I was instructed to make sure first that the original lesser offer, to expire in the next ten or so days, should be kept alive. For this purpose I was to obtain another letter from Esso confirming that their first, unfavorable offer was still valid. I could not believe that they could really ask for such a document, which seemed to me childish and completely lacking any business or logical sense.

I was almost ashamed to go back to Esso to ask for a reconfirmation of their original offer. Using much diplomatic skill, for which I had been told on some previous occasions that I have a natural aptitude, I managed to extract from them a reconfirmation, the necessity of which I blamed on red tape, not uncommon among large entities. The letter was in my hands the same day, and I could so advise my headquarters. At the same time I urged them again to act promptly. In my mind there was no longer any obstacle. It occurred to me, though, that their hesitance must have been prompted by a fear that a deal may have been lost altogether in the event that Esso had withdrawn the original proposal after I had suggested making an improvement.

The deal initiated by me was finally, and after additional delays, approved. I did not receive one word of recognition. On the other hand, I was proud of myself. As I was a man educated in economics and finance, it gave me satisfaction to know that later, upon my retirement, this amount would cover a great deal or all of my expected pension and that I truly had earned it myself.

J. Paul Getty never learned from me about the event. Then and in all future years in the group it was my principle to be absolutely loyal to my employer, the Tidewater Oil Company, and I never reported to Paul anything that would have put Los Angeles in a bad light; this was true even in the following years when I had official dual roles in both Getty Oil and Tidewater.

In 1962, when I was still a young executive, Jack Forrester introduced me to J. Paul Getty. Jack, an independent entrepreneur living in Paris, had been Paul's confidant for several years. Our executives in Los Angeles knew Jack as a shrewd businessman who sometimes meddled in their affairs in his conversations with Paul. They were polite to him but never felt any admiration for him. One of Jack's achievements, to Paul's pleasure, was his negotiation of a very favorable financial plan in connection with the company's construction of oil tankers. He managed to arrange an international monetary exchange transaction for the payment of the tankers. It resulted in a considerable cost saving for the company while at the same time enabled the other country's shipbuilding industry to create favorable conditions for its workers. Needless to say, Jack was generously rewarded by Paul in the form of a substantial commission, which he richly deserved.

Jack had met me during my first Copenhagen assignment in 1959. We became good friends when I was stationed there between 1962 and 1965. He had written about my handling of my assignments to both Paul and the Los Angeles office. Now, on October 21, 1962, I was given the opportunity to meet the legendary J. Paul Getty in his own lovely home, Sutton Place, southwest of London. He had bought the place to become his personal retreat as well as the official meeting location for executives of his group. Because of the latter, he enjoyed certain tax advantages.

Paul's executives bragged about, and sometimes feared, being called to the "castle." Sutton Place is not a castle but a huge and beautiful mansion. It was built in the Sixteenth century, purely as a place of rest and joy. Until then, feudal lords had been constructing real castles, equipped with fortifications, turret staircases, protective moats, and narrow defense windows. None of this exists at Sutton Place, with its gracious appearance amid carefully kept green lawns, trees, and flower gardens. It has a large number of rooms, including living quarters with renovated bathrooms, reception rooms, dining and kitchen facilities, pantries, and servants' quarters. Valuable paintings—Paul Getty's great weakness—were hung on prominent walls throughout the mansion, particularly in the Great Hall, the reception room, and his huge study.

On that day in 1962 I sat in the spacious reception room filled with exquisite antique furniture and priceless pictures. My mind was filled with a strangely curious expectation, but also with a degree of awe, to face, if not the richest, one of the richest men in the world and the master of the Getty empire.

After a few minutes Paul Getty entered. His walk was slow and measured, his torso rigid. Formalities were polite and kept to a minimum. He spent about half an hour with me, inquiring about the Danish operations, then switching to international oil affairs. At one point he brought up events concerning his Los Angeles top executives, of whom his eldest son, George, was president at the time. To my surprise, he started to share his misgivings with me about the executives' business acumen. After all, they were my superiors and I was only a relatively minor executive. It made me uncomfortable, and rather uneasy as to how I should react. One of his major complaints to me was that "they always manage to buy when prices are at the highest and to sell when they are at the lowest!"

Any diplomatic skills I may have had were called into use this time. Paul aired his grievances without my adding fuel to the fire. In later years it occurred to me that his trust in me may have been based, among other factors, upon my tact in general and my respect for him in particular. He must have had, too, a certain degree of confidence in my business abilities.

The room assigned me was the Butterfly Bedroom. This and the other guest rooms had been refurbished by Paul's beautiful and gentle friend Penelope Kitson. Every one of these rooms had been given a different name depending on its tasteful decoration. I sat down and reviewed in my mind the events of the day, including my impression of the Master. In my notebook I made the following entry:

> JPG—about 70. Strong profile, talking rather slowly, with contempt for bad management by his executives. Likes to use simple analogies in stressing a principle or point. Talks very precisely, knows what he wants. Is sometimes sarcastic about some executives who had not used common sense. But has something gentle and understanding in his eyes and expression in his face, when in agreement with other people's views. Never laughs freely or loudly, only smiles sometimes, but without a sparkle in his eyes. Eats modestly. Sits at the head of a sixty-foot-long table, in the ancient dining room with two huge fireplaces. The butler, Bullimore, serves the food. Gets up around noon for lunch, then has conferences until dinnertime. Thereafter goes back to his study and usually talks with guests or executives until late at night, often until the early-morning hours. In the evening a huge Alsatian dog called Shawn lies in front of the door leading to the study. He would jump at anyone not known to him. The castle is lit by

floodlights from the outside. No one moves around the park or across the lawns, day or night, for fear of the vicious dogs kept outside.

The evening meal was served around seven o'clock. We were the only two people in the room, Paul Getty sitting at the head of the long oak table and me occupying the chair next to him. Bullimore appeared at precisely the right time from the nearby kitchen, bringing in the food at precisely measured time intervals.

Paul Getty's eating habits were simple. He did not care for rich meals but enjoyed well-prepared food that would not adversely affect his health. We had a flavorful broth with crackers, followed by small steaks and boiled vegetables. Thereafter cheeses and a custard dessert appeared on the table. Bullimore filled our glasses with an excellent light wine, which Paul sipped rather sparingly.

Dim light coming from candles set in gold holders flickered on the walls and ceiling of the ancient room. The atmosphere was pleasant and warm. I could not help realizing that Henry VIII, the obese monarch himself, may have been sitting, eating and drinking in the same room centuries ago. Perhaps he sat in the same place where I was now enjoying my food. Henry the Eighth used to come to Sutton Place from time to time to pursue all the rich pleasures of life, regardless of the drain on his health. One of his famous wives, Anne Boleyn, spent many exciting days laughing, dancing, and flirting at Sudtone, as the mansion was known at the time. Her love affair with Francis Weston cost both lovers, as well as the owner of the mansion, their heads, in spite of the fact that Francis was the son of Sir Richard, a minister and respected member of the court.

During our meal Paul again asked only a few questions, mainly in connection with his Middle East and European business affairs. My personal life and my family's were never mentioned. Our conversation put considerable strain on me, as I had to be accurate and unhesitating in my reactions. Some of his queries made me think fast. Even if I could not know exactly, for instance, the price of heating oil in some obscure Danish village, I knew that he was testing me as he often did with other executives and I responded with a figure that was probably not exact but pretty close to reality. When the same question cropped up in some later meetings, I was aware that his famous memory would have retained the price, and so I repeated the same answer.

After dinner Paul rose and left the room, saying that he would see me later. I retreated to the little guest room close to his study. There was a television set, books, and a liquor cabinet. Around eleven o'clock I was called to see Paul again. I walked in carefully so that I would not excite Shawn, the big dog lying in front of the door. The story goes that one of Tidewater's vice presidents who stayed in one of the upstairs bedrooms rushed to the study, having been called for a conference. Midway, on the long corridor, he suddenly found himself face to face with the huge dog, who just would not let him pass by. The rumor goes that the vice president's only way to get past Shawn was getting down on his hands and feet and pretending that he, too, was a dog.

Paul was sitting in a comfortable easy chair, close to shelves containing a great number of impressive books. They covered the many subjects he had been interested in all his life: oil, art, shipbuilding, politics, antiques, history, the Middle East, and Europe. The knowledge he had acquired earlier through persistent studies in these and other subjects was formidable. My place was on a large sofa, about ten feet from his chair. Although this time our conversation was less formal, I thought it would not be proper for me to lean back or cross my legs as I would do at home. Instead, I sat rather stiffly, thinking this was the correct poise.

While he talked, Paul was busy handling a huge pile of mail and telegrams. It was placed on the floor on the side of his left armrest. He lifted the mass of papers and documents, one by one from the floor, glanced through it, and quickly made one of two decisions: throw the bulk of unimportant papers down on the floor next to his right armrest or keep the important ones—only a very few—on his right armrest to be dealt with later. Next morning he would dictate to his intelligent, efficient, loyal, and pleasant secretary, Barbara, appropriate responses. To outsiders his language was always proper and courteous. This was not always the case in his communications to his executives, particularly when he disliked their reports. He was often sarcastic, even to his own son, the president of Tidewater at that time. Sometimes he used phrases like "even a 6th grade student would know that" or "in this case a mature businessman would do so and so. . . ." The Los Angeles group would then spend days in researching the matter, recalculating the many figures and reports and trying to justify their actions. After sending off their now very carefully prepared answers, they, in most instances, never heard of the subject again. But Paul had his ways of keeping them on their toes at all times.

Around one o'clock in the morning I left the study. Paul's nod and faint smile assured me that he was not displeased with me. He inquired about my traveling plans and accepted my desire to leave the next morning. In fact, from my experience in visiting Sutton Place and staying there many times in the coming years, I became aware that he never suggested visitors leave early. On the contrary, he always seemed pleased when they themselves indicated that they would stay several more days or longer. I found out later that when executives stayed at Sutton Place, which was obligatory, the home office was charged a certain fee for meals and lodging. Apparently it was important to demonstrate that Sutton Place was indeed an official place of business.

The next morning someone knocked at my door. It was Bullimore, the aristocratic butler. He had been with Paul for about forty years and had previously spent several years with the Henry Fords in America. Bullimore brought me a typical English breakfast on a silver tray. It included fruit juice, boiled eggs, toast with butter and marmalade, and a pot of freshly brewed tea with a small container of cream, which is an absolute necessity in England. He took out my shoes and suit and returned after a while, having had them polished and pressed, respectively.

Paul's chauffeur took me back to the London airport in the midmorning hours. The ride took about an hour. We chatted during the drive through the beautiful green countryside. The driver, a pleasant and well-mannered man, talked about his family and the people living in the vicinity of the "castle." They all, he said, praised Mr. Getty for the mild and polite manners he always exhibited toward neighbors and servants, including his personal driver. To his visitors, particularly women, Mr. Getty always appeared kind and courteous.

When Georgine and our son Tom accompanied me one day to Sutton Place, he had his secretaries give them a delightful tour of the mansion and its gardens and expert information on the art treasures accumulated there. They were able to admire priceless paintings, such as Rembrandt's *Man with a Knife,* Rubens's *Diana and Her Nymphs,* Gainsborough's *Portrait of Lady Chesterfield,* and many other masterpieces.

When Georgine and Tom departed with me later in the afternoon, Paul expressed his pleasure with their visit, accompanied them to the front door, and waved to us as his chauffeur drove us in a Cadillac toward the park exit. The estate had two entrances that were protected by wrought-iron gates, with a little watch house where an employee checked everyone and all vehicles passing through. When satisfied with the identification, he or she opened the gate by pressing a button that activated the mechanism.

On other trips to the castle I sometimes arrived late in the evening. At one time I almost did not make the scheduled flight because of a heavy fog. The situation grew worse from the airport toward Guildford, a pleasant and charming little town close to Sutton Place. The taxi driver drove very slowly and carefully, although he must have known the way perfectly well. Toward the end we could hardly see two or three yards ahead. Finally we passed through the entrance gate. This time the watchman had to come out of his little house and identify us by almost touching us. We then proceeded toward the mansion, which we knew would be lit by strong floodlights. The fog, however, was so dense that night that after driving for some time we arrived at the iron gate on the opposite side of the park without having even noticed the mansion on our way, although it was only a hundred yards off the road.

For security reasons, and fearing possible kidnap attempts, Paul had installed elaborate means of contacting Scotland Yard in emergency situations. Among other precautions, his bedroom door had an intricate warning system and the windows were equipped with heavy iron bars. One of the bars, known only to him, could be lifted from the inside and removed in case of fire.

On one occasion I had the opportunity of looking through one of his bedroom windows down on the large well-kept lawn in front of the mansion. This was on the day that Princess Margaret came to pay him a visit. Paul's friends and notables from London and the castle's surroundings were invited. A visit from the royal family is always a festive and dignified occasion. I was permitted to make an amateur movie of the visit. Princess Margaret arrived in a military helicopter landing directly under the window behind which I was standing. I then followed the honored guests throughout the mansion and also captured the princess's departure on my film. Throughout the visit Paul behaved like a born aristocrat, starting with his greeting the royal party and ending with his waving farewell at their departure. After developing the film I sent a copy to Paul and was later told that he enjoyed reviewing it.

14

The weather in Denmark was different from that in California. During most of the year clouds were hanging over the city and the countryside. After the long winter months it is no wonder that Scandinavians were anxious to see the sun again. They flocked to the south for at least a week's vacation, trying to return with a healthy suntan, to the envy of those who could not make it. We, too, were looking for a change during the winter. Rather than going south, we went for an exciting skiing vacation in Norway. Together with our sons John and Tom, Georgine and I traveled to the Peer Gynt country in the north. The sky was blue and freezingly fresh, but invigorating. The mountains surrounding our Rondablik hotel had a special reddish haze in the early-morning and late-afternoon light, the same as our faces after skiing or taking a brisk walk through the snow. On one of our walks, we were near a little forest when Georgine remarked jokingly that there might be wolves in the woods. At that point Tom, about ten years old, suggested that we return to the ski resort, as it was getting dark.

After another skiing trip to Norway we enjoyed a vacation in the French Alps and later in Austria. These were happy days for us. We regretted only that Peter could not be with us. He was in California continuing his advanced engineering and physics studies and—on the other side—had decided to get married. I attended his wedding in Los Angeles. Sylvia, our daughter-in-law, is a sophisticated, lovely, and warm person. She had acquired a master's degree in Romance languages, while Peter had been working on his doctorate.

A number of Danes became our friends. We loved their clean homes and exquisite furniture. Their meals were always served in a festive atmosphere. Candles were lit and speeches made. Even in more modest households these rituals reinforced friendship bonds and family ties. After the meal everyone would be individually toasted: the hosts were thanked for the invitation and the excellent food and drink and the guests for honoring the home with their presence.

While stationed in Copenhagen I went on several occasions to Sutton Place to report to Paul. *My Life and Fortunes,* his autobiography, came out in 1963. He talked about his book and welcomed my comments. When I asked for his autograph he graciously wrote on its first page with his badly shaking hand: "To my friend, Arthur Wohlmut, with all best wishes from J. Paul Getty, Sutton Place, December 4, 1963." The book is a treasured item in my library.

Meanwhile in Denmark we also got to know a number of resident Americans from the embassy, including the ambassador and his wife. They invited us to numerous social and formal events. On two or three occasions we had mixed feelings when we had to exchange polite words with military attachés from the Soviet Block who also attended some formal events.

Georgine and I became members of the American-Danish Women's and Men's Clubs, respectively. Georgine soon became known for her outspoken remarks, her strong ties to our family, and her great patriotism, which seemed lacking in other Americans in foreign countries. Our guests always highly praised her meals.

The Men's Club held regular luncheon meetings, similar to the Women's Club. After the meal, a guest speaker presented his views. He was free to select any subject. Usually the audience was too polite or naive to offer any rebuttal. At one time a Danish radical blasted the U.S. government for waging an "aggressive and imperialistic war" against the peace-loving North Vietnamese. It was disappointing that none of the embassy people or military personnel present raised their voices in defense or reminded the speaker that during World War II the Americans were most welcome by his people when they helped to free Europe from another dictatorship.

After three years we left Copenhagen for Paris. This was in 1965. I became vice president of Veedol Oil Company, handling Tidewater's Algerian operations. My predecessor had difficulty understanding French, which made it hard to communicate with French companies that were also involved in our mutual association. He had also been quite generous to himself with his expense account. At one point he hosted, at our company's cost, the entire American community of Paris on the occasion of Thanksgiving. I learned during my stay in Europe that most of the executives coming from the United States on business loved to eat the most expensive food, drink the costliest wines, and enjoy lavish entertainment. I considered it an unnecessary waste of company funds, and I was just as happy spending only about half of what others did. My lean years during the war must have guided me in this respect.

In addition to handling the Algerian affairs as vice president, I also became the Europe and North Africa representative of Tidewater's international operations. In my latter capacity I made trips to Denmark, Germany, Italy, Spain, and Yugoslavia. There was little time I could spend with my family. My notes indicate that I flew on some thirty different airlines during those years. My various responsibilities called for crude oil sale negotiations, consulting, and even participating in long talks with about eighty small landowners in Spain in regard to a concession for tin ore mining. My work was so diverse that my salary and expenses had to be allocated to four different sectors of the company.

In Spain we were assisted by an efficient young lawyer, Tanis Chavez. Tanis and I became good friends. He used to be invited to hunting trips on General Franco's outings. Chavez's charm and intelligence made him a prominent figure in his country as the years went by.

My main assignment, however, was dealing with Algerian matters. The French and Algerians did not get along very well because of France's past strong rule of the country. The Americans adjusted themselves as the internal situation in Algeria demanded. One day the Algerians installed their own supervisory personnel in the offices of the foreign enterprises. Bank accounts were blocked. The companies' own crude oil had to be financed in advance, before shipping.

The U.S. drilling operations in Algeria were entrusted to Sinclair Oil, headed by an executive from Texas. He was as tough with himself as with his employees, many of them natives. One day their union representatives came to his office with some minor demand that irritated him. He disregarded their status as employee representatives of Algerian nationals and virtually threw them out of his office. He had to suffer for this. His stay in the country was declared undesirable by the government. On his departure at the airport on June 16, 1967, he was humiliated, being stripped, searched, and held for several hours.

It was also a sign that the Americans were not welcome in Algeria. This was only a few days after the Six Day War in the Middle East. The media were very hostile to U.S. citizens. As it happened, I was getting ready to depart for Algeria on the day the above-mentioned American arrived back in Paris warning everyone to stay out of Algeria. I considered postponing my departure but finally decided to fly there. It was imperative that I review our situation there with the newly appointed government "commissar" who was charged with supervising our operations. I spent the following days in the country and was fortunate not to encounter any hostility from either the hotel staff or the government people. Most pleasing was the fact that after hours of talks the Algerians agreed to make an exception as far as the blocked funds at the Central Bank were concerned. They let us use them against future shipments.

Our Los Angeles executives were pleased with my decision to travel to Algiers during those uneasy times, and with my achieving positive results in the difficult discussions with the Algerians.

From then on our relations with Sonatrach, the Algerian national oil company, constantly improved. Our respect was mutual. It had become clear, however, that they would insist on dramatic changes in the structure of oil concessions. It was hard for international oil companies to fully comprehend that this trend would be irreversible. They had in mind the tremendous efforts spent in various parts of the world, bringing in sophisticated crews and equipment, building roads to faraway deserts, working in inhospitable environments away from home, drilling many dry wells before discovering oil, transporting it hundreds of miles to the coast to be loaded on expensive tankers, shipping it to faraway complex refineries, and then finally bringing the products to distribution points. But the oil producing countries, now strongly organized in OPEC, were demanding a bigger share of the pie. We tried to understand their position and sympathize with them, hoping only that things would move in an orderly and mutually acceptable manner.

With the above in mind, I had once been asked to make a speech to a rather hostile audience in Copenhagen. One of the participants asked me why our gasoline was so expensive. He sat down quietly when I told him that after all the efforts described above he was getting gasoline at his favorite pump at a price much cheaper than the equivalent volume of a popular soft drink that contained mostly water and some rather inexpensive carbonating and coloring ingredients.

Getty Oil had been constantly looking at prospective exploration areas around the world. The chances for discovering large deposits were becoming thin. Paul, who himself had been successful in finding oil deposits in the USA and later in the neutral zone, kept referring to the top Los Angeles geologists as having been unsuccessful in some of their exploration efforts. He was aware, of course, that it is not only expertise, scientific knowledge, and sophisticated instruments that lead to discoveries but often sheer luck. The executives concerned kept accelerating their efforts, trying their luck in Spain, South America, the North Sea, Indonesia, and other faraway countries.

Consideration was also given to Algeria, where years earlier the French had had good luck in the Sahara regions. In fact, Sonatrach had been hinting on several occasions that they would not be averse to our exploration application, should we wish to present one. Our people looked to me for information about Algeria's political and investment climate, the safety of our assets there, possible contract terms, disposition of possible profits, monetary policies, and all the other factors that may have an influence upon any decision.

My general attitude was positive, although earlier I had not been happy in dealing with some of the Algerian government's representatives. I had, for instance, heated discussions and arguments with Mr. Belkacem Nabi, who later became representative in OPEC and a powerful energy minister of Algeria. He had always defended his government's actions vigorously, which certainly was his duty, but he could not hide his deep personal resentment toward foreign companies.

However, I made good progress in preparing the ground for serious negotiations. General concession terms were undergoing considerable changes as compared to the past decades, when the host countries depended almost entirely on foreign capital and experts. The newly suggested division of profits consequently had to lean in favor of producing countries rather than foreign companies. I was given to understand that any new contract with Algeria would have to be based on a 51 to 49 percent ratio in their favor. In view of the rapidly changing trend throughout the world, I recommended to our headquarters in Los Angeles that such a ratio be accepted as a basis for negotiations. We were the first company to accept Algeria's and other producing countries' new philosophy. Here again, this demonstrated Paul's wisdom and his respect for mutually fair business agreements.

On June 18, 1968, George Getty and I flew to Algiers for a meeting with Sid Ahmed Ghozali, president of Sonatrach, who was accompanied by his staff. With us was Honore Houel, the legal consultant whom I had hired in Paris. His record was quite colorful. Earlier he had been French deputy military attaché in Washington. He had also served in Vietnam, and at one time he had commanded a French camel unit in the Sahara.

Our meeting lasted from five o'clock in the afternoon until one-thirty the next morning. I remember it vividly, since we all were starving, not having been offered any dinner. Our glasses, however, were being filled constantly with hard liquor, which we did not speculate was being done on purpose. Well, the atmosphere became quite friendly. On our flight to Algeria, George remarked that he would prefer if I handled the various financial and pricing matters because I was thoroughly familiar with them. George, however, took over shortly after the meeting had started. He also outlined the areas in which we would be interested, and he accepted in principle some adjustments in the pricing structure that were not envisaged earlier. As a result a basic concession agreement was reached.

Three days later George telephoned me from Sutton Place to say that after talking with Paul Getty certain changes were required. I was still in Algiers, and so I got in touch with Ait Laoussine, top executive on Ghozali's staff. He presented the necessary adjustments to the minister of industry, Mr. Belaid Abdesselam, who agreed. In addition to George Getty's list of changes, I also added one that seemed important, namely, that the $2.25 million cash that was to be paid to Sonatrach upon the first 10,000 barrel-per-day discovery would instead only be credited to Sonatrach against the repayment of their 51 percent exploration cost share. This, too, was accepted. Upon hearing from me, George remarked, "Well, you're a better negotiator than I am."

On our part, the agreement was made in the name of Getty Petroleum Company, of which I was president. In this function I had exchanged numerous letters in French with Minister Abdesselam. These documents were an integral part of the accord. One of his letters to me stated: "This is to advise you that the control applied over your company by the Government since June 6th, 1967 is lifted as of today. Consequently, the assignment entrusted to the Government Commissar and his deputy is terminated."

Still, this was not yet the end of the negotiations. They continued with our legal, financial, and technical staffs, culminating in a special meeting in San Francisco weeks later. Finally, after some additional delays, the stage was set for a signing ceremony in Algiers.

On October 19, 1968, the signing ceremony took place in the Ministry of Industry. It required that two separate contracts be signed. One, with the ministry concerning all government matters, was signed by Minister Belaid Abdesselam and myself. The other, concerning Sonatrach, was signed by its president, Sid Ashmed Ghozali, and myself. In both cases I signed in my function as president of Getty Petroleum Company, a subsidiary of Getty Oil Company. The entire procedure, including the speeches, was broadcast on television the same night.

Two weeks before the signing, George had asked me to fly from New York, where we were having meetings, to Sutton Place to report to Paul and to explain in detail the terms of the two agreements. It was on October 7 that I booked my flight to London for this purpose. In midair the hostesses of Pan Am pleasantly surprised me when they came out of the galley carrying a lovely cake with candles, singing "Happy Birthday." This was the only time I celebrated my birthday high over the Atlantic Ocean.

Paul accepted my report with great interest. This time he even remarked that I had done a good job. He had been known not to acknowledge satisfactory performance all too often. He accepted the $20 million agreement cheerfully.

I had been to the Sahara on previous occasions, but I particularly enjoyed my trip there in 1966. Sonatrach was proud to have constructed a crude oil pipeline from Haoud el Hamra in the Sahara to the port of Arzew at the Mediterranean Sea. A big celebration took place, with President Boumedienne and his top ministers and executives attending. Among the invited oil executives I represented our company. We were flown on four government airplanes to the Sahara and given an extensive tour of the huge pumping station and the large crude oil processing plant. During the festivities we were greeted on the ground by proud tribesmen on horses who paid tribute to their president, his entourage, and the guests with salvos of ear-shattering shots from their antique silver-decorated muskets. We were also driven through a large oasis with natives standing in front of their huts. They were dressed in their traditional clothes in the blazing colors that only Arab women can design and weave. Later a performance by native dancers from the central Sahara followed. Their graceful moves and lilting music and song affected us deeply.

A big feast awaited us in the shade of tall palm trees. The president and his entourage were seated close to us. We enjoyed the same delicacies as they did. Algeria's specialty is couscous, a kind of porridge, often with pieces of lamb meat. I did not dare touch it, as only a few weeks earlier I did not feel well after eating it. An executive from Phillips Petroleum, a good friend of mine, looked at me with mischief in his eyes, waiting for me to take my first spoonful. He knew of my previous experience with couscous and amused himself by watching me.

The main course consisted of tender lamb meat. The lambs had been baked in deep pits for hours. There was one whole lamb on every table. No forks or knives were provided. It is the country's custom that everyone grabs with his fingers whatever piece he fancies directly from the lamb suspended on a stand. Without exaggeration I can state that such tender and delicious meat I had never enjoyed before.

The Sonatrach pipeline to the Mediterranean would be serving the country for years to come.

In October of 1968, following the historic Getty/Algeria agreement, a three-member Getty Group delegation was invited to meet President Boumedienne at his mountain retreat. George was accompanied by Earl Gray, vice president of the company's exploration and production division, and me. We waited outside the compound about an hour before being ushered into the reception room furnished in the Arabian style. The president and his closest aides shook hands with us.

Attendants brought us small glasses containing boiling water in which mint leaves were submerged. The tea was delicious, though very sweet. While we sipped from the hot glasses, the president spoke to us. Then he nodded to George to comment on the agreement. George was correct and polite, as the occasion demanded, but also businesslike. He stressed that we had signed the contract with the understanding that both sides would do their utmost to honor the true spirit of cooperation and that it was most important that Getty's aim of pursuing a profitable operation be looked at as natural and legitimate. President Boumedienne explicitly nodded in agreement.

After the audience we were escorted back to our hotel, where we mutually reviewed our impressions. We congratulated George on his handling the company's interests.

During the following months, preparations and building the necessary roadworks and actual drilling operations progressed as planned. One day Paul called me. I was to meet without delay Dr. Armand Hammer, chief executive officer of Occidental Petroleum, the world's largest independent oil company. The meeting took place in Dr. Hammer's office at Avenue Neuilly in Paris on June 11, 1969.

Dr. Hammer had impressed the world with his unusual business success. From relatively modest beginnings in the oil sector he had developed his enterprise to a powerful empire. In his younger days, following the Russian Revolution, he established friendly contacts with that country. Lenin himself befriended him, as the country was in dire need of supplies of various kinds that Dr. Hammer was able to deliver. In compensation, he acquired objects of art that at the time were considered of no significant value. Later, his reputation as an art connoisseur and collector would rival that of Paul Getty.

During Dr. Hammer's visit to Sutton Place the possibility of Occidental's acquisition of one-half of Getty's Algerian interests had been discussed. Both men's seriousness had been affirmed in an exchange of letters stating that each would recommend acceptance of the transaction to his respective board of directors.

In his office Dr. Hammer received from me all the pertinent information. This was followed by a number of visits by his top experts to Algeria, accompanied by our resident manager and me. My meetings with Sonatrach and with government officials brought about their consent. They stated that they would look favorably at an official application based on our own concession and presented in a proper manner.

The prospective transaction ended differently from what Paul had expected. At the end of June 1969, and after countless hours had been spent in meetings on both sides of the Atlantic, Dr. Hammer regretfully notified Paul that after a full analysis his board of directors had decided not to confirm the deal. This of course meant that Dr. Hammer himself spoke through his board, which was his full right. Politically, it seems, he was comparing our venture with his dealings with Libya and its king, whose terms he considered more advantageous and their situation more stable.

Paul expressed deep disappointment with the result. In his mind this meant that the terms we had agreed to with the Algerians must have been disadvantageous. He never said so explicitly, but his meticulous probing into the case clearly proved it. I was given the unhappy task to advise the Algerian government and Sonatrach of the situation. I did so on the occasion of a *mishui* feast at the government beach house on July 4, on the eve of Algeria's independence day. It was late after midnight when I finally had the opportunity to explain the unfortunate situation created by Occidental's withdrawal. I was glad to be assured that this would in no way cloud the friendship and respect that they had for us.

Even before concentrating on Algeria, exploration efforts had been directed toward the Middle East. On March 26, 1968, Paul advised Los Angeles, with copy to me, of the possibility of obtaining a concession in Abu Dhabi, at the mouth of the Persian Gulf. He had been approached by Sheikh Mohamed Joukhadar, former secretary general of OPEC and, at the time, legal adviser to a corporation called TRIAD. The company founders, the famous Kashoggi family in Beirut, envisaged a joint project by TRIAD, Getty, and the German company BOMIN. The purpose was to search for oil in the sheikhdom of Um al-Qui'am in Abu Dhabi.

Paul asked me to initiate negotiations in Paris with Sheikh Joukhdar and two of TRIAD's vice presidents. We conducted several meetings at the Hotel Prince de Galles between March 30 and April 11, 1968. I kept Paul advised about the progress. It was then necessary to move the discussions, which had become serious, to Beirut. An attorney was dispatched from Los Angeles to assist me.

Negotiations lasted for a full week. During that time we were also invited to the palatial residence of Mr. Adnam Kashoggi in the hills of the beautiful city, which years later would suffer terrible destruction. He was a gracious host.

My taxi driver in Beirut was a Muslim. He had a great personality, laughing and joking all the way. He stressed that contrary to some rumors, there was no problem in the relations between Muslims and Christians and that a true friendship existed between them. He pointed out to me hundreds of newly built luxury villas along the coast. Almost all of them were empty, unoccupied. The reason, he said, was that they had not been erected as living quarters but solely as an investment for those Middle Easterners who were drowning in wealth.

Our negotiations spread over several days. The ruler of Abu Dhabi, Sheikh Zaid Bin Sultan al Nahaiyan, was represented by Dr. Nadim Pachachi, a former Iraqi minister. A detailed concession agreement was prepared in Arabic and English. It contained several harsh conditions insisted upon by the ruler. They included among them hefty bonuses, stiff taxes and royalties, building an oil refinery and technical school once oil was found, and time schedules to be met. I advised our top Los Angeles exploration executives of the terms, the study, and preliminary approval of which were their responsibility. Shortly thereafter they telephoned me stating that they agreed in principle. They also requested me to convey their views to Paul and to ask for his approval. It did not take Paul long to give his consent. He was quite realistic as to the policy of oil producing countries, which had become more and more demanding as time passed. The concession agreement was now ready to be signed by all parties concerned.

As it turned out, Mr. Pachachi had also been holding discussions with a powerful Japanese group. In the final decision, the ruler decided to award the concession to the Japanese, who wanted it desperately and were willing to go to the extreme. We had mixed feelings at the time. Ultimately however, we were consoled by the fact that no oil was discovered in the areas under consideration. Ironically, this resulted in substantial exploration cost savings for Getty.

Meanwhile, Georgine, Tom, and I enjoyed our stay in Paris from 1965 to 1968. We found France a lovely country and Paris a beautiful city. General de Gaulle had ordered all homeowners to thoroughly clean up their buildings. The facades had to be sand-blasted to remove the centuries-old patina caused by burning coal and city dust and smog. The results were astonishing. The city looked like a newly born baby who had just been bathed and powdered. We strolled for hours through the lovely streets, visiting quaint shops, museums, theaters, churches, parks, and other worthwhile attractions. Concerts and shows had a special appeal for us. Often, whenever possible, we drove to the countryside to learn all we could about French customs, lifestyles, and culture.

On the other hand, my assignments took me away from home frequently. In fact, hardly a week went by without my being somewhere in the air on my way to Denmark, Italy, England, Spain, Germany, the Middle East, or North Africa. The Paris Metro, however, was so convenient that Georgine and Tom did not find it hard to get around while I was absent. They disliked the thought of driving a car in a city famous for its "mad" drivers.

Our life in France went quite peacefully until May of 1967, when the unrest fermented by strikes and demonstrations erupted in full force. Gasoline pumps were closed except for a very few that had to supply emergency fuel for doctors, hospitals, ambulances, and the police. By May 25 not a single letter had been delivered from or to France for the previous two weeks. Postal services within the country itself were nonexistent. Banks allowed their customers withdrawals of only pitiful amounts of fifty francs per family. Due to the shutdown of transportation, including airplanes, trains, trucks, buses, and most private vehicles, the Paris supply situation became critical. As in times of war, people tried desperately to buy bread, flour, sugar, and whatever else was still available.

Under the circumstances we decided to leave France, at least temporarily. With hardly any gasoline in my car I drove south through the countryside. The gasoline situation there was less critical, and with my gasoline tank filled we headed for Italy.

Meanwhile, the Paris mob and its followers all over the country demanded an immediate overthrow of the government. Workers occupied factories and hoisted red flags on them. While people behind the Iron Curtain were desperately trying to escape the red dictatorships, French workers and students who had been incited, no doubt by foreign agents, were acting like fools. It took President de Gaulle and Prime Minister Pompidou a great deal of patience and determination to calm things down.

My family then returned to our Paris apartment close to the Bois de Boulogne. We stayed there until the summer of 1968 and finally moved to Rome. The move had actually been indirectly initiated two years earlier when Paul called me to meet him at Fontainbleau, about forty miles south of Paris, while he was on his automobile trip to Le Havre. He had spent several weeks in Europe and was on his way back to his home in England.

We met at the Black Lion Inn at Fontainbleau on March 29, 1966. He had traveled with two of his secretaries and his personal chauffeur. During a pleasant, relaxed luncheon, Paul offered me the directorship of his Italian company, the Getty Oil Italiana, where I was asked to replace his son Eugene Paul and assume the top executive position. In Italy this function is called *administratore delegato.* A substantial salary increase was part of the package. I accepted the offer with the understanding that in my function I would be in full charge and report solely to Paul, and the position of president of Getty Oil Italiana, to which Dr. Georgio Schanzer of Rome would be formally appointed, would be an advisory one only. Georgio and I became the best of friends, and he always gladly assisted me with board meetings, legal problems, public relations, and contacts with authorities, with which he was of great help.

George was advised by Paul of my new assignment. He was delighted with my willingness to accept another difficult, responsible, and challenging assignment. He felt that with my tact and diplomacy in dealing with people I was building a successful career in the company.

In my new position I was to remain stationed in Paris. In addition to my responsibilities as European coordinator I also retained those over North Africa. Paul Getty envisioned that I would spend the initial period of a few months in Rome and then return to Paris. From there I would arrange my schedule so that I would spend about half of every month in France and the other half in Italy. In the beginning I tried hard to comply, but I soon had to give up. International business is such that emergencies, sudden meetings, negotiations, and government regulations and orders are not in the habit of occurring at neat, regular intervals. Consequently, irregular and very frequent trips in all directions became my way of life.

I started my assignment in Rome enthusiastically, hoping that my open attitude toward employees and people in general would be an asset to me. Eugene Paul Getty, from whom I took over my responsibilities, and his close staff displayed a lesser degree of joy, which was natural. Their way of handling their Italian affairs had been upset by Paul's decision. In many ways they tried to be helpful, for which I was grateful, but the naturally created distance between us could never be fully bridged.

In a few rather isolated instances I could not avoid feeling some animosity on their part. For instance, they had been using the services of the company chauffeur and car. This should have been assigned to me, but instead I was given a rather flimsy reason for their hanging onto the car: if Paul should travel to Italy, the car must be ready for him at all times, and therefore it must be set aside. I knew, of course, that Paul hardly ever traveled to Italy and that the car would be handy for them. I did not make a "federal case" out of it. I had more important matters in mind, and the simplest solution was to buy my own car with my own money, which I did. For this I never charged the company any expenses. No other Getty executive in a foreign country had ever bought his own car.

On another occasion I decided to move our offices, located on a narrow street with no parking facilities in the very old part of Rome, to the modern part of the city, called EUR (Esposizione Universale Roma). This was the section that had been built by Musollini between the old city and the port of Ostia. Magnificent marble-and-stone buildings had originally been designated for a world fair and later occupied by government offices, industrial and business enterprises, and prominent professionals. Among other oil companies, AGIP, the big Italian national oil corporation, had its headquarters there.

Eugene Paul's secretary, June, had a flat conveniently located close to the old office. She dreaded the thought of having to drive to our prospective new offices at EUR. Her private letter to Paul at Sutton Place described the advantages of the old location and the disadvantages of the new place. She had been on excellent terms with him, having assisted him whenever he traveled to Europe, performing secretarial services for him and doing research on valuable antique items when requested. Her Italian was perfect. Her letter did not stop our move to the new premises when he, as he usually did, left the decision to my own judgment. June was born and had most of her relatives in South Africa. On social occasions we used to discuss the almost insurmountable problems her country faced at the time and was likely to face in the coming years. She was apprehensive but could not offer any good suggestions as to the resolution of the dilemma.

Soon I found out that in Italy things could not be changed easily. The former management had hired a marketing manager, an Italian, who could not speak a word of English. This by itself was a great handicap in the international oil business, which had always been conducted in English. We needed to increase the export of our products. Replacing him at this late hour was practically impossible under the country's employment system. A dismissal would have cost the company several years of his full salary, notwithstanding the uproar it would have created. He was also vehemently opposed to the introduction of new business methods and procedures, as he had enjoyed complete freedom and power under his former bosses.

To make some progress I created a committee consisting of him, the refinery director, and a young Italian executive whom I promoted for this particular purpose. The two older executives deeply resented my idea. Instead of cooperating with the young man, who had modern and workable ideas, they made his life miserable. In spite of all this, we gradually made slow progress.

Late in 1967 a troublesome case arose. It concerned a certain Italian customs procedure that had to be followed strictly in order to avoid payment of heavy duties and taxes on oil shipped abroad. Under the former management, a certain employee was given the assignment of filing the company's claim for duty-free exports within the prescribed period of time. Without this claim, the company would be stuck with very burdensome payments.

The employee concerned maintained that he had presented the required forms to the government in ample time, although he actually did this on the last day of the one-year grace period, and the government clerk entered the application duly in the official register on that last day and assigned it the then-current number. An investigation by the government auditors revealed, however, that the registration had been placed ahead of another previous entry after the clerk had crudely erased the initial notation. The accusation stated that this was done deliberately so that Getty's former Italian management could claim that the application was filed on time. The government clerk was taken into custody, and a lengthy investigation took place. Our employee was steadfast in maintaining that he had nothing to do with falsifying the record. The government clerk admitted having erased the original entry, but only because he had made an honest mistake and had to correct it.

The case had never been fully settled, with both men maintaining that they had acted on their own and had not been influenced by anyone else.

Although this was clearly a case that had originated during the former management, Paul telephoned me numerous times during the investigation. He was extremely concerned as to his reputation in Italy. He had always taken great care in stressing to his executives that they must scrupulously adhere to local laws and regulations, even if this might result in the company's disadvantage. Although there were many other important items to be discussed, Paul kept hammering away, day after day, as to what actually had happened and why the former management waited until the very last day of the one-year grace period to file the proper customs forms.

I assured him that a problem of this nature would not occur in the future, as we had strengthened the procedures in our own company by introducing double-checking of all critical dates. Gradually I was able to put him at ease, having exhausted all possible means of finding out what had actually happened. Cases of this nature take years to resolve in Italian courts. The actual outcome of this case is still unknown to me.

The case made Paul even more apprehensive as to his possible vulnerability and reputation in Italy. He was determined to avoid anything that could harm his name. When an Italian friend of his, a skilled attorney, suggested that he would try to obtain from the Italian government a subsidy, the kind that had been provided for other enterprises in the impoverished Mezzogiorno area, where Getty's Gaeta refinery was also located, Paul liked the idea. He promised his friend a 25 percent reward. Paul did not expect, however, that a subsidy amounting to over $1 million would be secured and that the reward would amount to over a quarter of a million dollars. Paul got frightened that he would run into legal problems if he were to actually pay the reward.

Again I was drawn into the picture. Paul asked me to investigate the legality of such payment, while at the same time he disliked breaking his promise.

The problem came to a head one evening while I was at Sutton Place. During a lengthy discussion with me, Paul called his trusted British attorney, Robina Lund, to obtain her opinion. Thereafter he called his

New York attorney, Lansing Hays, who later became a trustee of the Sarah Getty Trust and a member of the Getty board, repeating his questions. Both were reluctant to advise Paul to go ahead with the payment.

The problem dragged on for three more weeks. I was in Los Angeles at the time and ran into Hays. He stressed that the commission case did not look good. Upon my return to Rome Paul telephoned me, having found a plausible and practical solution. He instructed me to get in touch with the best Rome and the best Naples attorneys, describe to them the problem, and ask them to clearly affirm or otherwise reject the legality of the reward payment.

I obtained from both attorneys a lengthy, affirmative dissertation, which was then readily accepted by Paul. The reward was finally paid.

The Italian juridical system disappointed me personally. Together with my sons Peter and John I drove one day from England across the Continent, down the Italian west coast, and home to Rome. Shortly before Florence, the *autostrada* made a sharp turn to the right. Just seconds earlier, a car driven by two Italians had hit the rail on the left side, bounced off, and overturned, blocking the road. There was no time for me to bring my car to a stop, although I used all the braking power available to me. There was no room, left or right, to avoid the crash. We hit the overturned vehicle on its side. Both our cars spun around. Fortunately, the other car had been lying on its roof, so the impact made it spin and slide rather than absorb the full impact of the collision.

Peter and John had braced themselves before the impact. Although they had painful injuries, these were not serious enough to require immediate attention. I had hit the windshield, cracked the glass, and suffered a painful head injury and a pair of black eyes. My hair was covered with glass dust from the broken window. Peter's and John's first thought was to protect the overturned vehicle from the oncoming traffic. We crawled out of our heavily damaged car, and with the help of other motorists who had arrived in the meantime and were able to stop in time we turned the other vehicle over and set it back up on its tires. After a while the highway police and ambulance arrived. They took the two Italians and myself to the Florence hospital, where we received first aid.

Thereafter I was taken to the police station to which our car had been towed. It was a complete wreck. The police put together a report in which it was stressed that the other car had hit the rail and overturned before we even reached the spot.

We took a tiring three-hour ride to Rome in a taxi. Georgine was shocked when she saw us, but we were all happy that nothing more serious had happened.

The next normal procedure was to inform my Italian insurance company and claim payment for the ruined car. Also, I had to file a claim against the two Italians involved in the crash. They maintained that it was I who had caused the damage. Italian insurance companies are very reluctant to pay damages to foreigners and generally act differently than we would expect from an insurance company in the United States. Their connections with the police are well established and friendly and particularly self-protective. This I realized when I received a police notice a few weeks later indicating that one of my car tires had been worn out. This certainly could not be true, as the car was almost new, for all practical purposes. The insurance company refused to pay compensation for my loss of several thousand dollars. My only recourse was to file a lawsuit. For years thereafter nothing happened. Finally the case vanished without ever being heard.

Under these circumstances, doing business in Italy meant the challenge of overcoming never-ending problems. If contracts were not met by buyers or if bills were not paid by them, if suppliers were late in deliveries, and if someone sued the company, these and many other difficulties could not be resolved with the necessary expediency. A few dishonest business partners took advantage of this, being fully aware that Getty would not be willing to have its name dragged through the courts for years and years. On the other hand, the great majority of business enterprises in the country were under hardworking, scrupulous management, and it was a pleasure and privilege to conduct business with them.

It was only natural that many prominent personalities made efforts to meet Paul in person. At one time an Italian aristocrat, Count Lequio, and his beautiful wife were introduced to Paul at Sutton Place. Titles had always impressed him. Furthermore, he had always had an eye for beauty and grace, antique or living. Before departing, the count indicated to Paul that he enjoyed valuable connections in the Italian business circles and that he could secure a favorable insurance contract covering our oil refinery at Gaeta, located on the beautiful coastline between Rome and Naples. In his mind he, of course, envisaged a sizable commission from the company run by me. Paul did not object to his submitting an offer. He had always encouraged deals that would improve the profitability of his various enterprises.

It just happened that our current insurance policy with a reputable company was about to be renegotiated. This was the proper time for me to secure the best possible terms for a new agreement. Foremost in my mind was the reliability of the insurance company to which a contract would be awarded. A fire or any serious disaster in the refinery could cause loss of life and millions of dollars in damage. This was a great responsibility. I wanted to be extra cautious in making the decision and, at the same time, respecting Paul's wish, helpful to the count. In order to be fair to all concerned, I decided to invite official sealed offers from the major insurance companies, and also from the count, giving him an even chance to present a bid supported by a reputable and knowledgeable insurance firm.

Under strict supervision we officially opened all the bids. While the general terms were about similar, the insurance premiums differed notably. The count's bid was the highest. I advised him on the telephone that, unfortunately, his offer could not be considered. He appeared in my office shortly thereafter, expressing disbelief about my decision. Among other remarks, he sharply criticized the way I handled the matter and that I had ignored the fact that Paul Getty was swimming in wealth.

I tactfully declined to change my decision. The count must have then called Sutton Place and talked to Claus von Bulow, reporting to him what had happened. At that time Claus was Getty's aide. Among other responsibilities, he used to handle some of the social schedules at the castle, and some of the antique purchases in London, as well as the related research. I had always respected him as a man of high intelligence and aristocratic manners. My dealings with him concerning company matters had always been friendly and pleasant. Once, while visiting Paris, he was a dinner guest at our apartment.

The day after the count had talked to him, Claus telephoned me in Rome, stating that it was strange that I did not award the contract to the count as Paul had envisaged. Claus did not mention whether or not he had discussed the matter with Getty. When I emphasized that sealed offers were the only way to ensure fairness and reliable insurance protection, Claus remarked that I could have revealed the lowest offer to the count, giving him the opportunity to adjust his offer. I could not agree with such reasoning.

Claus von Bulow had been born in Denmark under the name Claus Borberg. He was a valuable assistant to Paul for several years. Getty, however, had never been in favor of paying high salaries. To keep up with a decent living standard, Claus made efforts to improve his income. He was assigned the duty of the Veedol subsidiary manager for England, with the offices located at the Sutton Place estate, right next to the castle. He made efforts at one point to become a member of the board of our Danish Veedol subsidiary. Although he had been born in Denmark, this was not possible, as he did not reside in Denmark which was a legal requirement for any board member there. When our senior vice president at the Los Angeles headquarters asked for my views as to what could be done—I was European coordinator of our companies—I offered the thought that Claus could become an outside consultant for Denmark, to be properly compensated for every trip to Copenhagen made as a consultant. The whole affair was dropped when, perhaps, his association with Denmark became impractical.

Claus von Bulow later left Getty's services, marrying a wealthy Pittsburgh heiress, and moved to New York. Sometime in 1976 I was in New York with my eldest son Peter, to promote his patented invention of a high-speed laser-based video disc, recorded on regular black-and-white film. In spite of Peter's and his family's great sacrifices over a number of years, the invention never developed into a viable industrial enterprise, due to limited financial support. While in New York, I talked briefly with Claus to renew our old acquaintance. This was the last time we spoke to each other. A few years later the worldwide media reported at length about his trial and final acquittal in the case related to his comatose wife.

Before the merger of Getty Oil and Tidewater Oil, Paul's son Ronald handled Tidewater's marketing operations in Los Angeles. Later he was given the assignment of handling the company's European lubricating oil affairs and moved to Hamburg. I had several business dealings with Ronald, whom I had always respected for his businesslike and efficient handling of his responsibilities and his pleasant personality. Paul did not seem to be fair to him on some occasions. This became most apparent when Ronald was not treated well with respect to the wealth left after Paul's death.

While he was also in charge of the lubricating oil business in France, Ronald was accused by the competition of snatching from it some key employees, an action contrary to some old French laws and regulations. French newspapers made a big affair of the case. Col. Leon Turrou, a retired American security expert living in Paris, had been doing some work for Paul. One of Leon's assignments was the installation of a dependable security system at Sutton Place in cooperation with Scotland Yard. Leon became interested in Ronald's case and suggested various means to clear Ronald.

Paul, as he usually did, tried hard to disassociate himself from problems of his executives. When he learned about Turrou's proposition, he stressed in strong terms that the Veedol matter was entirely a Tidewater affair and that did concern Getty Oil—also, that Ronnie was fully competent to look after his own affairs and that he, Paul, had neither the time nor the strength to get involved.

Colonel Turrou was quite popular in the French security circles. At one point he was even given the French Legion of Honor award. I met with him on many occasions. He always tended to promote his personal publicity, in France itself as well as during his trips to Sutton Place, where he introduced, from time to time, some of his military or political acquaintances from the USA. Among the lists of his past achievements was his claim that he had been involved prominently in the solving of the "Lindbergh case."

After August 1968, following the occupation of Czechoslovakia by the Soviets, many Czechs left the country while it was still possible. Among them was a Mrs. Anna Hladka, who had been corresponding with Paul for some time. One evening she was invited to join us in the large dining room at Sutton Place. Paul explained that she was a journalist and that a ladies' group in Surrey was giving her moral support.

Paul encouraged us to speak in Czech. Our conversation covered general subjects, with only brief comments about the Czech and Soviet oil industry. As I had fled the country much earlier, in 1949, under very difficult conditions and was apprehensive about Czech official party journalists, my conversation with Anna Hladka was guarded and formal. I understand that she later rendered valuable services to Paul in the field of tracing origins of some of his art treasures.

In an effort to promote the sale of crude oil, I flew in May of 1969 to Zagreb, Yugoslavia, to talk to the state agency INA (Industrija Nafte) at their new headquarters at Proleterskih Brigade. The main purpose, as envisaged by Paul Getty, was to interest the Yugoslavians in the purchase of his heavy, high-sulphur Ratawi crude oil. This was as difficult assignment, as the Yugoslavians had been using almost exclusively types that did not have to be processed through sophisticated and expensive desulphurization processes. I stressed that Ratawi had been successfully mixed with lighter types in our Italian refinery and that this method might also work well in Yugoslavia. The reply was that they would have to build expensive mixing and storage facilities and that the Ratawi price, at $1.25 a barrel at the time, was too high to permit it. Finally, as a gesture of goodwill, they asked me to have a barrel of Ratawi dispatched to their Rijeka refinery for testing, which I arranged upon my return to Rome.

The result of my trip did not surprise me. Getty's crude oil had only one advantage over other types, namely, its favorable pour point. This, however, was far outweighed by its sulphur content. Paul was well aware of the problem but never admitted so openly. He kept maintaining that the oil should command a good price in the international markets. Reality proved otherwise. Although some of his crude oil was sold in small volumes to some overseas buyers, its main stream had to be directed to his own refineries in the USA, Denmark and Italy. Getty's personal ego and pride prohibited him from admitting that his neutral zone concession was, after all, not as favorable as he wanted his executives to believe.

He listened to my report about the Zagreb trip, expressing hope that the Yugoslavians would revert to the subject after they had tested the sample sent to them. He did not indicate, however, whether in such case he would consider granting them a reasonable price concession. In the end, not one shipload of Ratawi crude was ever sent to Rijeka.

The Suez Canal difficulties greatly influenced the cost of crude oil for European refineries. The long route around South Africa caused delivery delays and substantial cost increases. Soviet crude oil became quite popular in countries that had no restrictions on its importation. It was also cheaper than the Middle East crude oil, thus making our economic survival in the European markets even more difficult. Italian refiners did not hesitate to use the cheaper Soviet oil, but we could not do so, which hampered our Italian operations. Our State Department did not specifically speak out against it, but doing so would have created some political complications, in addition to affecting the reputation of U.S. refiners.

The Soviets made an effort to sell their crude oil to Getty companies. To this end, Mr. V. Sofinsky, counselor and cultural attaché of the Soviet embassy in London, together with his wife, a Mr. Tikhovov, and actress Ludmilla Savalyeva, paid a visit to Sutton Place in January 1969. Paul listened politely. Two weeks later he advised Mr. Sofinsky that in the future the matter of their crude oil might be directed to myself in my function as managing director of Getty Oil Italiana. To me, Paul stressed that, naturally, one would want to discuss purchasing Russian oil with the State Department and would not purchase it against its policy.

I considered it proper not to follow up on the matter myself until such time that a representative the Soviet embassy in London would approach me. Nothing happened during the next several weeks, so I considered it best not to pursue the matter further.

Italy had always fascinated Paul. He was very knowledgeable about its history, art, and people. From time to time he seriously considered settling there or at least spending several weeks a year there. It was for this reason that he bought a historic palace near Rome, the Posta Vecchia at Palo, on the Mediterranean coast.

Getty decided to spend more than $2 million for the restoration of the palace, the foundations of which dated more than twenty centuries back. The work was entrusted to the Roman architect Consiglio, who was instructed to stay in close consultation with Penelope Kittson, Paul's close friend and companion. The lovely and gracious Penelope was given the almost impossible task to furnish all the rooms of the palace with exquisite antique furniture, rugs, and tapestries. Often I found Penelope briskly walking the grounds of Posta Vecchia, talking to the architect and his skilled tradesmen, inspecting the work progress, or supervising deliveries of thousands of items to be placed in the palace. Her efforts proved most successful.

During their restoration, workmen discovered many architectural treasures dating from the Etruscan period, some six centuries before Christ. Among them were marble statues and columns that had been broken and scattered over the centuries. The Italian laws call for a strict preservation of such treasures and their registration. Paul Getty, himself a devoted art connoisseur, was more than pleased to honor this requirement.

At the time of the purchase, the palace was a mere shell without a roof. Fortunately, the thick stone walls and some arches had defied the salty air and the storms that battered the palace since its last occupants, probably popes, noblemen, or merchants of the Middle Ages, had abandoned it.

It is said that Pope Pius IV and Pope Leon X of the Medicis stayed in the palace on several occasions. Records indicate that Muslim ships raided the coast. One of the popes had to flee the palace in the sixteenth century when Turkish pirates sailed their ship along the coast. Earlier, in the first centuries of Christianity, the area surrounding Rome was overrun and heavily damaged by Huns, Vandals, Visigoths, and other hordes that inflicted heavy damage on the Roman Empire and its trade and development.

After the restoration, the palace became a showplace to any visitor who had the privilege to be invited. It was a pleasure to walk through the spacious, exquisitely furnished rooms, including the large dining room, several sitting rooms and halls, and a great number of guest rooms. The kitchen itself was restored to its original appearance. It was a huge place with ancient brick and stone walls, wrought-iron tools, and oversize ovens that in the past had witnessed many a wild celebration and feast.

In one corner of the palace, facing the sun and sea, a large indoor swimming pool was installed. Paul stayed at the Posta Vecchia only on a few occasions when the weather was warm. During his visits I drove from Rome to see him. My last visit was in the summer of 1971, before my family and I left to relocate in the USA. I shall refer to it later.

Next to the palace is the historic castle belonging to Prince Odescalci. Paul had rented some of the rooms and had restored the castle's old kitchen at considerable expense while the restoration of Posta Vecchia next door proceeded. I took a few pictures of the palace and sent them to Sutton Place.

Madame Mary Teissier, a Russian-born art expert, was a close friend of Paul for years. Mary was known to friends for her claim to be related to the Romanov dynasty. Paul never expressed any warm feelings toward women in the presence of other guests. Mary sometimes showed her affection regardless of circumstances. Once we were all in the sitting room watching television when Mary slid down to the floor next to Paul and fondly put her arms around his legs. It was difficult to judge whether this was genuine affection or a move to demonstrate her closeness to Paul.

Mary was also very fond of Italy. The English weather was sometimes depressing. Sutton Place was not always a place to warm one's bones. The heating system could not cope with the many large, high-ceilinged rooms. Paul sometimes sat in his working room and library with his collar turned up. Mary used to urge him to spend several months every year in the south of Italy, close to his Italian officers and refinery. In the fall of 1967 she learned about the availability of a small island a few hundred yards off the coast of Naples. A spacious building stood on top of the rocky island. The place could be reached by small boat only. This, Mary reasoned, would be an ideal place from a security viewpoint.

Apparently it was not difficult to persuade Paul that this would be a good investment. The island belonged to Mr. Agnelli, chairman of

FIAT. His ownership was through a company called Societe MAGIORA-LFRA. The villa's name was Gayola.

It happened that I was at Sutton Place at the time. Paul was anxious to close the deal promptly. Prompt payment was required for the MAGIORALFRA's shares to be transferred to Getty. Paul asked me to stop in Zurich on my way to Rome. The price to be paid for Gayola was set at $225,000. He instructed Los Angeles to transfer this amount promptly to Credit Suisse in Zurich at my direction so that I could make payment against the transfer of the MAGIORALFRA shares without delay. I handled the transaction and the subsequent accounting formalities.

At that time, the price for the property was not cheap. Even so, Paul never set foot on his small island. He had always been afraid of traveling by boat or air. The only access to the Naples island was by boat. This may have been the main reason for his reluctance to go there. He would cross the English Channel to travel through Europe only when he felt reasonably sure that the weather and sea would be calm. Even then, his secretaries had to inquire each day before his departure as to whether conditions were favorable before he made up his mind. Often the trip had to be postponed several times because of deteriorating weather conditions, to the dismay of everyone around him, who had to unpack and change all kinds of schedules. His secretary, Barbara, once told me that after several cancellations she finally got tired of them. When Paul instructed her on the morning of the anticipated departure to read him the weather forecast of the *London Times* that day, Barbara covered up the bad news about a storm and "read" instead imaginary lines about a calm sea. His fear of sailing further intensified at the time of the sinking of the passenger ship the *Andrea Doria* on the high seas. Flying was even more frightening to him. He explained that during World War II he had a "near-miss" in one of the planes at the Spartan Aircraft company he had been managing.

My family and I used to go for a vacation to the USA every year. Whenever I stopped at the Los Angeles headquarters to report on the European business and my various negotiations, I was always asked: "... and when is Paul Getty going to come to the USA, particularly to California, his previous home?" I would always reply with certainty that Paul, in my opinion, would never do so. The executives concerned were skeptical about my view, as Paul in almost every interview with reporters and conversations with friends stressed that he certainly would travel to California.

One of his Italian noblemen friends once proposed to Paul a membership in an exclusive Italian social club, the Circolo della Caccia. Paul certainly did not initiate this step but was rather flattered by it. He was later very much hurt when it became public that some of the club members, for some unknown reason, voted against his membership. Over and over again he expressed his anger about the affair, stressing that he was not in favor of the unsolicited membership in the first place. In meetings in which normally pressing business affairs would be discussed, Paul brought up the subject of the Italian club again and again. This sometimes went on until the early morning hours. George and I were relieved when during one of these meetings we were finally allowed to withdraw to our living quarters. The next day Paul spent the day in London at some social function. George and I were watching television in the sitting room when we suddenly heard Paul's car being driven into the courtyard. At that moment George signaled to me that we should immediately rush to our own rooms to be spared another lengthy meeting with Paul and to avoid hearing again about his Italian club adventure.

The Getty Group was not in a favorable position to establish a solid marketing base in Europe. In all the European countries most locally owned oil companies had grown in size and importance. In France and Italy, state-operated companies had become very large and powerful. Branches of major U.S. oil corporations, which had already enjoyed long years of prosperity and growth, began to feel increasing pressure of local competitors, some of whom used large quantities of Soviet oil sold at comparatively low prices.

Slowly the idea crept into Getty's mind that disposing of the company's assets in Europe, in time before sizable losses might be incurred in the future, might be prudent.

Doing business in Italy became increasingly difficult. The company's undersized refinery could not reduce its operating cost to the level enjoyed by the large refining plants of our competitors, who were subsidiaries of the huge international oil conglomerates as well as big enterprises created and run by local businessmen and financiers.

A friend of mine explained to me how one of the private entrepreneurs had made his fortune. I could not believe this bizarre story but was assured that it was true. According to my friend, the businessman concerned acquired a small refining plant, with the intention in mind of taking advantage of the law that permitted duty-free exports while charging exorbitant duty rates for gasoline shipped for local consumption. The entrepreneur allegedly filled the export ships with plain water from the refinery. The customs officer duly entered the volume of water in his export register as gasoline, thereby freeing—probably unwittingly—a corresponding quantity of actual gasoline for domestic use. The businessman knew that if he could use the gasoline in the local market without paying the stiff duties he could earn millions. The only problem was how to get the material out of the plant without going through customs. To solve the problem, he led an underground pipeline from a large gasoline tank at the plant to a facility located outside. From there his trucks merrily loaded the stuff and took it to prearranged marketing outlets. His profits grew enormously month after month. When he exhausted the original volume, he repeated the process by exporting another shipload of water.

Together with our Los Angeles technical experts I proposed to Paul a sizable expansion of our refinery. After numerous conferences, economic studies, and reports by outside consulting firms he finally agreed.

In addition, a partnership with a reputable industrialist was proposed for building an oil pipeline from Gaeta to Rome to reduce transportation costs. Our executives were not keen to commit themselves to this project. The matter was referred to Paul. He talked to me about it on the telephone and was satisfied when I assured him of its soundness, but again he was not willing to give his explicit personal approval. Instead, he authorized me to use my own judgment, which I promptly did upon my return to Rome. I approved the costly project and proceeded with the formulation of a proper partnership contract. Our California management must have been puzzled, but probably also relieved, when I told them it was I who made this important decision, with the backing of Paul Getty.

Those executives were not always on the best of terms with me, although our relationship in general was smooth enough. In my heart I recognized their handicap insofar as they were bound by U.S. laws and customs, while I, in my European function, could not ignore the local laws and "old-world" approaches to many problems. On frequent occasions an attorney or another executive sent to assist me would hamper rather than facilitate the work. Once we negotiated a contract in London. It was initiated in a personal conversation between Paul and the Honorable Sir Frazer of the British Petroleum Company. In the beginning I was leading the negotiations. The role of the California executives present was not clearly spelled out. This proved a handicap in the talks with the British executives. Every now and then my colleagues would give me a strange look suggesting a different approach to the specific matter being discussed. I got tired of it and finally shifted the responsibility to them. At one point it happened that they overlooked an important item in our favor. In the heat of the debate they walked out on the other party, thus signaling the end of the talks. That evening in our hotel I pointed out their error. Negotiations were then resumed and then successfully concluded.

Meanwhile in Italy things started to move. The expansion work in the refinery and the pipeline to Rome created new interests in Getty's Italian assets. Word reached Paul that the powerful independent Attilio Monti Group had expressed interest in the acquisition of his refinery and in the partnership covering the Rome pipeline. Monti's involvement included sugar refineries, newspapers, and huge oil refining plants in Northern Italy at Ravenna and at Milazzo in Sicily.

Paul looked on the prospect of the sale favorably and told me to commence discussions. Dr. Georgio Schanzer, formal president of Getty Oil Italiana, introduced me to Bruno Riffeser, the son-in-law of Monti and the head of his huge enterprises. He was a man of refined manner and at the same time an efficient and dedicated administrator. We developed a straightforward and fair business relationship. Several weeks were spent in preparing a rough draft of a prospective agreement. Our efficient chief accountant, Pompeo Borlone, rendered me invaluable services. It was he who was the most familiar with the thousands of items that had to be considered in the preparation of the price and terms of a possible transfer of assets. They included outstanding financial and legal items, pending lawsuits, unfinished government and marketing business, and complicated taxes.

The draft was prepared under Riffeser's insistence that it must be based upon mutual trust and respect rather than cumbersome legal phrases such as those used in similar situation in the United States. Riffeser stressed that if we were to spend several months in writing and rewriting every single paragraph a deal would not be favored by him. He added that even if attorneys tried to cover every unimportant item in minute detail, there would always be the possibility of challenging the contract and consequently spending years in the courts.

In this respect it is of interest to note Paul's attitude concerning the role of the Los Angeles headquarters. He stressed that Getty Oil Italiana, of which I was managing director, was legally and factually responsible for running the entire business and that any possible recommendations by the headquarters should be considered suggestions only, not orders.

Paul also made it clear that Getty Oil Italiana and Getty Oil of Delaware were two separate companies and that their individual officials had no mutual authority.

Now, in 1969 Paul, in fact, asked me, contrary to expectation, to handle the sale of his Italian assets, a matter clearly in the sphere of the parent company. I was flattered. At the same time I recognized that this was the only way in which a sale would be concluded. This became very obvious when a staff attorney from Los Angeles joined me to work on the legalities. As he had been used to, and also instructed by his bosses, at the very first meeting we reviewed the wording of the contract and began dissecting every word and sentence. A paragraph of some six lines took more than two hours before he approved the final wording. I could not blame him. From my experience, I was aware that while American business leaders make important decisions, they often shift the responsibility to the attorneys who must take the blame if unpleasant lawsuits come up later.

Bruno Riffeser observed our attorney for a while and got increasingly unhappy about his "nit-picking." After consulting with Attilio Monti, whom he introduced to us one day, he made the firm statement to the effect that the deal was off if we continued in such a manner. Thereafter things proceeded with due speed and efficiency. Our attorney's input was kept to a minimum.

The draft covering the multi-million-dollar transaction neared completion, although some technicalities, including the actual proposed transfer date, remained open. Such a date was of great importance, since every business, financial, legal, and technical item had to be cut off on such date. The matter kept me busy, as I had to keep in touch with the Monti people, Paul, and Los Angeles, to make certain the agreement had no serious flaws. A formal review was made by the foremost Italian firm of attorneys in Rome.

During a lull in the negotiations during the summer of 1969, I took my family on our yearly vacation to Hawaii. My oldest son, Peter, lived there with his wife, Sylvia, and sons Kevin and Kyle. Together we built a modern home in the Aina Haina hills overlooking Honolulu and the Pacific Ocean. Peter was working and studying at the University of Hawaii, where he later earned a doctorate in high-energy physics. We always had a good time fishing and swimming in the warm waters of Hawaii.

Sometimes our vacation was interrupted by urgent business calls concerning European matters for which I was responsible. There was no exception this time. On August 4, 1969, Paul directed me to return to Rome and to "push" the sale of the company's Italian assets.

My vacation had to be cut short. Back in Rome I resumed serious talks and then advised Paul that the Monti Group was prepared to conclude the deal, details of which I had outlined earlier. The machinery was set in motion.

On September 2, 1969, I was able to inform Los Angeles that after having reviewed the matter with me, Paul, having considered the effect upon the sales of his Neutral Zone crudes, had instructed me to bring the prospective deal to a conclusion.

The transfer took place in Milan on October 30, 1969. Half of the shares were acquired by the Italian METRA company, the other half by the Panamanian TRANSOIL EUROPE Corporation. Complicated transfer procedures were applied, taking into account regulations of the countries involved. After completing the Italian part of the procedure, including the necessary change of company names, we all flew in Monti's executive jet to Zurich, crossing the Alps, to finalize the remaining half of the deal.

Cash was paid in lire for the first half of the shares. Our Los Angeles comptroller expected to have substantial dollar countervalue available at the company's bank account the next day, so it could immediately earn interest. It was unfortunate that a strike prevailing in Northern Italy at the time prevented a prompt transfer. Then followed a weekend when no banking transaction could take place. Los Angeles became nervous and demanded a lengthy explanation from me. I convinced them that to convert the lire into dollars required a purchase of the latter during a working day and that the Italian bank authorized to do so could handle the transaction only when the foreign exchange institutions were open for business. The matter ended in a satisfactory way for all concerned when the comptroller, at my suggestion, made sure that any U.S. banking house would have had to go through a similar and lengthy process.

The transfer to TRANSOIL was effected against its four-year promissory note guaranteed by the Swiss Credit Bank. Again, there were sizable Italian lire amounts. They carried a 7 percent interest rate that had been personally determined by Paul. The notes were paid in full during the next four years. At that time the value of the lire had stayed at a high level. Their conversion into dollars brought the company an extra profit of several hundred thousand dollars. I was relieved, as during the four years Los Angeles expressed repeated concern about a possible devaluation of the Italian currency. This did not happen. Had it occurred, the blame would have fallen squarely on me, as I had recommended to Paul that he accept the lire payment demanded by the Monti Group.

A serious, but in my view humorous, situation developed in connection with the Panamanian notes. Our comptroller had sent out the usual year-end requests to all larger debtors to confirm the accuracy of the amounts as carried on the Getty books, as required by the auditors. He must have gotten the shock of his life when his letter addressed to Panama was returned by the postal authorities stamped "addressee unknown at the given address." At that point our auditors must have suspected the worst.

The problem had been created due to bureaucracy, which is prevalent in most large businesses. The Los Angeles executive management had failed to advise the auditors that in one of my confidential reports I had specifically pointed out that the TRANSOIL matter should be handled exclusively with a specific director of the Swiss Credit Bank in Zurich. The affair was satisfactorily cleared up in a day or two.

This was just one of the several occasions when I was in variance with some headquarter executives. Other "incidents" were related to legal work routines of their attorneys that were not always in line with methods applicable in other parts of the world. Upon my return to Los Angeles in 1971 I worked closely with these attorneys on a variety of occasions and learned to appreciate their difficult task in handling complicated U.S. cases where they had to face equally tough other American lawyers. On one occasion, however, their legal skills did not help. It was a case involving an agreement between Getty Oil and another major U.S. oil company covering product supplies for our Philippine operations that were under my jurisdiction. In the New York meeting my boss and a member of the legal department, both experienced lawyers, participated. The afternoon session was exhausting. At dinner that evening both my colleagues stated strongly that in their opinion our case was hopeless.

The next morning I continued to negotiate. With me this time was only an attorney from our legal department. I was determined not to give up. My persistence paid off when the other party's vice president finally offered a settlement in our favor amounting to almost a half a million dollars. The result was highly praised by our top executive management.

15

Contrary to some reports, Paul Getty was not a petty, selfish man. It is true however, that he had no sympathy for anyone who expected something for nothing. He insisted, rightly, that people should be paid for their work and pay for their needs. He disliked those who asked undeserved favors of him. Somehow he was unable to express his love for his sons, although I am certain he was very fond of them. He wanted them to go through hard times in order to prove themselves. Even when they had grown up he often treated them like immature children, to their dismay.

Sometimes he has been criticized for having installed a pay telephone at Sutton Place. Again, this confirmed his principle that everyone should pay for the services they require. The telephone was not meant to be a convenient gadget, and it certainly was not. To place a long-distance call from it, the caller had to have two handfuls of small coins ready, with no place close to the telephone to put them down. This was just like any other public telephone in England at the time. I myself had the greatest of difficulties one time making a long-distance telephone call from the London airport. It took great effort to obtain the necessary change in the first place and to finally get the right connection.

Paul was a highly intelligent man. At one time he had studied at Oxford University together with his friend Edward, the Duke of Windsor. The duke sometimes visited Sutton Place to chat with Paul about the good old days and usually signed the guest book. Once, when I arrived at the castle, the guest book lay open on the desk of the big hall. I automatically signed it without realizing the duke's signature was directly above mine. I would not have thought of it twice had it not been for a photograph published in *Town and Country* magazine of July 1964 depicting the open guest book, with the following caption: "Paul's guest book, which has been signed by the world's great. The page is opened to Edward, Duke of Windsor, which is not bad for openers. The Duke and Paul went to Oxford together." I certainly do not consider myself one of the world's great but deemed it unnecessary at the time to send a disclaimer to the famous magazine.

In his travels through Europe, Paul and his staff usually stayed in first-class hotels. He always liked the European atmosphere. He was often a guest in palatial homes where he could relax and enjoy weeks of a sort of vacation from his usual Sutton Place routine. While in Paris he sometimes stayed at the grand residence of Paul Weiler at the rue de la Faisandrie. We spent several hours there on one occasion reviewing some personal and business matters.

While in Germany, Paul was sometimes the guest of Baron Heini Thyssen, who had built a powerful business empire after World War II. The baron owned a number of magnificent palaces throughout Europe. One of the most famous ones was the Villa Favorita on Lake Lugano in Switzerland. The huge grounds of the estate were landscaped and almost "manicured" by an army of gardeners. The villa housed art treasures of immense value, which on certain weekdays were on display in a number of separate galleries. Baron Thyssen was said to own the largest private art collection in the world.

After the transfer of Getty Oil Italiana shares had been completed, together with Bruno Riffeser of Monti and a few others who had participated in the transaction I visited Paul at the Villa Favorita, where he had been staying as Baron Thyssen's guest. Paul listened to our report and comments but talked very little himself. Later he and Bruno Riffeser conducted a private conversation at the swimming pool. While they talked, Countess Marianne von Alvensleben of Dusseldorf, a close friend of Getty, offered to give me a tour of the villa and its treasures, about which she was most enthusiastic. She had good reason for her enthusiasm, as I found out. The treasures were so numerous and beautiful that they boggled the mind.

The countess had always impressed me as being a cultured and well-mannered lady. Earlier I had had the opportunity to take a picture of her strolling with Paul through the gardens at Sutton Place. It proved to be one of the best pictures of Paul. The countess requested several copies, and I was happy to oblige.

Paul was in the habit of strolling through the estate with his friends and visitors in the late-afternoon hours whenever the weather permitted. On one such occasion I had the opportunity to introduce him to my oldest son, Peter, with whom he exchanged a few polite sentences.

My son John did not have the opportunity to meet Paul. While we lived in Paris, John spent a few years in Copenhagen, where he studied music at the Royal Danish Conservatory, under the guidance of the famous Professor Rasmunssen. John's basic education in the United States had been in the field of engineering, in which he proved himself to be an outstanding student. His stay in Denmark, however, brought out in him the finest qualities of a born artist and human being. Georgine and I often listened to his playing the piano with our eyes closed and a feeling that his gentle fingers were transmitting to us warmth and joy. We sometimes regret that he could not pursue his musical talents after we returned to the United States. The fast lifestyles in America guided him toward a more practical field. His intelligence and adaptability enabled him to become an expert in high-tech computers and landed him a responsible and respected place in the related industry. His lovely wife, Debby, was of great support to him in the early years of their marriage, when every dollar counted. Debby is now able to stay home, taking care of their two beautiful sons, Patrick and Nicholas.

In the summer of 1971 Paul spent a few weeks in Italy at the Posta Vecchia. After his major Italian assets had been sold, it was time for me and my family to move on. There was some speculation what my next assignment would be. After nine years in Europe, Georgine and I, as well as John and Tom, were anxious to return to America. When Paul called me on the telephone to come and see him at Posta Vecchia, I had the feeling that the talk would, among other subjects, include my future. I was right.

The talk took place in the huge sitting room. It was a damp day, with the wind blowing from the open sea. The room was cold and unfriendly in such an atmosphere. Paul sat opposite me. It was obvious that he was feeling cold and perhaps even ill. He had raised the collar of his coat so as to protect his head from the creeping humidity. At one point he asked me to close the huge door, from which he felt a draft.

Paul asked me first whether I was really determined to return to California. I had heard from other sources that he had mentioned earlier the possibility of my moving to England or assuming the position of general manager in his neutral zone oil fields in the Middle East. I confirmed that indeed it was my desire to return to the States. He then suddenly posed a direct question that I had not anticipated. I had thought that he would indicate to me what the company had in its plans. Instead, he asked me to tell him what I would like to do when I returned to the Los Angeles headquarters.

At this moment the events of the last nine years flashed through my head. I had been so much involved in a different way of life, of doing business, of charting mine and my family's lives and an unprecedented freedom of action under Paul's wings that I suddenly became apprehensive of fitting properly into the habits and lives of Getty's American executives, with their regular social events, their golf games, their stiff business and legal procedures, and their special standing in the community.

This time I failed as a businessman in my reply to Paul. I should have asked him whether he had any special assignment in mind. Instead, and in view of my general feelings about the Los Angeles headquarters, I said, "I am not after a career in the company, but—as always—I shall be happy to work in any responsible capacity in which I could make myself useful."

In later years I sometimes felt that my reaction to Paul's question was ill-chosen. I will, of course, never know if he had a position close to the top of his empire in mind or whether he merely respected my attitude concerning a "career" in the company.

Upon my returning to Los Angeles, I was given the position of head of international marketing operations, with a worldwide staff of over eight hundred employees. Georgine and I bought a comfortable home in the suburb of Westwood, a charming area not far from the University of California. Our youngest son, Tom, completed his studies at that university, graduating with honors in film production and direction. Expanding his work in this field with the latest developments in video electronics, he later established his own very successful enterprise. They specialize in the production of educational, training, and promotional films and videotapes for heavy and medium industries and businesses, as well as educational institutions. His wife, Michele, and daughter, Katie, as well as Peter's daughter Colyn, are great assets to our families.

In my new assignment a great deal of traveling was again required of me. My position took me on frequent trips to Europe, Canada, South America, and Japan and other countries of the Far East. I made several trips to Hong Kong, Singapore, and Taiwan. One of my major responsibilities was the Philippines, where Getty had a strong marketing subsidiary.

On one of my trips to the Philippine island of Mindanao, I was introduced to Benigno Aquino, then an important political figure in the country. The use of guns was so widespread then that the whole country was, in fact, an armed camp. Politicians could not travel without armed guards. When Aquino stepped out of his car to say a few words to me, two armed men with automatic weapons immediately followed, ready to defend him if necessary.

The situation in the Philippines later became so tense that President Marcos had to order the confiscation of all arms owned by civilians. In Manila alone it was reported that more than half a million handguns were surrendered following the order.

Georgine and I had the opportunity to meet Benigno Aquino once more when the then-senator gave a political speech at a reception in Los Angeles. He impressed me as a man of high principles and morals. I did not realize then that in the Philippines political rivals did not fight it out with words but often with guns. It was a sad day when Benigno Aquino several years later, following medical treatment in the United States, was brutally assassinated as he stepped from the plane on his return to Manila. No one could have predicted that his widow, Corazon Aquino, would in February of 1986 take the oath of office as president of the country, after Marcos had, in fact, lost the election, his friends, and power.

In my job I was also given the privilege of joining prestigious clubs where our foreign visitors could be entertained. Among my memberships was one in the Foreign Affairs Council, which arranged for monthly business luncheons where invited dignitaries made their speeches. Once we had a speaker from the Soviet Union. It was Georgy Arbatov, then a member of the Soviet Academy of Science and later a member of the Communist Party's Central Committee in Moscow and key advisor to Soviet leader Mikhail Gorbachev.

Arbatov, in his acceptable English, spoke from a raised platform while several feet to his left sat two members of the Soviet consulate of San Francisco. The audience was listening politely and even nodding their heads as Arbatov poured lies and insults at them. He stressed that he had to have a special permit to travel to Los Angeles. The audience was appalled at that, believing it was unfair that such a nice man could be under such severe restrictions. Arbatov, of course, did not state that Americans traveling to the USSR are subject to much more stringent restrictions or that even the Soviets themselves cannot travel freely in their own land. He continued to say that America would surely one day adopt communism with all its advantages, but he omitted to state that during the seven decades of communism in the Soviet Union more than

20 million innocent citizens were executed in order to create a "paradise on earth." He also criticized America for having waged an "aggressive and imperialistic" war in Vietnam. Finally he stressed that all the "real" people in the world should get together and demand peace. He conveniently omitted to say that the Soviet people cannot get together with other people simply because they are not allowed to travel freely or mingle with foreigners.

For me it was pathetic to watch the audience and observe how politely and sympathetically they listened to the lies. No one stood up to ask any embarrassing questions of the speaker. In their naïveté they must have accepted his untruths and insults as facts presented by a nice foreign gentleman. Although we Americans enjoy an almost unlimited freedom, we often do not know or believe that such freedom does not exist in some other countries. We are embarrassed to express our true patriotism when it is badly needed.

During the luncheon, I was the only person who stood up and opposed Georgy Arbatov. Among other points I made was my question as to why similar meetings with public participation, where, for instance, the brutal occupation by the Soviets of Hungary and Czechoslovakia could be aired could not be held in Moscow.

Mr. Arbatov is a clever man. Without hesitation, and with an approving nod from his consulate colleagues, he stated with a straight face that in the Soviet Union open public debates embracing "all kinds of subjects" were held regularly.

At that point I remembered my friend Dr. Peter Zenkl and wished that he were present. His confrontation with Arbatov would have been priceless. As mentioned earlier, Zenkl was a two-term Lord Mayor of Prague. As a great patriot he was arrested by the Gestapo and spent six years in the Buchenwald concentration camp. After the war he became deputy prime minister in the Czech postwar government. As a staunch anti-Communist, he was again arrested, this time by the secret police of President Gottwald. Zenkl was heavily guarded, but his friends managed to free him and smuggle him across the border and arrange for his departure to Washington. From there the Zenkls came to visit Georgine and me while we lived in San Francisco. The *San Francisco Chronicle* carried an article about them, saying among other things: "Zenkl and his wife plan a brief visit with Mayor Christopher. They will be guests of Mr. and Mrs. Wohlmut." In my presence, Mayor Christopher gave Peter the keys to San Francisco and offered us a police escort through the city. Before his return to Washington, we received their photograph with their personal inscription: "To the dear Wohlmuts, with devotion, from Peter and Paula Zenkl. August 1957."

I wonder if Mr. Arbatov read the booklet *Peter Zenkl. Champion Anti-Communist;* by Bracket Lewis (Chicago: Beseda J.V. Fric, 1956). The two page preface in the booklet was written by Edward R. Murrow, who concluded it as follows:

> The years in prison and in exile have served to intensify and strengthen his intolerance of injustice. He knows that in a world where there is no security for little nations, there is no security for big ones. He is a quiet man, with a truly ferocious faith in freedom. And there will come a time when school children in his own country—and I hope in mine—will read the story of Peter Zenkl, his life and his works, and will draw from it the pride, inspiration and respect for human rights which is the diet on which individuals and nations must survive.

During another session of the World Affairs Council at the Ambassador Hotel in Los Angeles, I met the Apollo 16 astronauts. It was June 26, 1972. With John W. Young and Thomas K. Mattingly was Charles Duke, lunar command module pilot. I have a photograph of Duke and his charming wife talking to me. Meeting the astronauts who participated in the historic moon landing was a privilege.

Paul had always been interested in the space program. On April 17, 1970, two Los Angeles executives and I sat with him in his television room watching the Apollo 13 splashdown that had almost ended in disaster. We all sighed with relief when the astronauts' lives were saved.

My association with Paul's business transactions frequently offered opportunities to meet and confer with prominent people. Among them were George D. Woods, then president of the World Bank in New York, and Baron Wolters, chairman and managing director of the powerful Belgian oil company PETROFINA, with whom I met in Geneva. While I was in Rome, a distinguished visitor from Tokyo came to see me: Mr. Fujioka, the wise and gentle president of Mitsubishi Oil Company, the fourth largest Japanese oil company. Getty Oil had a 50 percent share in Mitsubishi at that time.

16

On one of my later trips to Europe, in 1974, I stopped on my return trip to Sutton Place. Paul was sitting in the TV room together with Lady Ursula d'Abo. It was known that she had been a train bearer for Queen Mary at the coronation of George VI. When I entered, Paul got up and gave me a warm welcome, clasping my arm with both his trembling hands. I was moved, seeing his frail frame and tired face. We exchanged a few polite sentences. When he withdrew to his study and we said goodbye to each other, it was the last time I talked to him. Lady Ursula kept our conversation going. She showed unusual interest in worldwide oil affairs, soliciting my comments to possibly refer to them later in her conversations with Paul.

Paul's son Gordon was closer to him than his other sons. This was particularly true during the last few years of Paul's life. While in Europe I was with Gordon several times. We became well acquainted. Paul used to give him specific business assignments, such as studies of particular phases of oil marketing and economics. With his brilliant mind Gordon used to prepare scientifically well-documented and extremely detailed reports. His father did not always apply them in his business but rather used them to provide Gordon with a good exercise session.

Once I spent several days with Gordon at Sutton Place. In our free time we played tennis on the covered court. At the dinner table Gordon diplomatically reported, "Arthur played well, but I beat him." Being aware of my limited skill, I considered it a compliment. After dinner Gordon gave me a copy of his musical composition "Seascape," on which he inscribed: "To Arthur—Gordon Getty."

Gordon's talents encompass not only a business acumen but to a greater extent a great love for music and art and a passion for the scientific search for the origin of man. He is an unusual, highly intelligent, mild-mannered man on whose shoulders had, through recent years, rested a heavy burden of the Getty Trust.

My relationship with George, Paul's oldest son, had always been pleasant but businesslike. George enjoyed life, but from time to time he seemed engrossed in worries. On occasions he tended to become somewhat irritable with his executives when things took a different turn than he had expected. After the Getty Oil/Tidewater merger he was bitter about the fact that his father did not allow him to become president of the new conglomerate but instead kept that title to himself. George's grievance in this respect was indicated to me on the occasion of my signing the Algerian agreement. The 1968 Getty Oil Annual Report showed a picture of me depicting me as president of Getty Petroleum and George F. Getty II as executive vice president of Getty Oil. My position was, in fact, much lower than that of George, but to outsiders the distinction was far from clear. George certainly fully deserved to be president of Getty Oil Company, the parent company, but there was no way of inducing Paul to give up the title and become chairman of the company.

Sometimes George opened his heart and talked freely about his private life. Georgine, Tom, and I once had dinner with him at the famous Roman restaurant called Georgios. It was a happy occasion. He talked about his life, stressing that at the moment he was a free man who enjoyed his friends, the California sun, and the parties at his beach house. Then, after a while, he confessed that he had decided to remarry and asked us what we thought of it. I replied, half-jokingly, that even when enjoying the greatest of freedom a man always seemed to look for some sort of lasting commitment, although it might invariably be connected with complications in life.

A few weeks later his marriage to Jacqueline Manewal Riordan in Beverly Hills was announced on May 20, 1971.

George maintained a stable of horses. In 1968 he listed seven brood mares, three yearlings, six foals, four horses in training, and five stallions. Although proud of his stable, he was somewhat apologetic for this "extravaganza." I told him that it would be a shame if a man in his position and with his stature could not have such a worthwhile hobby connected with his love for animals. He promptly corrected me, saying that this was a profitable business and that he had always been careful to stress that to his father.

In my position as international marketing manager George used to direct to me various articles and magazine clippings pertaining not only to marketing subjects but also to items covering OPEC, international and domestic crude pricing, and developments in the stock market. On June 5, 1973, he directed me to a copy of a voluminous report on oil issued by Laird Incorporated. George wrote on the copy, in his typically strong left-handed writing: "MR. WOHLMUT." That same evening he became fatally ill under mysterious circumstances that were never fully explained, was taken to a hospital, and died several hours later. Only those who were with or around him during the last day of his life know the circumstances surrounding his death. The full truth will probably never be known. I was saddened, as I had been acquainted with George for more than seventeen years. He had been designated by Paul Getty as his successor and chief executive of all the Getty enterprises, but fate dictated otherwise.

Having reached the age of sixty-four, I asked for early retirement from the company. Its international operations had been curtailed year after year. I missed the challenges I had enjoyed working for nine years under J. Paul Getty in Europe. A warm farewell luncheon was given me by my closest friends and colleagues. It was held at the California Club in Los Angeles on July 18, 1975. During the luncheon a treasured, touching thought was conveyed to me from Paul, expressing appreciation for my good work for the company and wishing me happy years in retirement.

Less than a year later, on June 6, 1976, J. Paul Getty died of cardiac failure at Sutton Place. Through his death he was finally able to return to his beloved Malibu home in California, where he is buried. On behalf of the J. Paul Getty family, Gordon Getty, who had been close to Paul during his last months, thanked many for the numerous expressions of sympathy. To me Gordon also recalled, at the time, the happy memories of the old days.

The many communications between Paul Getty and myself will always be treasured by me. In connection with his later dreams about returning to California, he sent me a copy of his book *The Joys of Collecting* with his personal inscription: "To Arthur Wohlmut with best wishes from J. Paul Getty—Mar. 25, 1970."

The original Getty Museum in California had become too small to house his many treasures. In the same year, 1970, he ordered the construction of a large new building, and he so advised his associates and friends, including myself. Paul was proud that the original J. Paul Getty Museum had been opened in December 1953 to show the public the collections of artworks assembled earlier. The newly constructed museum opened at 17985 Pacific Coast Highway in Malibu, California.

Many contradictory reports have been written about J. Paul Getty. Some of them were based on one-time short interviews, various press articles, or repeated reviews of printed materials. Many articles have stressed the darker side of his life and character, as if none of us ever had a thing or two to hide.

Often emphasis has been put on the business sense he displayed while amassing his vast fortune, particularly the way he had always foreseen business and economic trends. This is certainly appropriate, but it is unfortunate that his true sense of fairness, honesty, and straightforward financial dealings have never been stressed.

Once at a dinner at Sutton Place I observed that he was wearing a belt that looked rather heavy. It was stuffed with heavy pellets, causing the body to involuntary exert a certain effort while moving around. The belt had been given to Paul by his son, George, who himself wore a similar belt, in addition to miniature belts around his wrists and ankles. George knew his father was a health buff.

Although I was aware that this was the latest fad introduced by exercise addicts, I teased Paul. When I jokingly remarked that I thought he was carrying his money in his belt, Paul erupted in a hearty laugh. In fact, I had never before observed him laugh so uninhibitedly.

Our conversation then turned to the subject of his wealth. It had never been said to the public, I remarked, that his wealth had been accumulated through hard work, consistent policies, and foresight, rather than by shady deals or charging high interest rates, like others who had made huge fortunes. I added that through his wisdom and understanding thousands of families were able to lead good and happy lives. Paul was visibly moved, the expression in his eyes was warm, and he thanked me and said, "I would hope that would be said of me."

17

Georgine and I are now spending our golden years of retirement in the foothills of the Sierra Nevada Mountains, surrounded by pine and oak trees. We are enjoying the clear air, beautiful weather without fog or smog, and peaceful surroundings. It is a far cry from the hectic days we encountered during the more than four decades of our marriage, through upheavals and unrest, through storms and sunshine. We have lived in countries ruled by monarchs or democratic presidents, but also by Nazi and communist dictators and other ruthless men. We have experienced political and physical terror that taught us that the search for freedom is worthy of any, any sacrifice. Our experience always makes us feel sorry for those in the general public as well as in high political circles who sneer at the sacred need for freedom for individuals as well as for whole countries. They will learn one day that tyranny and oppression may threaten their children and grandchildren in their own country in the same manner as they threatened our life and future.

The arrival from time to time at our mountain retreat of our three sons and their families is always a special treat for us. A few years ago, my brother, Bruno, was able to visit us from Prague. It felt good to reinforce our brotherly ties and to recall our adventures during our young life at the time of World War I.

Life is such that past events cannot be relived. They only pass through our minds and evoke pleasant or painful memories. When I close my eyes I, too, see vivid pictures racing through my mind. Sitting in my chair surrounded by silence, I wonder why the past events occurred and what or who caused them to run in the sequence they did. As in the beginning of my story, tranquillity engulfs me and my head slowly sinks like a leaf in a gentle breeze.